LANGUAGE AND CULTURE

Language

NEW YORK

and Culture

HERBERT LANDAR CALIFORNIA STATE COLLEGE AT LOS ANGELES

OXFORD UNIVERSITY PRESS · 1966

Library of Congress Catalogue Card Number: 66-14478

PRINTED IN THE UNITED STATES OF AMERICA

To my Parents and the Memory of their Parents.

Οὗ μὲν οὖν ἐστιν ἡ ὄψις, τοῦτ'
ἐστὶν ὁρατόν, ὁρατὸν δ' ἐστὶ
χρῶμά τε καὶ ὃ λόγῳ μὲν ἔστιν
εἰπεῖν, ἀνώνυμον δὲ τυγχάνει ὄν·
δῆλον δὲ ἔσται ὃ λέγομεν προελθοῦσι.
—*Aristotle,* Π.Ψ.Β.7.

ACKNOWLEDGMENTS «

A number of institutions and individuals have contributed to my education. The foremost of these, on the institutional side, are Yale University, Cornell University Medical College, the RAND Corporation, the Social Science Research Council, and the Research Institute for the Study of Man. My debt to individuals is more difficult to specify. There is a general obligation to my students at Reed College and the California State College at Los Angeles, students who induced the continual reshaping of my "Language and Culture" course until the present synthesis was reached. Particular obligations, however, are so numerous as to tie one's tongue with circumspection and end the naming of names in advance. Of those who will find their influence in these pages I must, nevertheless, gratefully distinguish Bernard Bloch, Floyd G. Lounsbury, and Eric Hamp.

CONTENTS «

IV. CULTURE: BOAS

V. CULTURE: SAPIR

FIGURES

PREFACE «

This book asks what relevance the careful study of language may have for the careful student of culture. It provides an answer which the author believes will be of interest to social scientists and humanists alike, to all, indeed, who for one reason or another find the study of human sign behavior compelling.

The author's answer is fairly technical, and requires an interpretation of the history of the study of anthropology, particularly in America, from natural-historical beginnings to present attempts to formalize, and make interesting discoveries about, the learned sign behavior which we call culture. To facilitate the exposition, a format based upon short lessons has been adopted. The book, however, has been written to be read and understood as a whole.

Some contemporary theories in linguistics have great scope. Katz and Postal, for example, have gone beyond the early transformationalists to embrace semantics. They describe the entries in a semantic dictionary and the rules for deriving the meanings of phrase markers. They provide for the semantic as well as the syntactic interpretation of any given sentence. A generative grammar has a syntactic component which generates strings, a semantic component which semantically interprets sentoids (sentences with their structural descriptions), and a phonological component which provides the phonetics of utterances. In this general approach lie seeds for creative attacks upon larger, extralinguistic problems.

Theories of great scope are liable sometimes to be controversial. An effort has been made to characterize controversial positions fairly, and at the same time to raise questions about them. This is the case, for example, with issues in comparative linguistics. It is important, one theme of this book goes, to qualify inferences from linguistic data. The formation of broad hypotheses about ancient events can beggar rapid documentation. If Boas lies at one extreme, the cautious conservative, it is not difficult to find others who lie at the other extreme. In the matter of the classification of languages, and inferences about ancient migrations and culture history which follow from such classification, the testing of genetic hypotheses is a function of the collection of acceptable data, ordinarily a slow process.

Linguists such as Sapir and Swadesh have formulated challenging theories of genetic relationship. Such theories, however, cannot be anything but controversial in the absence of adequate data. In the American case, Swadesh has supposed that the major phyla, separated by at least forty-one minimal centuries of divergence (excepting Beothuk in North America and Tinigua, Omurano, and Nambicuara in South America), are Macro-Mayan, Macro-Quechuan, Macro-Arawakan, Macro-Carib (Macro-Cariban), and Basque-Dene (Bask-Dennean). To the last-named phylum he assigns Kutenai, Wakashan, Na-Dene, Eskimo-Aleut, and other languages mentioned in Chapter 21. A less audacious formulation, restricting attention to America north of Mexico, prefers to deal with seven major groups: Macro-Algonquian, Hokan, Iroquois-Siouan (Macro-Siouan), Aztec-Tanoan, Penutian, Eskimo-Aleut, and Na-Dene. Even this more conservative estimate has controversial aspects.

Once reconstructions are available, with a basis in systematic recurrences of phonemes, the comparison of grammars begins to make sense, and the broader theories may be tested. For *Macro-Algonquian* one can list—with an asterisk to show that reconstructions are available—*Algonquian-*Ritwan, *Muskogean, Natchez, Chitimacha, Atakapa, Tunica, and possibly Tonkawa. For *Hokan,* *Palaihnihan, *Yanan, *Pomoan, *Yuman, *Salinan, *Chumashan, Karok, Chimariko, Washo, and possibly *Shastan, Tequistlatecan, Seri, and Esselen. For *Iroquois-Siouan,* *Iroquoian-*Siouan, and possibly *Caddoan, Catawba, and Yuchi. For *Aztec-Tanoan,* *Kiowa-*Tanoan and *Uto-Aztecan. For *Penutian,* *Sahaptian (Sahaptin and Nez Perce), *Coos, *Yakonan, *Takelma-Kalapuya, *Yokuts, *Chinook, *Miwok, *Maidun, Cayuse, Molale, Klamath-Modoc, Tsimshian, and possibly *Wintun-Costanoan and Zuni. (Swadesh prefers to assign Zuni to Macro-Quechuan.) For *Na-Dene,* *Athapaskan (including Eyak), possibly Tlingit, and perhaps Haida. While Swadesh groups Kutenai, Wakashan, Na-Dene, and Eskimo-Aleut under the Basque-Dene rubric, many scholars regard the Wakashan, Salishan, Chimakuan, Kutenai, and other groups or isolates as of problematic status. An awareness of such problems is protection against premature speculation.

This book deals with various sorts of speculation. It suggests that the facts of experience must be recognized before speculation can be validated. Take the example of the assumption that a lexical form may represent categorical meanings in antithetical contrast. Carl Abel (*Über den Gegensinn der Urworte* [1884], pp. 37–65) misinterprets contrasts such as Arabic *ǵaunun* 'white/black,' Egyptian *xeft* 'for/against,' Old English *blaec* 'black/white,' in postulating 'a time when the mind could not conceive the one notion without contrasting it with its opposite.' A more sensible interpretation, I think, is that a marginal meaning may stand sometimes in paradoxical opposition to the central meaning of a linguistic form, but only as the result of historical shiftings of sense.

Two assumptions seem to underlie the claim of semantic inversion: first, that the meaning of a lexical form is static; second, that logical antithesis may characterize two polysemes or senses of one form. The assumption of static meaning, however, is a convenient fiction; for Bloomfield this was indeed the basic assumption of linguistics, but for all of that it was still a convenient fiction. And two senses or readings cannot really be rated as equivalent in any psychological interpretation which affirms that linguistic responses are based on experience.

An attempt to verify Abel's English example reveals that his *blaec* represents a homonymic pair which produced accidental semantic expansion. The *Oxford English Dictionary* gives 'black' (OE *blæc, blāce, blācan*) versus 'shining, white' (OE *blác*), thirteenth through fifteenth centuries. It is possible to show, moreover, that data contradict Abel's notion of antithetical polysemy, even when the notion seems to have some support, as with *wan.*

Between about 1300 and 1400, fluctuation occurred among (1) 'dark,' sb., (2) 'darken,' v., (3) 'pallid,' sb., (4) 'pale and wan' (from about 1374), as shown below. (Dates are from the *Oxford English Dictionary.*)

700 / 8 / 9 / 10 / 11 / 12 / 13 / 14 / 15 / 16 / 17 / 18 / 1900

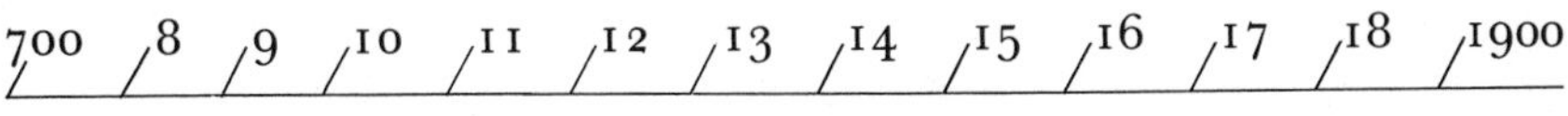

(1) *c.*700–1655

(2) *c.*1000–1400/50

(3) 1300–1883

(4) 1374–

(5) 1582–1906

(5) 'pale,' v., developed after (2) had been obsolete about 150 years. (1, 2) and (3) competed for about 75 years, with (3) initially in marginal status. Unequivocal (4) reinforced (3) and probably helped in the loss of favor for (2), which was lost about 25 years later; compare the loss of (1), despite almost 1000 years of use, about 75 years after (5) appeared. With this example we conclude that unpredictable fluctuation conditioned by analogic use of existing linguistic forms is hardly a basis for postulating unqualified antithetical polysemy.

This brings us to the question of cultural relativism. Aside from an attempt to show how linguistics contains the seeds of creative attacks upon larger, extralinguistic problems, the author wishes to develop the theme that there are two kinds of cultural relativism. The baser sort has grown out of the baser part of post-Socratic teachings; the nobler out of the nobler part. The baser sort deals in primitive tribes, of primitive mentality, doomed by their primitive languages to primitive world-views. The nobler sort deals in the higher cultural contributions, the most humanistic ones, which are transcultural and not restricted by time, place, or the nature of philosophical language. To understand how properly to reject the one is to understand the value of the other.

Los Angeles H.L.
November 1965

LANGUAGE
AND
CULTURE

1

Writing

A once-established opinion, however delusive, can hold its own from age to age, for belief can propagate itself without reference to its reasonable origin, as plants are propagated from slips without fresh raising from the seed.

—Sir Edward Tylor, *Primitive Culture* (1871).

1

The Sociology of Knowledge

The proper understanding of the transcultural equivalences of all cultures begins with the sociology of knowledge. The sociology of knowledge is concerned not simply with such forms of deception as false dichotomization, the all-or-nothing mistake, by which binary choices between easy extremes obscure the value of contextual clues in the formulation of rational decisions. It concerns itself also with the situational determinants of binary decisions.

The utterances of language, in general, are considered in isolation for analytical purposes, because the policy of science is to divide and conquer, but one cannot lose sight of the intimacies and interconnections of all phases of cultural life and the enormous importance of a wise synthesis of human experience. A sentence, no less than each of its parts, is a creature of social convention and part of a larger and grander sociocultural perspective.

The sociology of knowledge takes the broader social context as its province and tries to understand how communication and social interaction are related. As an academic field, it is in its infancy; but since ancient times philosophers have attempted to work out the truths concerning the transmission of knowledge among small groups. The academic work thus has some basis in past speculations.

An example of early academic work is Georg Simmel's. In arguing that human nature is dualistic, Simmel pointed out that every relationship presupposes mutual knowledge, and that, while words imply a sharing of conventions, one should realize too that speakers can have different socially conditioned backgrounds. Only one of two speakers who are interacting has certain private information, and that figures in his motivation.

Learning a language means learning social conventions. Language, having cognitive, expressive, and value aspects, qualifies as an institution, a cultural institution in the Parsonsian sense. The sociology of knowledge, which spotlights the kinds of private information that interacting people have as they manifest sanctions and role-expectations, is thus a prime tool in addressing the problems of a universal institution. How do people form images of what others expect? How do they decide upon their own reactions as determinants of the reactions of others? Such questions help us to evaluate this universal institution, language.

An actor's role is part of his orientation to reality which is built on a knowledge of expectations. These expectations are held in a given context of interaction. Ego has one or more alter egos or alters who take appropriate complementary roles. Culturally imposed sets of values, dynamic themes of the society, govern each system of reciprocally integrated role-expectations. There are various institutionalized roles which a speaker may play, now as addresser, now as addressee. And since such roles are learned within a given culture, we should not be surprised that there is variance from one culture to the next. Discovery of this variance leads to culture shock, as it is called, as well as to false notions about the way people of other cultures, speaking other languages quite different in structure from our own, actually look at the universe. This variance, which the good sociologist of knowledge easily discounts, is therefore one of the culprits responsible for the false notion that language molds thought in dramatic ways.

This false notion, advanced by such writers as Cassirer and Whorf, is one of the great self-deceptions of our age. More scholars held to it in the last century than hold to it at present, a time in which misinformation based on inadequate records and vulgar apprehensions is withering away. Yet to repeat the doctrines of scholars of the past, after their theories have fallen from respectability, is a not uncommon failing of the untutored layman. The best protection against the outworn doctrines of cultural relativism is a healthy skepticism, one with a basis in the sociology of knowledge.

The sociology of knowledge tries to understand how communication between one group of people and another is affected by the various pressures of social institutions other than language. It asks how communication between *A* and *B* while *C* is actually or potentially present is affected by such institutions. It studies not only literary self-deception, then, but literate deception in general, in contemporary propagandistic contexts and throughout the ages, in all societies and for all groups of which written records are available.

The linguist or anthropologist is concerned primarily, perhaps, with the formal and semantic relations and properties of empirically verifiable cultural elements. The structure of a language provides a context, in a certain sense, for its own study. The sociologist of knowledge, on the other hand, often takes language as an institution; in exploring the value of language to the preservation of social cohesion and the stability of social systems, he is likely to pay more attention to context, and to find more significance in contradictions and silences, at least for the moment, than his anthropological confreres. He lives in greater danger of attack or thoughtless ostracism, and perhaps tries to conceal his teachings in jungles of verbiage.

Despite their style, philosophical sociologists have contributed much to an understanding of the role of language in culture. They have directed our attention to that form of culture which often is mistakenly thought to be indentical with language itself, writing. Writing is a form of culture which has more often been studied by the historian of culture than by the historian of social relations. It is a form which has both structural and functional values of the greatest social importance. The use of language, in a literate society or in a primitive society where writing is not unknown, cannot be understood very well without some attention to the use of writing.

2«

Writing

The student of language works with various symbols. If he is studying English, for example, he wants to free himself from the bondage of an imperfect system of spelling, some conventions of which have come down to us from the fourteenth century, and he uses symbols for entities called phonemes or morphemes. A phoneme, taxonomically considered, is a class of phonetically similar and noncontrastive allophones (variant sounds); a morpheme is a class of semantically similar and noncontrastive allomorphs (so that we are compelled in setting up a morpheme for *wife* to add to the class the form *wive* broken away from the plural *wives*). Phonemes are written as symbols inside of slashes: we say that the stop phonemes of English include /p t k/, or that /f/ represents a labiodental spirant phoneme. Morphemes are written as symbols inside of braces: we say that the morpheme {*wife*} has two allomorphs, /wayf/ and /wayv/. There is a technical term reserved also for a contrastive class of characters or letters used in writing: the grapheme. Graphemes, as might be expected, have predictably positioned variants called allographs. Graphemes are written as symbols inside of pointed brackets: ⟨**a**⟩.

Writing can be considered as an invention. For the anthropologist the study of inventions is a compelling passion. Given an invention, a composition of cultural traits, can one, in considering what appears to be the same thing elsewhere, discover any evidence that the compositions were made independently of all others? Similar compositions, not independently invented, offer the possibility of diffusion. And students of anthropology are not loath to speculate about specimens of writing in terms of independent invention versus diffusion. For evidence of such speculation one need only turn to Kroeber's *Anthropology,* Diringer's *The Alphabet,* or Gelb's *A Study of Writing.*

Writing can also be considered as something that needs reforming. Idealists claim that if the rules of English spelling were to be simplified, children could learn to spell and read more easily. Some suppose, indeed, that if the rules of English grammar were to be simplified, or if an artificial language with simplified rules were to be created or propagated, then all men would share common experiences linguistically in the cause of some form of moral brotherhood. Thus far the work of the reformers has succeeded only in multiplying the number of proposals for reform. Yet one must admire all efforts to replace anecdotal laws with rational ones, including the efforts of the reformers.

Writing can be considered in another, very special way. Writing, and the characters used in writing, may concern us not simply as ends in themselves or matter for a history of invention and diffusion or a beginning of reform. There is a rarer kind of writing, found between the lines of the actual writing, between the graphemes as it were, decipherable and understandable from clues provided in the texts at hand and in the contexts reconstructed for us by the alert cultural historian, if not directly advertised by the sociologist of knowledge.

There are three ways to discuss language, within the framework of the social sciences and the humanities, metaphysical dualism aside. The oldest way is in the natural historical tradition. When anthropology began to flower, when Tylor began training students at Oxford and Boas began training students at Columbia, late in the last and early in the present century, cultural traits often were regarded as museum pieces, objects to be reported and examined in and of themselves. Aristotle, who composed a natural history by mixing shrewd observations with widespread popular beliefs, can be taken as an early anthropologist in the natural historical sense. And language, which is a microcosm within the macrocosm of culture, has objects perhaps too easily examined as museum pieces.

After Bloomfield's *Language* (1933), and studies by Bloomfield's followers, had appeared, it became increasingly difficult for the serious anthropologist to ignore certain basic assumptions of linguistic science, central among them the assumption that objects have their existence by virtue of contrast, on a given level of analysis, or else they do not have commensurate status. In contrast to the simple natural historical approach, the structural approach came to the service of students of culture, with powerful impetus from the studies of sophisticated linguists. And anthropologists like Lévi-Strauss have followed linguistic leads in characterizing cultural systems in structural terms. In his short book *Totemism,* for example, Lévi-Strauss shows how fruitless were early representations of totemic customs, and how productive it is to ask not why there are so many animal totems in a given culture but why and in what respects these animal totems are set in contrast with each other by carriers of that culture.

The structural or taxonomic approach, as developed in America, has produced what some call stratificational analysis. In linguistics, it is possible to collect data from an informant and to analyze a corpus of data level by level, classifying the elements studied on one level into sets of higher-order elements, beginning, for example, with the phones or sounds represented by the symbols of a phonetic alphabet, say symbols for shades of the *t*-sound, proceeding by definition to a grouping of phones into phonemes, the *t*-phones then being called the allophones of the /t/-phoneme, proceeding then by definition to a grouping of allomorphs into their respective morphemes, and so on, until the sentence, as the highest-order element, has been reached, and the varieties of sentences themselves have been determined. Stratificational analysis has even been extended by some scholars, notably Lamb, to the semantic domain. The possibilities of rigorous procedure offered by taxonomic linguists have deeply impressed many anthropologists, one of the most important of these being Kroeber, who was trained in his formative years by Boas. The admiration which Kroeber had for linguists as students of the most easily described part of culture has been translated into penetrating contemporary anthropological studies.

These structural studies, however, while not natural-historical in any vulgar sense, still repose in the natural historical tradition. The tradition of mathematical linguistics, drawing heavily upon the contributions to the philosophy of science of Carnap and the applications of positivistic logic and also of mathematical semigroup theory to linguistics by Chomsky, offers a third way to discuss language, and a third major theme in the construction of anthropological models of culture. This final way, insofar as it involves absolutely rigorous axiomatization of a deductive theory of culture, takes one as far as it is within the power of logical positivism to go. Whether this is far enough, or the highway to a blind alley, is a question of vital concern to the humanist.

In rejecting taxonomic linguistics, Chomsky and other generative grammarians have emphasized the importance of theorems about competence which cannot be tied, except by means of logic, to the directly observable objects which engross the interest of the natural historian of culture. This is not to say that linguistic propositions cannot be derived inductively from empirical data, only that two different traditions are at stake.

One must not suppose, however, that linguistic propositions that are not self-apparent can be explained in two ways, by relating them logically to propositions or axioms that *are* self-apparent, in a scientific deductive system, or by deriving them inductively from empirical data. For some linguistic propositions must be explained in a third way, in terms of social forces. A better understanding of these propositions depends upon information provided about writing by the sociology of knowledge.

3«

Ancient Writing

The sociology of knowledge, in contradicting the view that cultures are somehow prisons of sense and outlook, asks whether there are not some universals which cut across cultures, only dividing the rational from the irrational, not the Hopi or the ancient Egyptian from the sophisticates of modern urban society. The existence and nature of cultural universals have become a challenging problem for anthropologists; Kroeber and Kluckhohn on the ethnological side and Greenberg on the linguistic side have among others been particularly interested in this problem. We know that all people, regardless of cultural diversities, share sexual and alimentary dispositions, religious or doctrinal enthusiasms, some division of labor in recognition of the basic sexual division, and certain taboos. Incest is deemed uncouth universally, though some societies permit it in special circumstances. And no society exists in utter alienation from reliance upon language; we all share certain linguistic customs. Some of these customs involve writing. Is there evidence in ancient writing which would support the claims of the sociologists of knowledge? This question can be answered best against a background of the oldest known of scribal inventions.

Napoleon took Egypt from England for a few years, just as the eighteenth century was turning into the nineteenth. During Napoleon's stay in Egypt the Rosetta Stone was found there. This tablet is inscribed with Greek, demotic, and hieroglyphic writing. Knowing Greek, Champollion and others deciphered the Egyptian writing. Decipherment has permitted the partial and incomplete capture of ancient Egyptian history and culture. The better the Egyptologist, the fewer the claims he is willing to make about temporal frames of reference, but we will offer the following frame as a point of departure.

Neolithic Egyptians worshiped a mother goddess, but we are not aware of the language of worship. From around 4000 B.C. the language was Proto-Egyptian. After 3000 B.C. a Proto-Dynastic period began. For three or four hundred years prior to this period, the language had taken on the characteristics of Old Egyptian. Some historians count thirty-one dynasties. Dynasty I saw union of Upper and Lower Egypt under Memphis, and the first hieroglyphic writing. Dynasty II began about 2850 B.C., and was marked by disunion. The Old Kingdom saw the building of many pharaonic pyramids, especially opulent in Dynasties III, IV, and V. Dynasty III, from about 2780, was a time of reunion. Royalty prospered in Dynasty IV, from about 2600. About a hundred years later the period of the Middle Egyptian language began, along with the Vth Dynasty. In Dynasties V and VI, the power of the priests increased, and then feudalism appeared. The First Intermediate Period, which, with the Second Intermediate Period, may be put in the Middle Kingdom, began around 2250 B.C., and includes Dynasties VII, VIII, IX, and X. This was a time of political anarchy, followed by the establishment of two kingdoms, the stronger at Thebes. The Middle Kingdom proper includes Dynasties XI, XII, and XIII, and dates from around 2160 or 2050 until about 1788 B.C., when the Second Intermediate Period begins. The Middle Kingdom proper saw union again, under Thebes. In the Second Intermediate Period (Dynasties XIV, XV, XVI, XVII), Egypt suffered invasion and was dominated by Hyksos intruders. The New Kingdom was established under the XVIIIth Dynasty, a Theban dynasty, around 1580 B.C., about eighty years after the *terminus a quo* of the New Egyptian language. In this dynasty the Hyksos were driven away.

Priests of the high god Amun gained power and contended with monotheistic Akhenaton. The XIXth, XXth, and XXIst Dynasties saw the Empire wax and wane. Breasted observes a Decadence from the latter part of the XXth through the XXVth Dynasty, 1150 through 663 B.C. Then came the Renaissance of 663 through 525 B.C., in the XXVIth Dynasty.

From about 1320 B.C., Amun had been restored and the lore of Osiris prospered especially after the end of the fourteenth century B.C. The Exodus of the Israelites may have taken place in the thirteenth century under King Merneptah of the XIXth Dynasty. This was a century in which Egyptians and Hittites, Hittites speaking a language not unrelated to English (both having a common parent), contended for power.

Cambyses conquered Egypt for Persia from 527 B.C. The dynasty of Cambyses is counted as the XXVIIth. The language in this period is called Demotic. In 332 B.C., Alexander the Great, once a pupil of Aristotle's, took Egypt. After Alexander died, the rule of Egypt fell to Ptolemy and his heirs (332–30 B.C.). The period of Roman domination began with the suicide of Cleopatra and the triumph of Augustus Caesar. At this time, the Egyptian language was in its Coptic stage, a stage which endured for several centuries after Christ. Coptic writing used Greek letters and seven characters of Egyptian origin; this language and writing system was taken up by Christianity in Egypt, and the Scriptures were translated into Coptic.

Coptic fell into disuse after the Saracens began the Arabic conquest in A.D. 540, and other Arabic tribes spread in earnest after A.D. 641. Arabic dialects replaced Egyptian dialects in North African communities.

That much of Europe was conquered by notions of cultural relativism justifies this long account of Egyptian history. It was Hegel to whom many cultural relativists looked in arguing that some cultures, the more civilized, were better than others, the more primitive and archaic. In his work on aesthetics, Hegel propounds a theory that the course of art was and must be evolutionary. There are stages of history in art, one of which is the Egyptian. At that stage of history, and we can see now how enormous the Hegelian oversimplification of history was, art could not be anything but the austere, rather defective creation of an austere, rather defective people.

It has been argued that Hegel must be read between the lines, that he has a vulgar or popular teaching and also a hidden or secret teaching, and that those who repeat his popular teachings, his Egyptian stereotypes, for example, are propounding a form of decayed Hegelianism. Such an argument illustrates an inference based in the sociology of knowledge. It implies an assumption that there are prudent uses of nonsense, and strengthens the assumption that cultural universals will prove to be more significant in human history than cultural differences.

4 «

The Roots of Writing

The pictorial came before the calligraphic and probably both were early pressed into the service of the gods. Prehistoric cave paintings showing animals dear to the hunter are supposed to have had magical importance. The picture, just like the word that named the thing, was an act of capture, to the glory and salvation of the artist-priest. The Egyptians had their pictures too, covering walls of inner rooms in tomb and pyramid with scenes of cosmic importance. Hieroglyphic writing, dramatically pictorial, embodied myths and spells. The office of the scribe was holy; just as he, the scribe, wrote letters at the behest of the king, so the god Thoth, perhaps not more holy than his human counterpart, wrote letters at the behest of the supreme god.

His writing brought into service pictographs or pictograms, cues to utterance, stimuli to verbalization, as well as pictures, ideographs or ideograms that symbolized events and were not cues to utterance. His writing, in short, was pictographic but was augmented by ideographic determinatives. Eventually there were twenty-four symbols which represented an initial consonant and then the vocalic remainder of a syllable. We must conjecture about this vocalic remainder; the Egyptians did not separately represent their vowels. The twenty-four symbols were used syllabically, not alphabetically. They were used along with almost five hundred scribal characters. The writing of Thoth and his human counterparts was the property of the gods and their priests: there is no contradiction between the exclusive nature of the rulers of ancient Egypt and the esoteric nature of their sacerdotal records.

Older evidence of writing than the Egyptian has been found in certain Mesopotamian and Chinese logographic developments of line drawings. The drawings were simplified in the course of time often beyond recognition. Cursive attrition and the exigencies of cuneiform impression contributed to this simplification. The progression from a linear Mesopotamian star ✳ to a cuneiform sign and later is typical. (The line with a triangular head represents the impression of the tilted edge of a stylus in clay: one shows the impression as .) The Sumerians, having perhaps learned to write from Mesopotamian teachers lost to history, used writing to enhance the culture which they developed in southern Mesopotamia, a culture, strengthened by the centering of intellectual life in cities, which may have flourished as early as 5500 B.C. When Semitic rulers extended their dominions after 2600 B.C., Sumerian writing was brought into Babylonian life. The Babylonians spoke Akkadian, a Semitic language not relatable to Sumerian; but the cuneiform or wedge signs could be adapted to Babylonian purposes. Later, the Babylonians passed their knowledge on to the Hittites, whose language is relatable to those of the Indo-European group. The Sumerian scribe, confronted by the sign , might say [an] without thinking of a particular meaning for this syllable, or he might say *an* for 'sky,' or he might say *dingir* for 'god,' according to context. The Babylonian scribe used the sign for 'god' too, but he read it as the Akkadian word *ilum.* In writing, the sign for *ilum* was buttressed with an ideographic determinative *lum,* which he looked at but did not pronounce. The form of this word in the dative case, the case indicating 'to' or 'for,' in Akkadian is *ilim,* in Hittite is *karimni* 'for the god.' The Akkadian sign *lim* came to be used with the Sumerian sign *dingir* and a sign for the Hittite dative. The resultant form was pronounced *karimni* and signified 'for the god.' In some scholarly works, however, in classical scribal fashion, the Hittite word is represented as DINGIR-*LIM*-ni. That could be referred to as *igi* and could mean 'eye,' 'face,' 'first,' or 'opposite' to a Hittite scribe, depending upon context, merely confuses the issue. A more important observation is that writing in its most ancient metropolitan forms was difficult, perhaps intentionally difficult, to master and was a private vehicle beyond the reach of the unlettered multitudes.

To study the Hittite language, which has lost its natural speakers and was unknown to nineteenth-century pioneers in Indo-European linguistics, one must come in contact, then, with a variety of writing systems, some ancient, some modern. The Hittites had relations during their tenure as a military power with various tribes and nations, for example, trade relations or raid relations. It would be misleading to give precise dates for such relations. When we say that Columbus discovered America in 1492, our dating is precise and a matter of careful record. When we say that the Hittites entered Cappadocia about 2000 B.C., our dating is approximate and may be in error by one or two centuries. The dating of events in ancient history or prehistory generally involves considerable uncertainty, despite any explicit or implicit claims to the contrary. It is convenient, however, to take 2000 B.C. as a time of contact between invading Hittites and retreating Assyrians. The Hittites could have learned something of cuneiform writing from Assyrians. The Assyrians, like the Babylonians, spoke a Semitic language called Akkadian. The Assyrians left Babylonia as colonists some time around 2000 B.C., by some accounts, and were slavish emulators of Babylonian culture. The Babylonians, as we have said, were able to profit from Sumerian culture; part of the profit came through cuneiform writing which manifested itself historically as a series of inventions (in the technical, anthropological sense, which considers an imaginative collation of cultural traits or elements an invention) going back to the first Sumerian pictographs of about 3500 B.C. The Hittites raided the Babylonians about 1758 B.C. and could have learned to write from Babylonians then or earlier, rather than from Assyrians. The fortunes of the Babylonians waxed and waned at various times. Under Hammurabi, around 1720, Babylon reached a peak of power as it nestled close to the Euphrates. Egyptian warriors contended with Semites and Indo-Europeans at various times: Thothmes III (1501–1447), for example, brought war to the Hittites. The 1400's were a time of war also for the Assyrians, who attacked the Babylonians repeatedly; by 1400, however, Assyrian power was on the wane. The Hurrians were a power to contend with in the fifteenth and fourteenth centuries, but the Hittites ruined them at last. Hittites continued to fight with Egyptians, for example, Seti I (*c.* 1313–1292) and Ramses II (*c.* 1292–1225). The Hittites lived in city-states under kings who at first had been chosen by lords, and who ruled by right of human law rather than divine revelation. For this reason, perhaps, the Hittite empire gave way to Phrygian, Thracian, and Assyrian assaults around 1180 B.C. In the same century, however, around 1120, Tiglath-pileser I led his Assyrian warriors from the Tigris to the Euphrates and took Babylon.

Only by means of written records can one substantiate a history such has been sketched briefly above. How many cultures and languages and tribes have been intermixed in struggles for power in areas and at times which had no writing? How many ancient peoples vied with each other in the hundreds of centuries before the Sumerians created their pictographs of 3500 B.C.?

The theory of the monogenesis of writing gives a Mesopotamian inspiration to Egyptian writing, on the basis of which other forms of writing with which we are more familiar have developed. The culture of Mesopotamia reached Egypt in dramatic fashion around 3000 B.C. Egyptians came to use the potter's wheel, cylinder seals, new styles in brick and pottery, and Sumerian pictographic writing. It was a case of stimulus diffusion, perhaps, rather than slavish copying, a case of the imitation of basic principles of writing.

Of the priority of Akkadian cuneiform writing to Hittite cuneiform writing we can be certain, as well as the priority of Sumerian to both of these; of exact dates we cannot be certain. The Hittites wrote as early as 1600 B.C., or perhaps later. The Akkadians wrote as early as 2500 B.C. Proto-Sumerian pictographic writing began approximately 3100 B.C. From this, on the monogenetic theory, other systems developed, the Egyptian (from 3000 B.C.) and from it the Proto-Semitic syllabic writing (1700 B.C.), whence Phoenician syllabic writing (1500 B.C.) and the Phoenician alphabet (1000 B.C.). From this last came Old Hebrew writing (900 B.C.), Punic writing (400 B.C.), Aramaic writing (900 B.C.). Indic writing came from this source too. So did Greek writing (900 B.C.), whence Latin writing (600 B.C.). It is for the archaeologist to establish the claims of the monogenetic theory. Our chief interest at the moment is in the writing of the Egyptians.

The progression from Egyptian hieroglyphic realism by way of hieratic simplification to Phoenician syllabic signs is shown in Figure 1.

FIGURE 1 Hieroglyphic and other writing

The hieroglyphs were used in monumental writing from about 3000 B.C. The cursive hieratic script, from which demotic or more cursive writing evolved, was used from about 2500 B.C. for legal documents, letters, and other sorts of writing. On the first line of Figure 1, to the left (first column of three's), we see stages in the ancestry of our letter A. First we see Phoenician *'aleph* 'ox,' then its hieratic precursor, and finally the ancestral hieroglyph, an eagle. The B or crane line shows Phoenician *beth* 'house' and its ancestral forms. The C and G or throne line shows the ancestry of *gimel* 'camel.' The D or hand line shows the ancestry of *daleth* 'door.' The E or fretwork line shows the ancestry of *hē* 'window.' The F or horned asp line shows the ancestry of *waw* 'peg, hook'; our F, U, V, W, and Y all derive from *waw*. The hieroglyph of the H line is a sieve; of I parallels; of K a bowl; of L a lioness; of M an owl; of N a wavy water line; of P a shutter; of Q a knee; of R a mouth; of S a garden; of T a lasso; of X the back of a chair; of Z a duck. Scholars do not all agree that O, from Phoenician O *'ayin* 'eye' goes back to the hieroglyphic eye seen in the lower right corner of Figure 1. Nevertheless, this eye invites special mention.

This eye represented a real 'eye' in hieroglyphic writing, as well as such objects, events, properties, or relations as shared one or several criterial attributes which were agreed upon by the scribes as suitable metaphorical extensions of a real or fancied eye. Thus the eye could stand for the Mediterranean mother goddess, an apparently bizarre association which, however, makes perfect sense in terms of ancient Egyptian religious beliefs. The eye also represented the hot or angry sun. If the student has a dollar bill handy, he will find a green eye whose ancestral form is shown in Figure 1, shining atop a pyramid, in testimony to the profound antiquity of some of our American cultural roots.

As with the eye, so with the other hieroglyphs. The star at the extreme lower right, for example, meant 'star' but also was imbued with deific overtones, since dead kings or pharaohs (*cf. per* 'house,' *'o* 'great') were supposed to journey to the sky after death and become stars. The paraphernalia on the eye line, the palette, bowl of water, and reed, meant 'scribe's equipment' or 'scribe' or 'what a scribe does.' The Egyptian vowels are not recorded, and some scholars do not write them in transliteration: hence *zš* serves for this hieroglyph, whose reference can be nominal or verbal, 'writer' or 'to write.' Lower Egypt, near the Mediterranean, is rich in papyrus plants. The five papyrus stalks of Figure 1, next to the eye, stood for Lower Egypt. (Upper Egypt is represented by a plant of unknown species with five branches.) Some hieroglyphs were cues to pronunciation and others were not. The hieroglyph might prompt utterance of a meaningful word or of a syllable in such a word, as with Sumerian *an* 'sky,' pronounced [an]. The art of reading was complicated by multiple possibilities of interpretation as well as by the fact that writing could be horizontal and vertical. Some scribes helped the reader by aiming the heads of birds, asps, and other creatures at the starting-point for the reader's eyes.

Above the eye in Figure 1 are two lines of letters which illustrate correspondences of Greek, Hebrew, Arabic, Brāhma, and more recent Sanskrit forms. The alpha line shows forms pronounced [a]. The next line shows forms pronounced [ta].

An example of a hieroglyphic text is given below. This text is from a stela, a kind of gravestone. It contains praise of Osiris:

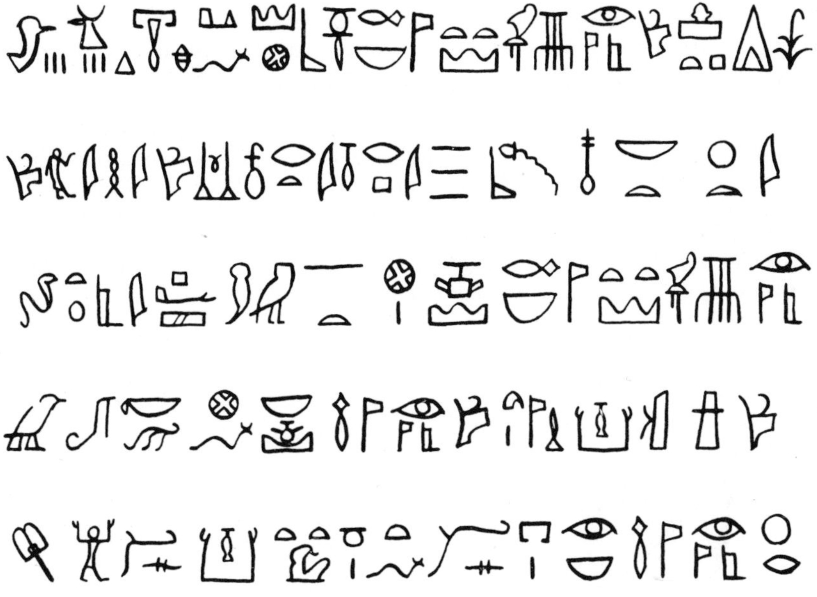

FIGURE 2 Writing from the Stela of Netempeashese

> An offering which the king gives to Osiris presiding over the West, the great god, the lord of Abydos, that he may give a mortuary offering of beer and bread, oxen and geese, everything good and pure, wine, milk, and clothing to the musician of Osiris presiding over the West, the great god, the lord of Abydos, Netempeashese [=Sweet is the Call of Isis], deceased, son of the *ymy-yz,* the *ḥzk*-priest, the high priest of Osiris the great god, the lord of Abydos, Fektihor [=Whose Head is Shaved for Horus], deceased, worthy in the presence of Osiris the great god, offspring of the house mistress Nesitefnut [=She Who Belongs to Tefnut] and the *ḥzk*-priest Nesikashuti [=He Who Belongs to the Lofty of Plumes].

This text reminds us that to the extent that we are ignorant of the context of a communication, of the surrounding roles and goals, expectations and pressures, to that extent are we outsiders, alien to the culture in question. Our hypotheses about ancient cultures and our reading of ancient writing are based upon our own experiences and cultural conventions. In the midst of so much praise of Osiris, we find a scribal error, unrectified, contrary to the dictates of the ancient religion.* Was this a blunder, or a sign of heresy, ironic commentary on the scribal occupation? Behind this question lies the eternal human capacity for dissent in the face of power, and the enduring, transcultural contrast between vulgarity and wisdom.

*To win the favor of three deities, a deified pharaoh and Onuris-Re and Horus, Huerhetef ordered the erection of a round-topped limestone votive stela. Huerhetef's scribe was expected to decorate the stela with 'Live the good god, the Lord of the Two Lands, Menkheperre, given life forever,' 'Utterance by Onuris-Re, lord of the sky,' and 'Utterance by Horus the son of Osiris.' The scribe wrote the word 'Utterance' the second time facing in the wrong direction. Then he erased it. Then he wrote 'By Horus the son of Osiris,' with 'By' in place of 'Utterance.'

5 «

Cultural Relativism

Two questions invite the attention of all serious students of language and culture. First, what is universal in all of human experience regardless of languages? And second, what is unique in the special human experiences of particular tribal societies by virtue of their languages?

In suggesting that there might be private aspects to ancient Egyptian writing, one touches upon the first question. It was not simply lack of historical perspective which led Hegel to posit various stages of art, the most primitive being an architectural stage which went best with the most primitive minds, the next a stage of sculpture whose earliest exemplars, turning out expressionless stereotypes, were the ancient Egyptians. Or perhaps it would be better to say that having historical perspective, Hegel knew that primitive types of culture are changeable rather than stable, and yet he posited a myth to the contrary. This view rests on the assumption that there might be private as well as public aspects to Hegel's writings, just as with those of the ancient Egyptians.

The question of esoteric writing amongst primitive peoples did not escape the attention of Franz Boas, the godfather of American anthropology. He took the position that the esoteric teachings as well as the exoteric or popular doctrines of American tribal societies existed in a mutual and inextricable interrelation, and that esoteric teachings arose in attempts to systematize heterogeneous beliefs of the tribe. Such teachings, he held, are marked inevitably by internal contradictions and inconsistencies. Boas says, 'In such cases the contradiction between the general scheme and special ideas often escapes entirely the notice of the native philosophers.' It is easy to understand the view that esoteric teaching must be understood against a background of ethnically more general exoteric doctrine, but not so easy to admit contradictions as blemishes of the best of literate thought.

hat is a contradiction in one context may not be in another. To rstand writing or for that matter the product of an oral tradition, one must understand it as the author or composer understood it. One must examine the context as well as the content. Many writers of various times and cultures have resorted to ambiguous remarks to point the way to esoteric doctrines, particularly political ones, while prudently expressing orthodox views. Some writers have larded orthodox declarations of the most forceful sort with ambiguous remarks, blunders, contradictions, and other clues that can be interpreted by thoughtful independent readers as veiled criticism.

The philosopher Mêng-tzŭ (Mencius) was a contemporary of Aristotle. Mêng-tzŭ asks:

> Is the arrow maker less benevolent than the maker of armor for defense? And yet, the arrow maker's only fear is lest men should not be hurt, and the armor maker's only fear is lest men should be hurt. So it is with the priest and the coffin maker. The choice of a 'profession' is, therefore, a demand for great caution.

For 'profession' one might as well read 'doctrine' in the Chinese text. Was Mêng-tzŭ for the priests or against them? Shall we equate the priest with the arrow-maker, who wants men to be pierced and killed, and the coffin-maker with the maker of armor, who wants men to be well shielded? Or is it the other way round, with the priest bound to keep men alive and unhurt, and the maker of coffins anxious for men to go on dying and contributing to his business and success? If there is universal need for the wise man to be prudent, there may be some substance in a search, here and elsewhere, for esoteric meanings.

Before returning to this problem, let us consider the second question. Some writers, following Wilhelm von Humboldt (who, in the early years of the nineteenth century, argued that a language veils the world for its speakers*), deal in ill-considered stereotypes and would find it easier to say what they know about primitive tribes than how they know it.

A rash of American linguists of the nineteenth century—undeterred by the midcentury warning of the eminent statesman Albert Gallatin, who concerned himself with the classification of American languages after his political career was behind him—thought it fair to rank

*See H. Steinthal, *Die sprachphilosophischen Werke Wilhelm's von Humboldt* (1884).

tribes on the basis of whether the language in question had a copula. Gatschet used aesthetic judgments, for example, as well as the copulative criterion, in making negative judgments about tribes of Oregon, where he had done some field work. Powell, head of the Bureau of Ethnology of the Smithsonian Institution (where Gatschet worked), propagated similar sorry notions of cultural relativism.

Contemporary writers also present questionable views about tribesmen. One of these, for example, creates a primitive myth-making mentality which seems a caricature of his own. For him, the primitive mind thinks only subjective thoughts about concrete matters, thoughts so colored with emotions that abstract reasoning and sober objectivity are impossible. Language for such a primitive mind is a vehicle of daily intercourse, not a vehicle of reasoning, problem solving, or scientific thought. His notions of reality are mythical and timeless. Time, for modern civilized man, is linear, with moments strung one after the other along a continuum without beginning or end. Time, for the primitive, is cyclic, durative, renewable. In its periodic aspect, time is timeless, eternal. If asked for proof of this primitive experience of time, the author of this view perhaps would refer us to the writings of Whorf, whose linguistically supported thoughts on Hopi time are suspiciously like his own.

Whorf came to the study of American Indians from the study of the secrets of the Book of Books, which he hoped to unlock with a linguistic key. As a chemical engineer employed by a fire insurance company in Hartford, he traveled to Yale to undertake formal linguistic studies, to tool the key which the lock still resisted. He sat at the feet of Edward Sapir, a brilliant specialist in American Indian languages, one who had studied anthropology with Boas at Columbia and languages of the Pacific Coast, the Southwest of the United States, and Canada at first hand for several decades. Sapir steadied Whorf's hand, but not enough. It was Sapir's curious gift to hint at profound truths affecing the basic questions of language and culture while at the same time insinuating possibilities too easily misunderstood.

Here is a famous observation of Sapir's which is sound as long as it is not misunderstood:

> Though language is not ordinarily thought of as of essential interest to the students of social science, it powerfully conditions all our thinking about social problems and processes. Human beings do not

> live in the objective world alone, nor alone in the world of social activity as ordinarily understood, but are very much at the mercy of the particular language which has become the medium of expression for their society. It is quite an illusion to imagine that one adjusts to reality essentially without the use of language and that language is merely an incidental means of solving specific problems of communication or reflection. The fact of the matter is that the 'real world' is to a large extent unconsciously built up on the language habits of the group. No two languages are ever sufficiently similar to be considered as representing the same social reality. The worlds in which different societies live are distinct worlds, not merely the same world with different labels attached.

Sapir's 'merely' leaves room for referential equivalents such as the numerals used in scientific calculations. But it is quite true that each culture has its own associations and symbols. There is evidence, for example, in psycholinguistic experimentation with colors, to support the view of referential or associational relativity which Sapir derived from Durkheim and social psychologists before Durkheim.

To take a single example of associational relativity, some Germans regard the *Weihnachtsbaum* as an apparition, an object which mysteriously appears for Christmas and just as mysteriously disappears on January 6. The American associations for 'Christmas tree' may involve decorations, gifts, or the smell of pine needles, but not the mystical aura of the *Weihnachtsbaum.* To translate the German word with the English phrase is to confirm the aphorism, 'Translator, traitor.'

In referential relativity we find the best evidence of hope that some day scientists will be able extensively to document the existence of special human experiences from culture to culture. Whether such special human experiences powerfully affect cognition or problem solving is another question for which only negative answers have been provided so far by the best of psychologists.

Whorf posed two questions that are not entirely alien to those which open this discussion. First, 'Are our own concepts of "time," "space," and "matter" given in substantially the same form by experience to all men, or are they in part conditioned by the structure of particular languages?' And second, 'Are there traceable affinities between (a) cultural and behavioral norms and (b) large-scale linguistic patterns?' In answering these questions, Whorf claimed that such notions as 'time' or 'matter' are given by experience to men of different languages in different ways, ways dependent upon the 'nature of the language.' This 'nature' concerns not simple systems like tense or nouns taken alone. It concerns fashions of speaking, systematically integrated. It concerns vocabulary, morphology, syntax, and various other vocal factors.

Voegelin in *Hopi Domains* has shown that Whorf's Hopi data, upon which his claims about the relativity of concepts as a function of fashions of speaking largely rest, were misleading and imperfectly understood, partly because Whorf's Hopi informant was imaginative, that Hopis do in fact have words for temporal units (missed by Whorf), and that Whorf's conclusions from unreliable data may be called to question. Whorf attempted to develop some suggestive points in Sapir's work, but side-stepped the substance of Sapir's message.

In answering the second question, Whorf said, 'There are connections but not correlations or diagnostic correspondences between cultural norms and linguistic patterns.' Anthropologists sometimes echo Whorf's claim that there are connections and sometimes they go further, rejecting Whorf's view that causal correlations cannot be established. In either case, they are operating with undefined terms, a fact which seems to cause little embarrassment.

The Navaho Indians of the Southwest, neighbors of the Hopis, figure in a rejection of Whorf's second view. Hoijer, hoping to find a diagnostic connection between cultural norms of the Navahos and their linguistic patterns, has pointed out that culturally the Navaho is relentlessly concerned with motionful activity. He is always strikingly attentive to the nature and quality of actions and motions of objects. The Navaho language is action-happy too. The verbal system forces a speaker to consider an action in various ways: action in progress, for example, or action at an instant, action now and again (consider a dog having puppies), past action, action delayed until some time in the future, future action on the brink of happening. There is even a category of verb, the neuter, which indicates 'the withdrawal of motion.'

In reporting Navaho parallels of language and culture, Hoijer says:

> Navaho verb categories center very largely about the reporting of events, or better, 'eventings.' These eventings are divided into neuters, eventings solidified, as it were, into states of being by virtue of the

> withdrawal of motion. . . . Parallels to this semantic theme [of motion] may be found in almost every aspect of Navaho culture taken as a whole.

Whether this interesting parallelism, which deserves further careful study, amounts to a diagnostic correlation depends, of course, on one's interpretation of Whorf's term.

Let us return now to the first question, that of universal human experience. Here lies part of the answer to the question of linguistic relativity. Is there a sense in which the Navaho headman and, let us say, a sociologist of knowledge immersed in the philosophy of Kant are akin? Can both share experiences, and not simply biological experiences but intellectual ones, that have to do with universal human wisdom? Perhaps we can begin the answer to this question with an account of Kant's view of reality.

Kant's two kinds of reality are phenomenal, based on what we see, and noumenal, based on what we fail to see. And what we see must be seen in Time and Space. The human mind creates its reality when it imposes such categories as Time and Space on its phenomenal experience, or such other categories as Substance, Accident, and Causality, catalysts, as it were, of objects, properties, and relations. And the way to a clear absolute knowledge of the world for Kant is through dispassionate reasonable examination of phenomenal experience, not through fruitless sallies into noumenal speculations.

We know that bees see ultraviolet flowers and dogs hear ultrasonic waves of sound, that the spectrum of color extends away from our human vision just as the range of sound goes beyond our human hearing. We can infer from the reactions of bees and dogs that some of their experiences are real but beyond us. But that reality beyond any animal experience, what of that? We have to believe it exists, to avoid the solipsistic claim that the world we know by experience is known because of the nature of the human mind. This world beyond the world is a world of things-in-themselves, a world of what there is, the hidden reality, unknown but indubitable, that the mind transfigures in its acts of apprehension.

The central contradiction which Kant built into his philosophy, his description of a secret reality, of things-in-themselves which cannot be described or even be said to exist, has been taken by some philosophers as a fault. Not every blunder, however, is read by the sociologist of knowledge as unintentional, and it may be asked whether Kant blundered on purpose. If he wished to indulge in Socratic impudence, to hint at a transcultural reality in the face of vulgar apprehensions, would he not be disposed to say that denumerable unknowable entities of the noumenal world caused the content of experience to be what it is? This is just what he did, claiming first that the categories of Plurality and Causality—along with ten other categories which form the structure of experience—could apply only to spatiotemporal phenomena. And if Kant was serious in a disguised fashion, would there not be room in Kantian exegesis for the serious perpetuation of misunderstood blunders?

That our language has sentences of the form, '*X* is *Y*,' where proper names, actors, may be substituted for *X*, led Kant to suppose that the mind cannot avoid attention to individuals and properties, governed, therefore, by the categories of Substance and Accident. Cassirer extended Kantian explorations into the realm of language, developing this and other positions that Kant had half seriously defended, and some of Cassirer's observations, perhaps mixed with the linguistic speculations of Lord Russell, have filtered down in popularized form into the contributions of I. A. Richards and other literary critics, some to be satirized by Orwell in *1984*. It is this watering down of the subtleties of Kantian philosophy which accounts in part for speculations among modern linguistically minded popularizers of the nature of language and its influence on thought and the cognition of reality.

If Whorf took from Whitehead much of his inspiration in addressing questions of Time and Space, as Voegelin has indicated, and if he was led away from sorrier notions of cultural relativism by the teachings of Boas and Sapir, we can still discern in the Whorfean approach something of the great Victorian popularity of the decadent part of Kantian philosophy. What links the Navaho headman and the German philosopher across time and culture, it might be insisted, can be discovered more in Socratic temperament where it exists, in an awareness of the human condition, than in the most intricate of intellectual perambulations.

II

Theories

Une langue philosophique, bon Dieu! qu'est-ce qu'une langue philosophique? La Nature a fait les langues comme elle a fait les fleurs et les fruits, en donnant à l'homme et aux plantes le pouvoir et les moyens de les produire. . . . Et nous, faibles mortels, nous voudrions surpasser les ouvrages de la nature et de l'Etre suprême! Une langue philosophique!

—PETER DUPONCEAU,

Mémoire sur le système grammatical des langues de quelques nations indiennes de l'Amérique du Nord (1838).

Science and Behavioral Models

Just as there are two central questions for serious students of language and culture, so there are two basic approaches to the data which such students wish to characterize. These approaches are, simply, the scientific and the unscientific. The latter may bring in supposed theories, classifications of all sorts, intuitive insights, dogmatic beliefs, and a variety of intellectual perambulations. The former, however, must bring in real theories and also an attitude which offers truth conditionally, not all at once but by successive approximations.

Paradoxically, a scientific statement can be disproved. It is so carefully framed that, if mistaken, it can be dismissed in favor of one more accurate, more in accord with the facts. Not all statements about language as a vehicle of or from culture are scientific. Some are not impeachable. There is no way to test them. Given the proper metaphysical basis, any statement can be true and beyond challenge, beyond test. It becomes a fact raised to the power of pugnacity.

Science confronts us, therefore, with a distressing dilemma. It deals with facts in the real world, the phenomenal world, in less than satisfactory fashion from the point of view of the humanist imbued with awareness of the world's wealth and variety. It narrows vision, ignores complications, and works for control of limited funds of data. The picture with which the scientist replaces the world is a formalization. But that picture is the best that can be obtained, for the data in question, without abdication of intellectual dignity.

A scientific theory of culture (which would include language as part of culture) must have certain formal properties. It must be tied to and dependent upon real facts. Given undefined terms or primitives *A*, *B*, and *C*, these must be co-ordinated by a set of co-ordinating definitions with real facts. The primitives of the theory must be related by axioms. (An axiom is an unproved relational statement.) There must be rules of inference which apply to primitives and axioms to generate theorems, higher-order relational statements sometimes called hypotheses. The truth of the axioms depends upon the justice of the rules of inference and the co-ordinating definitions. The beating heart of a theory is in its application, its truthfulness to reality. In terms of such requirements, no theory comprehending all of learned sign behavior, that is, all of culture, may at present be deemed to be scientific.

The study of languages, it should be noted, has brought formalization into the social sciences. A language, as an exemplar of a universal social institution, may be characterized by a formal theory. Chomsky and others at M.I.T. have made notable contributions in this direction. Just as the accomplishments of structural linguists in past decades moved anthropologists to sharpen their techniques for the collection and assessment of cultural data—but yet within a taxonomic or natural history tradition, despite etic-emic sophistication—so in the present decade we can predict that anthropologists will construct formal theories of culture, perhaps not at first with the hope of comprehending all of human sign behavior, but with the hope of applying abstract structures or theories by means of co-ordinating definitions to limited areas of experience, following the lead in studying other institutions that linguists have provided in the most scientific study of languages.

The term 'theory' has been used by some in the loose sense of 'model.' Part of our concern in this text will be with models, ways of assembling or presenting data. The academic study of culture has a history rich in models, but spare in true theories. The true theories can scarcely be understood unless presented, as we propose to present them, in the context of the interesting but largely outmoded models which have preceded them.

One of the most comprehensive of models is the Peircean. Charles Sanders Peirce (1839–1914) worked in physics, mathematics, and logic. He taught at Johns Hopkins and Harvard. He made signal contributions to pragmatism, to the doctrine—so powerful a stimulant to William James, Josiah Royce, and John Dewey—that the meaning of an idea is the story of its consequences or series of results. For Peirce, all necessary reasoning is mathematical, and no mathematical reasoning is not diagrammatic. The reasoning, however, is not concerned with the diagram itself, but with the diagram as an icon or image of more general observations. The diagram is iconic of a hypothetical state of things, whose truth is at issue. It represents general relations by analogous visible relations.

In *Existential Graphs,* Peirce considers a symbol as a species of sign. An icon is another, and an index a third species of sign. (In the special language which he favored, the term 'representamen' is used for sign.) An icon is an image of what exists in consciousness, the sign itself or the object that excites the image. It is an appearance based on past experience. 'A pure icon can convey no positive or factual information; for it affords no assurance that there is any such thing in nature. But it is of the utmost value for enabling its interpreter to study what would be the character of such an object in case any such did exist.'

An index is a real-thing sign, tied to an object in present experience, a tag, for example, or a reassurance. A special kind of index, because it has an icon incorporated into it, is a photograph.

A symbol is a sign that one is disposed by rule or habituation to tie to its target. Symbols have their replicas in written words, and their beings in the satisfaction of certain conditions. Every sign which depends on conventions, be it word, sentence, book, or other representamen, is a symbol. A symbol is an active law. And that law may be purely symbolic, with no iconic or indicative force (consider the words *and, or, of*), or with iconic force, a summoning up of imagery (consider *dog, cat, pane, pain*), or with indicative force, a summoning up of ropes, threads, or reins, as it were (*that, this, I, you, which, here, now, yonder*). In neat and logical fashion, Peirce observes:

> The value of an icon consists in its exhibiting the features of a state of things regarded as if it were purely imaginary. The value of an index is that it assures us of positive fact. The value of a symbol is that it serves to make thought and conduct rational and enables us to predict the future.

Just as Kant supposed that sallies out of the phenomenal world are fruitless, so Peirce supposed that signs alone are the subject of cognition. It is nonsense to discuss the uncognizable, the world beyond the universe of signs.

In developing some aspects of Peircean philosophy, Charles Morris has focused attention upon three ranges of experience: the syntactic, the semantic, and the pragmatic. The first range deals with signs in relation to signs, the second with signs in relation to things signified, and the third with signs in relation to their users. The development of a true theory of culture along Peircean lines, that is, the formalization of the Peircean model, is presently under way at the University of Texas. Pendergraft's work is of key importance in this connection.

While some models lead towards true theories, others simply function as icons of experience. To illustrate this observation, let us consider some diagrams. The first suggests that linguistic data implicate three components of language: expression, content, and vocabulary. Phonemes and morphemes are important forms of expression; the student of expression studies the patterns of such basic units. The key forms of content are basic semantic units; the student of content studies patterns of semantic units. And the student of vocabulary studies interrelations of expression and content.

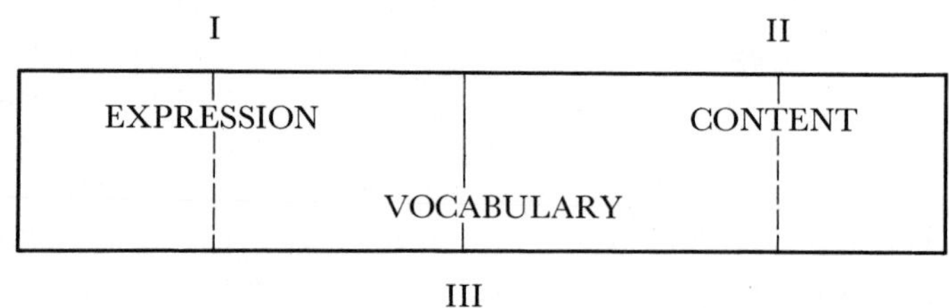

FIGURE 3 A tripartite model

This model includes or overlaps with others. Let us consider by way of illustration the word *father.* This word has its place in the vocabulary of the English language. On the expression side, we have a morpheme {*father*} in the class of nouns. The morpheme is represented by a sequence of phonemes. On the content side, morphemes and phonemes are not our concern. Our concern is with semantics.

One model of semantic analysis uses Boolean algebra and defines kinsmen in terms of basic semantic components. How this model works will be clear after a few remarks on common means of mapping relationships. Starting with ego as the center of consciousness we can see how ego relates to consanguineal or blood relatives and affinal or marital relatives in Figure 4 (a), and to agnatic kinsmen, consanguin-

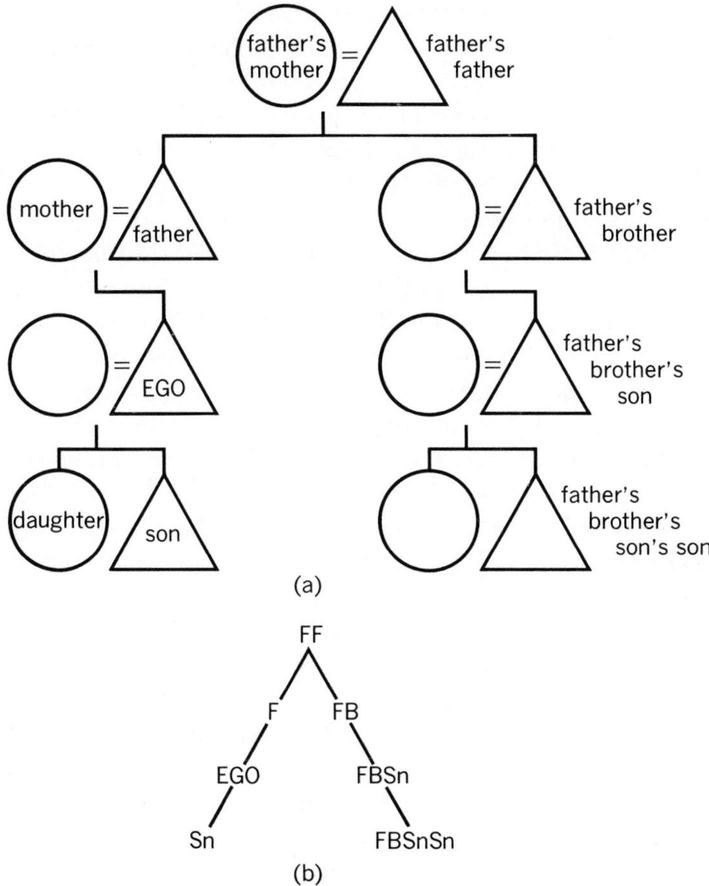

FIGURE 4 Kinship diagrams

eals whose relationship to ego is traced entirely through males, in Figure 4 (b). (Ego is taken as a male.)

Basic dimensions for distinguishing kinsmen include sex of kinsman; symbols are ♂ for male, ♀ for female. It is not enough to say that father is a male; this component fails to distinguish him from uncle, brother, son, grandfather. The symbol represents the class of all of ego's male kinsmen. Within that class there is another, men of the first ascending generation. Suppose we use G for generation, with a superscript numeral to indicate the proper level: G^0 indicates ego's own generation, G^1 indicates the first ascending generation (father, mother, father's brother, father's brother's wife, and so on); G^2 indicates the second ascending generation; G^{-1} indicates the first descending generation; and so it goes. Can one represent father with the formula $♂ \cdot G^1$? (The formula says, 'The class of male kinsmen, restricted to those of the first ascending generation.') No, the formula does not exclude father's brother. Would it help to suppose that one of our basic distinguishing dimensions is 'agnatic generation,' whereby we could isolate generation categories as subclasses within the class of agnatic kinsmen? Let $A^1 = A \cdot G^1$, indicating the class of agnatic kinsmen of the first ascending generation. Then is 'father' fairly represented by the formula $♂ \cdot A^1$? Perhaps for some other language, but not English.

If we have made a good start with $♂ \cdot G^1$, we need a measure which will show a single step or link between ego and father. Let $D =$ absolute genealogical distance, the number of links between ego and the kinsman in question. Does any kinsman other than father fall into the class symbolized by D^1, a distance of one? Yes. That is why the formula for father must have the first two components first: $♂ \cdot \mathrm{G}^1 \cdot \mathrm{D}^1$. (The finished formula says, 'The class of male consanguineal kinsmen, limited to those of the first ascending generation, and further limited to those whose absolute genealogical distance from ego is one link.')

Componential analysis applies, of course, to other than English data. Suppose that an ethnographer working with the Tequistlatec of Mexico collects a list of kinship terms for all the people in an informant's family, exhausting the informant's experience, memory, and predictions. For ego's father the ethnographer records *ƚaɔáy*. Eventually he discovers that this term applies also to father's father and other kinsmen. By eliminating repetitions, the ethnographer arrives at classes based on native terminology. Thus he finds that *ƚaɔáy* refers to a class of kinsmen including ego's father, ego's father's father, and others. Then he identifies the distinctive semantic components of each kin-class. For an unmarried ego he identifies criterial components of *ƚaɔáy* as sex of kinsman (male, ♂), generation (any ascending generation, G^+), and collateral distance (the number of links from ego to common ancestor or from kinsman to common ancestor, whichever is smaller, here of zero degree, C^0). The Boolean algebraic formula $♂ \cdot G^+ \cdot C^0$ then is used to represent the distinctive features of the class referred to by the sign *ƚaɔáy*. Any male consanguineal kinsman of the first or higher ascending generation, who has a collateral distance from ego of zero, ego calls *łaɔáy*.

Using labels suggested by Morris, a Tequistlatec Indian's father is a denotatum of the sign *łaɔáy* when ego uses the sign. He uses *łaɔáy* to denote his father. Each denotatum belongs to a class whose description is called the designatum of the sign. The designatum involves a full range of possibilities, all cases designated by the language-sign. Thus *łaɔáy* designates ego's father, his father's father, his father's father's father, and others, and *łaɔáy* is or may be any one of these. The defining features of the designatum are the significatum of the sign, in our simplified case, ♂ $\cdot G^{+} \cdot C^{0}$.

Let us now consider two more models, shown in Figure 5. Six

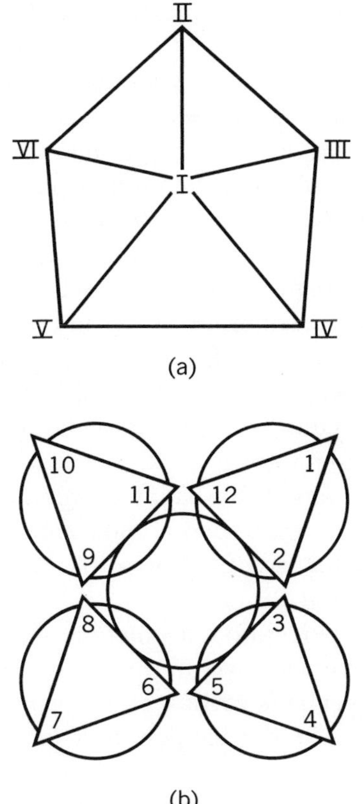

FIGURE 5 Communicational models

communicative functions are represented in diagram (a). These are (I) a source, the speaker or addresser; (II) a code, discrete elements which can be manipulated in various patterns, relatively free of context; (III) a message, composed of elements of the code by the source; (IV) a designation, the context for the message, the realm of open and guarded language; (V) a channel, the contact medium for the sound waves carrying the message; and (VI) a destination, the hearer or addressee whose reactions are expected.

Twelve variables are represented in diagram (b), based on Doob's theory in *Communication in Africa.* Doob, as a psychologist, is interested in these aspects of communication:

(1) the communicator, a teacher let us say;

(2) his goals, say to teach that 2 + 2 = 4, and to show wisdom;

(3) his basic media of communication, say his words and gestures aimed at attaining his goals;

(4) his extending media, when his presence is indirect, say a tape recording of him saying "2 + 2 = 4" played by an assistant;

(5) his spatiotemporal locus, his situation in time and space, say in a noisy classroom by a railroad station at a place and time when it is difficult to hear him saying that 2 + 2 = 4;

(6) restrictions upon his expression, a function of contextual, situational, or group regulations (in Orwell's *1984,* 2 + 2 = 5 and 2 + 2 = 4 is heresy, a communication not to be made publicly);

(7) the communication itself, a message whose contents elicit a response, and can be analyzed rigorously, context aside for the moment (2 + 2 = 4, context aside and social overtones gone, is said to be universally translatable);

(8) the addressee's mood, his frame of mind, emotional states, or dispositions to respond, at the time of the communication (2 + 2 = 4 has smaller effect on Johnny if tomorrow is Thanksgiving than if he expects a test tomorrow);

(9) the addressee's perception, a function of attributes of the communication and motives or drives of the respondent, as when Johnny, distracted from the teacher's writing of 2 + 2 = 4 on the board, sees a winter owl flapping at the window and fails to comprehend the teacher's message;

(10) the addressee's reactions, once he has comprehended or apprehended the communication, in terms of what Socrates in the

Philebus calls pleasure and pain, the presumption being that 2 + 2 = 4 brings pleasure to the young student with average predispositions and response chains, before he realizes how complicated mathematics can be;

(11) changes in the addressee, which may be of little value or of enormous value in affecting his actions, whether at once or after a time; and

(12) feedback, informative clues, such as Johnny's being unable to answer the question, 'What is 2 + 2?' This inability may come in clearly and lead to revision of variables, or it may not come in at all. The triangulation of variables in this model is a function of intimacy of connection. Doob's formulation is tentative and subject to revision.

As our review of models indicates, different models serve different purposes. It is possible to rank models or arrays of data so that one can be seen as better than another: the touchstone is command of data. One analytic model is better, more logical, less mythological, than another, if it is more iconic, more indicative, more symbolic of empirical facts than a rival.

The best models rest on the greatest amount of data. Before a student can speak responsibly of language and culture or models in this field, he must control much more data than can be collected in a summer season or a room full of musty books. When Bloomfield said that the only useful generalizations are inductive, he was stressing the importance of data as a corrective of imperfect models. With open petulance at vulgarized models, he reminded men that those models drift least which have firm empirical anchors.

7 «

The Meanings of Meaning

If Bloomfield was impatient with vulgarity, Wittgenstein was impatient with such schemata for analysis of meaning as were touched upon in the last section. He took a Socratic stance in his later days, and, in my view, has to be read between the lines. It is accurate, however, to take at face value his urging that one should tease out the material meaning, undiverted by side issues.

An opposing argument might run: Who will do the teasing? Are there no advantages in limiting the range of phenomena to be inspected? Does one not thereby avoid the Scylla of reification and the Charybdis of relativism? The reificational confusion of words and their referents is a widespread token of monolingual culture bondage if not of charismatic policy. The practice of relativistically condoning indeterminacy of explanatory solutions to problems is also widespread. And another kind of relativism, built on dogmatic and thoughtless assertions about the customs of others, presents stereotypes where one would be happier with qualifications and restrictions as seasoning for generalizations.

A rejoinder to this argument might be based upon the sociological analysis of meaning. The sociology of knowledge forces the student to confront not only statements which purport to be scientific, but also the motives and social orientations of those who make them. It is too simple to view science as independent of social orientations. The direction of research and the nature of models reflect the milieu of the scientist. Leaps and discontinuities in nature became a preoccupation of scientists once differential and integral calculus, quantitative and qualitative chemistry, electromagnetic theory, and physical anthropology had brought process and growth to science. And once Darwin's hypotheses of biological evolution had been popularized, scientists concentrated on the implications of structural systems in the process of gradual transformation. Pragmatists or operationalists, of whom Peirce was a giant, identified man's progress with his experience operating in the service of his needs.

The achievements of Newton and Locke prompted men toward optimism about an age of enlightenment and a universe free of mystery, freed by mathematical physics and *tabula rasa* psychology, but later developments such as the non-Euclidean geometries of Lobatchevski and Riemann or the theories of relativity set forth by Einstein have prompted some thinkers to consider theirs an austere and gloomy age, one fit for quantitative as opposed to qualitative studies. Some of the latter are labeled positivists, or conventionalists (Poincaré), or phenomenalists (Ayer), or logical atomists (Russell); and many, Russell and Wittgenstein excepted, avoid questions about the nature and relation of things; and most turn away from the study of change in nature and society, seeking to use logic and mathematics divorced from sensations and the use of common sense.

The danger of common sense lies in the claim that all men have it. It is only common sense to be dismayed, a student might say, by the disagreements of linguists about such basic units as phonemes and morphemes, syntactic structures or transformations, or to be dismayed by the observation that scientific statements are not received truths impervious to challenge. This selfsame common sense can reject reason after giving it a try, like the younger Unamuno; it can turn to decadent transcendental doctrines, as the older Unamuno did, and seek truth in intuitions and intimations. It can justify aimless eclecticism.

Einstein rejected common sense on the one hand and classical physics on the other. Positing invariance, he negated orientation as absolute. He resorted to an aesthetic notion, that of invariance: a snowflake exhibits invariance with respect to rotations by sixty degrees and at least part of its beauty lies in this sixfold symmetry.

Natural laws written mathematically permit of transformational rewriting; substitutions for equational variables do not change the invariant forms of the laws. The causal laws of physics, for example, are invariant with respect to temporal and spatial displacements. When one of two frames of reference moves with constant velocity respecting the other, they form an inertial system. Suppose now that we wish to transform a law of nature, say the law of light propagation, from one inertial system to another. Would we discover that the law is invariant against transformations? Devotion to tabulations in the Baconian tradition would mislead us here. We would suppose with the classical physicists that certain changes in the variables were needed, Galilean transformations permitting passage to a new frame of reference. But Einstein followed an aesthetic lead and imaginative insights, turning away from old classifications and tables of comparison.

Both the proposition that one's frame of reference is crucial in an investigation of meaning, and the suggestions made by contemporary students of language and culture that their models are marked by symmetry, simplicity, and elegance are to be understood as responses, in part, to Einstein's contributions to the study of the universe. It is not enough, however, in analyzing meaning, to advertise the relativity of frames of reference. Language is an infinitely nuanced instrument for socialization and the preservation of cultural inventions. The individual, in the process of learning his roles and statuses and achieving some measure of control over the inventions in his environment, finds definition for his important life situations; but his cultural environment sometimes handicaps him. It supplies him with themes, propositions which he has learned to support unthinkingly. He may repeat unperceptive but damning criticism which he has read or heard from authorities. He may adhere to one or another fashion of scientific theorizing and may be persuaded that what is adequate in one model is wild presumption in another. He may be required by canons of faith to accept certain truths *a priori,* not to be challenged. He may be like the lover of a fine old Vermeer who, one moment, reveres it as a masterpiece, and later, after discovering that it is an incredibly good forgery, despises it as garbage.

Thematic resistance is accompanied generally by interactional resistance. The latter sometimes stems from the relatively low social status of the innovator, as compared with that of accepted and authoritative professionals. Sometimes specialists are annoyed at the pretentious theorizing of an outsider, a maverick, who then suffers from what Robert Graves has called the scholarly disease of 'academic xenophobia.' The specialists suffer from the disease, but the innovator, accused of fathering a naïve or poetic rather than a scientific theory, also suffers as a victim. In other countries, younger scientists also suffer from the conservative or inept policies of learned societies or journals, or the so-called 'closed minds' of their elders. In our own country, on the other hand, we have many encouraging themes and many older workers in science who champion innovation. Sample themes are: 'It is good to be open-minded.' 'Objective tests validate scientific discoveries.' 'We are not allowed to project our wishes on physical and biological nature.' And social mechanisms encourage competition among old and new ideas.

In Europe, things have not always been so encouraging. Under the rubric of thematic resistance we would have to mention the reception which disappointed Copernicus when most of the astronomers of his time, including the prestige-laden Brahe, as well as many non-scientists, rejected his work, his heliocentric theory. Similarly, Thomas Young's theory that light moves in waves was resisted in the early nineteenth century because of the popularity of faith in a corpuscular model. That Liebig and others insisted fermentation is a simple chemical process led to rejection of Pasteur's theory that fermentation involves bacterial action. Mendel, with a theory of separate genetic inheritance of characteristics, was buried under an avalanche of disapproval when he introduced it in 1865; Mendel's theory and Mendel himself had to be dug out of oblivion later, but only after his theory was rediscovered independently by the Dutch scholar de Vries, the scholar Carl Correns, working in Germany, and the Viennese scholar Erich Tschermak, all in the first year of this century. Resistance was the lot of the scientist Arrhenius, though later his theory of electrolytic dissociation won him a Nobel prize. Resistance was the lot of Roentgen's theory of the X-ray: Lord Kelvin, the eminent scientist, suspected that X-rays were a hoax. Kelvin also resisted the Ramsay-Soddy theory that helium can be produced from radium, and Rutherford's theory that the atom has electrons. For Kelvin, the atom had no moving parts. The student, therefore, must be alert to the possibility of a clash of theories, pitting one man against another. Such clashes occur within linguistic anthropology as well as elsewhere. A clash of theories within a man is a special case: we have already mentioned the subclass of deliberate contradictions, as with Aristotle on his theories of the nature of the universe; and sometimes a scholar may entertain contradictory themes because of carelessness or inattention. He may look right through an object without noticing its existence. He may discover evidence which challenges a received view, and yet ignore it. An instance is the discovery that the enzyme papain causes a rabbit's ears to flop. The discovery was neutralized by the theme, 'Cartilage is inert and uninteresting.' Later, the theme was discarded and the victim cured of what Robert Graves has called the scholarly disease of 'apoblepsia.'

A clash of theories may be reduced sometimes to a clash over methods. The adequacy of evidence, the value of models, and the utility of mathematical formulae need to be considered here. Proof requires facts, facts which can be called true or false, facts which move consistently without contradictions toward a conclusion, consistent facts which are accurate and adequate. Men can more easily agree if facts are facts rather than metaphors or exhortations, and if they are consistent, than they can about the adequacy of the facts which support a theory.

In disparate opinions on the adequacy of evidence, in interactional resistances and thematic doctrines, in scientific fashions of constructing or evaluating models which apply to larger or smaller ranges of phenomena, in the intricacies of cultural associations, the essence of symbolism and the key question in language and culture, in all of this there is such richness and variety that many frames of reference are implicated, not just one. Even granting Wittgenstein the priority of material meaning, it must be admitted that there are meanings of meaning, never 'the' meaning. And so, if one is to implement the scientific policy of divide and conquer, one can be content with no single program for the study of meaning.

8 «

The Study of Meaning

In the verbal aggressions which scientists have hurled at each other it is difficult not to find the word 'school.' We hear of a Whorfist school, a structuralist school, a transformationist, generative, or M.I.T. school, a Prague school, a Vienna school, a structural-functional school, or a phonemic school, a Copenhagen school, a Geneva school, an American or Yale school. It is easier to supply dates for the names often identified with these schools than to mistreat the contributions of these men by giving them easy labels. B. L. Whorf (1897–1941) is identified with the Whorfist school; Zellig Harris (1909–) with the structuralist school; Noam Chomsky (1928–) with the transformationist school; Nikolai S. Trubetzkoy (1890–1938) and Roman Jakobson (1896–) with Prague and Vienna; Louis Hjelmslev (1899–) with Copenhagen; Ferdinand de Saussure (1857–1914) with Geneva; Leonard Bloomfield (1887–1949) and Edward Sapir (1884–1939) with the Yale school. It is better to deal not in good and bad schools but in good and bad programs of research of particular individuals.

Aristotle was a master of research programs. In *De Anima* 2.7.418a26–28, he echoes his general theory that each of the five senses has an object when he says that the object of sight is something visible. And the visible is color, and something that has no name but can be described, that is, a nameless cognitive category. To reject the proposal that, as 419a2–6 indicates, he meant phosphorescence, is to hint that Aristotle belonged to the Socratic school. His program of research, then, would have two parts, one public and taxonomic, the other private and esoteric. He would be an exemplar for Kant, just as Plato was an exemplar for him. Only one wise man appears in any of Plato's dialogues; the researches of Socrates, when he is that wise man, are researches among men who are not wise. Speculations about meanings in Plato or Aristotle, notions about the relation of language and culture, need not be taken at face value. To philosophize on the human condition requires more than a narrow interest in linguistic forms, it requires the study of meanings, the various relations obtaining among signs of various sorts. Since these relations are registered upon and by the senses, it requires also the study of perception and cognition, sensation and reactivity. It requires psychological research.

Much of modern psychological research in verbal behavior betrays the impact of taxonomic linguistics and, less widely, the impact of generative or truly theoretical linguistics. The impact of the former has been manifested partly within the semiotic frame of reference. Charles Morris, in *Foundations of the Theory of Signs* (1938) and elsewhere, has dealt with signs in terms of semiotic analysis. His program involves three kinds of analysis, which have to precede semiotic synthesis. The final synthesis is very important, but analysis must come first, with apologies to the impatient.

The syntactic aspect of semiosis treats of signs in their relations to other signs. On a given level of syntactic analysis, a sign exists by virtue of contrast with at least one other sign. Structure, in other words, may be interpreted as a network of relations defined by contrast. The syntactic aspect of semiosis is the province of the descriptive linguist.

The semantic aspect of semiosis treats of signs in their relations to things signified outside of the linguistic or syntactic system. Phonemes and morphemes are syntactic signs considered apart from sememes of the real world. As soon as we ask what are the qualities or attributes or distinctive features of a particular speaker's {*rose*} at a particular time in his life, we are no longer in the province of descriptive linguistics. We are companions of the ethnologist and the psychologist and the sociologist of knowledge. We study situational stimuli which produce or dispose one to produce linguistic responses. We are free then to consider meaning apart from the convenient fiction of the sememe, as a variable rather than as a constant.

The phonologies of languages have been studied more thoroughly than their morphologies; the relations of constructions to other constructions or transformations have been studied relatively little. But the syntactic aspect of semiosis has been studied more carefully than the semantic, where much work remains to be done. And the last aspect, the pragmatic, has been studied least of all. Here the semiotician deals with the relations of signs as stimuli to the responses which they elicit.

A basic text, which the beginner should read from cover to cover in his attempt to understand some of the programs implicit in the semiotic trichotomy, is a work edited by Charles E. Osgood and Thomas A. Sebeok. The title is *Psycholinguistics: A Survey of Theory and Research Problems; Report of the 1953 Summer Seminar Sponsored by the Committee on Linguistics and Psychology of the Social Science Research Council* (1954). This work was issued as a supplement to the *International Journal of American Linguistics* and as a supplement to the *Journal of Abnormal and Social Psychology;* it was reprinted in 1965. The student should study section 7.2 with special care.

The term 'sememe,' used a moment ago to mean a 'tag,' has other meanings in other contexts. In stratificational grammar, it refers to a category of semons, semantic components like those which we have examined in connection with kinship terms. For Bloomfield, however, sememe means 'tag (used with a given morpheme).' So anxious was Bloomfield to avoid problems of meaning, he left it to the zoologist to define *whale,* and reserved a place for the definition by means of a tag. Such tags, of course, often turn out to be inadequate vehicles of meaning. It is bad enough when we move from English *blue* to Navaho *tootłˀiž,* since the Navaho word refers to a continuum of color stimuli that range from green through blue into purple. How much worse it is when we move from English to ancient Greek or from ancient Egyptian to English we cannot say, for our records of contexts are very poor. Our understanding of ancient cultures is bound to be worse than our understanding of modern cultures, in spite of our readiness to reconstruct on the basis of human universals.

Bloomfield's definition of the meaning of a morpheme as a sememe underscores the fact that meaning is understood in various senses depending upon context. Different definitions of meaning reflect attention to different elements of the total context. Some linguists, for example, try to discover morphemes which are fused units, part form, part meaning. Most American linguists, I would guess, do not. They follow Bloomfield, and rely primarily upon differential meaning, though they are assisted sometimes by involuntarily accepted situational clues. Semioticians do not look for fused units, matching a 'piece' of meaning to a 'piece' of form. Such matchings at times are impossibly complex and have suggested that analysis of formal structures and of semantic structures should be carried out separately, as a prelude to any study of how formal units and semantic units are correlated by members of a particular culture. In the following sections, we will show how complex the study of meaning has come to be.

9 «

Aspects of Symbolism

A rose by any other name would smell as sweet. But to change the name of the rose would be to violate not only aesthetic sensibilities but also symbolic conventions. Once a society makes its members parties to an agreement to use a certain string of phonemes representing a given morpheme or morphemes to refer to certain facts of the world, once a sign finds arbitrary connection with its referent, society then also establishes symbolic conventions, and subgroups of society establish subsidiary, often hermetic sub-conventions, as poets all know. If Wittgenstein could claim to tease out material meaning, perhaps what he was after, in view of the diversity of possibilities, does not deserve to be called 'the' meaning of a postulated entity. There are two popular ways to discuss meaning. One is to say that a meaning is there. The other is to say that a single meaning is a fiction, convenient perhaps, but an oversimplification.

Let us consider the second way first. Its proponents argue that meaning is an abstraction from experience. One cannot form a mental image of a rose which is the meaning of the rose. Indeed, meaning is the total disposition to respond to a given stimulus; the description of the meaning of *rose* is therefore too ambitious a project. Subordinate projects are much more to the point.

All the stimuli which fire neurons in a speaker's nervous system function as signals of 'the speaker's situation.' When the stimuli are linguistic and audible and produce in the hearer a certain word, we have 'the hearer's response.' Bloomfield defined meaning in one sense as the speaker's stimulus and the hearer's response. On this definition it is obvious that only a very small part of the history of an utterance can be available to an investigator. With no means for defining most meanings, Bloomfield postulated a fundamental assumption, 'the fundamental assumption of linguistics,' giving a constancy available in no other way: in a given community of speakers who share a language, speech forms will sometimes be alike. There will be a form or arrangement of phonemes, say for the Cree /misatim/, and this form will have a certain constant meaning represented by the tag 'horse'; and the same form and meaning will recur in the community. A different form will have a different constant and specific meaning. Thus *fast* and *swift* are not actually synonyms, because each has its own constant and conventional meaning. The linguist can operate with Bloomfield's assumption, which is true only within limits (as Bloomfield was first to admit), even though he cannot define meanings in the broadest sense. He cannot tell anyone what the total relevant context of a sign is, but as far as the requirements of his discipline go, he does not have to.

It has become apparent that linguistics cannot deal adequately with the problem of characterizing grammatical competence unless the range of phenomena with which Bloomfield was content is extended. Bloomfield's work, some thirty-five years ago, had a vitalizing effect on linguistics. If some of his views are now judged to be outmoded, we must not lose sight of the importance of his contribution, that of a rational man in a not always rational world.

Bloomfield's linguistics dealt with the convenient analytical fictions of vocal features of utterances which are alike, such as *Osiris* spoken by a priest and *Osiris* spoken by a doubter. These are said to be *same forms.* His linguistics also dealt with the stimulus-reaction features of these forms only insofar as they are alike; faith and doubt are excluded: we say that the stimulus-reaction features of the two cases of *Osiris* which are alike are *same meanings.*

Bloomfield's assumption freezes meaning. Unfrozen, infinite variety is the rule; frozen, the rule is absolute sameness. The unfrozen meanings of *rose* vary from speaker to speaker and from context to context. The same meanings of the one who says *rose* and the one who hears *rose* facilitate communication; what is shared in the experience of two who say *rose* helps them to interact efficiently. There is a difference in their experience of *rose.* Records show that meanings change through time. How can a form take new meanings if not through multiple shifts or differences of context? And yet, by the fiction of formal and semantic sameness, there can be no change. There can be no frequency or probability curves of referential importance.

In guiding linguists to look at meaning as outsiders, Bloomfield did not reject various scientific ways to study meaning. He did not reject the views of psychologists, for example, that meanings can be explained in terms of various stimulus-reaction systems. Bloomfield simply absented himself from their discussions. He admitted that his basic assumption does not hold true for the historical change of language. He also extended his basic assumption to include *partly* alike forms and meanings, and then by a commutational test he isolated minimal meaningful forms or constituents (the *straw* of *strawberry,* the *blue* of *blueberry,* the *cran* of *cranberry,* for example). The ultimate constituents he called morphemes. The description of a morpheme, he observed, could be carried out in terms of its phonemes, but not in terms of its meaning, as far as linguistic science is concerned. Its meaning is a sememe. Let us restrict ourselves to one idiolect. In a given idiolect, the morpheme *rose,* more properly {*rose*}, by a convenient fiction is said to have a sememe, a constant and unique meaning, a feature of the real world that is pointed to or signaled about by one or more phonemes. The linguist deals with the phonemes. He leaves to the psychologist, the botanist, or the poet, specimens of thorny plants and blossoms golden as bees' fur, pale as snow in moonlight, or redolent of lovers' jubilations.

Suppose that the linguist operating with frozen meaning offers to contribute to the study of how signs relate to signs. What can he contribute? How can he get along without worrying about the deeper meanings, the more fleeting symbols? He can contribute operations based on *differential* meaning, on informants' judgments that given forms are different in meaning. His distributional analysis and classificational work then is relatively free of what once was considered a deterrent to truly scientific work in linguistics.

Another kind of meaning comes from distributional analysis. Let us say that a sign is discovered by a linguist as it occurs in one context of signs: *Osiris* (is king). The linguist next finds other contexts of this sign, linguistic contexts made up of forms:

Osiris (is king).
Osiris (eats rice).
Osiris (is my dog).
(Good for) *Osiris.*
(Horus avenges) *Osiris.*

Eventually the linguist may identify certain criterial attributes or distinctive features or components of the collected contexts: in the sample, the immediate contexts are predicates following a subject, or objects, once of a preposition, once of a verb. A list of the most frequent general frames or contexts of *Osiris,* as opposed to a complete or infinitely long list of actual contexts, constitutes for some the syntactic function of the linguistic sign. Given a new context it is then possible after study to determine whether *Osiris* is privileged by custom to occur there: (I pray to) *Osiris* puts the sign after a preposition as its object and the linguistic meaning of *Osiris* is not extended. One meaning of meaning, in sum, is 'linguistic meaning.' While some speak of the linguistic meaning of a morpheme, not as any Bloomfieldian sememe but as the set of conditional probabilities that it will occur in context with all other morphemes, most intend to indicate the distribution of forms, which is the same as the function of a part of speech.

Now let us come at meaning in a slightly different way, concentrating upon dimensions. Situational parts of the total context, more precisely all relevant speech or nonspeech stimuli of the total context of a form, constitute situational meaning—as opposed to behavioral parts, all caused or causable speech or nonspeech responses, the behavioral meaning of the form. Relations of signs to things signified may be studied as situational or designative meaning (as by lexicographers or ethnologists); relations of signs as stimuli to the responses which they elicit or express, as behavioral or expressive meaning (as by psycholinguists or ethnologists); and relations of signs to other signs within a system of signs as implicative or linguistic meaning (as by mathematically-oriented linguists). Another dimension of meaning involves location, intramural versus intermural. Meaning for some linguists or psychologists may implicate internal or mediational variables which cannot yet be observed directly. Others denounce introspection and deal only with externally observable situations or responses. Some men speak of meaning mainly in terms of situational contexts, whether contiguous to a sign or remote from it and whether determinable or indeterminate, which give meaning to the sign. Others focus upon overt, objectively recordable responses. Still others stress contiguous or remote responses which are not overt and which cannot be recorded objectively. Their techniques for the description of their particular meanings of meaning vary, depending upon each investigator's conservative or radical propensities.

An investigator may concentrate on the external or extra-organismic stimuli which contribute to the production of a particular linguistic response. Or he may investigate not extraorganismic but intraorganismic events, some with a cortical locus, some with a somatic locus. In the case of cortical activity, we have a sense of covert cognitive meaning, reported on the basis of introspection applied partly to circumstantial linguistic evidence, observation of overt behavior, and instrumental stimulation or recording of such phenomena as electrode-resuscitated memories, galvanic skin responses, or records of brain waves. In the case of somatic activity, we have a sense of affective meaning, measurable by appropriate instruments. Subliminal movements of speech organs during reading or thinking yield a type of covert linguistic meaning with intraorganismic locus.

In most of such research into dimensions of meaning, the Bloomfieldian fiction is maintained. Let us come back now to the first way of discussing meaning. Here we find the same fiction. Freudian psychologists read meanings into dream symbols according to a grammar of symbolism in which mushrooms and javelins, wells and fireplaces fall into different parts of speech. The rules of the grammar are supposed to involve semantic universals, yet there is something private allowable in dream symbolism, that cannot be understood without personal associations, the recounting and analysis of personal experiences. But given the proper history, the right confessions rightly understood, and the meaning of a symbol becomes transparently clear.

With poets, symbolism has obscurer aspects. Wallace Stevens typifies the obscurer poet. He wrote beautifully cadenced, moving, esoteric poetry in Connecticut. He was eclectic and dialectic. He saw the universe, however, as the property of imagination working upon the perceptions of his material consciousness. He supposed that the universe, which could only be sampled and not fully comprehended in any realistic way, the only way that he accepted, was nevertheless a totality in process, a 'heaven' or 'supreme fiction' of growth and change, its existence predictable by dialectical logic. Even logical method, he supposed, has a future; formal logic is itself predictable by dialectical logic as a moment in consciousness of flux and growth. The imagination is a dialectical engine, given to endless syntheses. It is also a creative engine, making pragmatic assay of the work of perception. In 'Notes Toward a Supreme Fiction,' for example, Stevens is dialectic in method; the poem has three major parts: first, *It Must Be Abstract,* second and by way of antithesis, *It Must Change,* and third, in ultimate synthesis, *It Must Give Pleasure.* Elsewhere, Stevens shies away from polarities and natural laws, and stresses in pragmatic fashion the unity of human wants and experiences, and the limitations of consciousness, wherein, as he says in 'A High-Toned Old Christian Woman,' fictive things 'wink as they will.' He hoped for answers to the ontological queries, 'What are things like, and how are they related?' And he hoped that the answers would take meaning from eclecticism.

Eclectic though he is, he has made it possible for critics to read his symbols in terms of frozen meaning. Stevens, the critics might chorus, Stevens the poet is a seer and sayer for the universe of experience. Within a comprehensive system of metaphysical symbolism he constructs subordinate systems, an important system of nature symbolism, one of color symbolism, and lesser ones of seasons and personae. A system itself is symbolic of the nature of imaginative creation. Within a given system, which may crosscut other systems, less comprehensive symbols or *tropes* are used, some as simple as the equation of birds and poets.

An oppositional grid of tropes reflects the grand metaphysical opposition of Reality, things as they are, and The Imaginary, things as they seem. Opposed terms are earth-heaven, sun-moon, solid-non-solid, day-night, north-south, winter-summer, nature-art, body-mind, green-blue, musical instrument-music itself, darkness-light, black-white. The earth-heaven opposition is part of the system of metaphysical symbolism. A poem is a symbol of God, the imagination, the supreme fiction. The term heaven requires its tropes, furniture of Christian symbols reinterpreted and tied to earth by an Adamic poet.

The winter-summer opposition is part of a system of season-symbolism, itself part of the system of nature symbolism. Winter is the time when the imagination, that relentless composer of new images, is at its barest; summer, the time of its fullest creativity; and spring heads toward the peak of imaginative work, while autumn is the time of its decline.

The green-blue opposition is part of a system of color symbolism, also involved in nature-symbolism, in which tropes figure once more: red for what is old, green for what is primitive, blue for what is imaginative; and shades and areas of the spectrum pertain to these and other points of color reference. Pink is less old than red, and more faded; purple is on the other side of blue imaginativeness from primal green.

Important in the cosmic symbolism of Wallace Stevens are the colors black and white. Black stands for non-formulation, chaos or unlit nothingness, reality not touched by the imagination, flux or dissolution. Tropes for nothingness need not be black, however; some are glass, air, ice, light, winter cold. Illuminated bareness, 'lit nothingness' as it were, pertains to white, the color of formulation, whose emblems are snow, ice cream, a shroud.

One of Stevens's books is *The Auroras of Autumn.* Auroras are shining lights, hence tokens of The Imaginary. Autumn indicates the time of imaginative decline. Seasons, colors, and metaphysics—systems in interplay—glisten together in a stunning amalgamation, a dazzling symbolic production, in which minor inventions add sparkle—a guitar, a guitarist, a red Rabbi, a peacock with autumn leaves in its tail, all blown by the wearying wind of time. In the creations of the poet, where criticism has worked out the poet's recurrent private associations, even here the profundities of symbolism shine beyond the reach of scientific analysis.

10 «

Semantic Variables

While some aspects of symbolism are too profound to give promise of yielding soon to scientific techniques of analysis, such techniques have immeasurably improved our ability to follow the subtleties and nuances of human communication. Even an approximate statement of the variables of a situation is better than the vague description of an even vaguer 'feeling' about the situation. In this section we shall consider possibilities inherent in both analytic and synthetic approaches to such variables.

A sign occurs in a context: I utter the word *cat* as a stream of sound waves analyzable into phonemes which represent two morphemes, if we count intonation as a morpheme. In linguistics as it developed into the 'fifties, a distinction was made between segmental phonemes and suprasegmental or prosodic phonemes. Many languages have phonemes of stress (degrees of loudness), pitch, and juncture (terminals, terminal contours). It was debated if English idiolects have three or four stress phonemes and four pitch phonemes. In one interpretation, there are primary, secondary, tertiary, and weak stress phonemes, noted respectively as shown: /á â à ă/. (Weak stress is not written by some.) Pitches are indicated by small raised numbers with /^{4}/ for a speaker's highest, and most amusing or embarrassing, habitual pitch and /^{1}/ for his lowest, with /^{2}/ as his commonest pitch of sentence attack and /^{3}/ as a pitch often used for emphasis: ^{2}*I sàw a* ^{3}*cát*^{1}. Compare ^{3}*Í* ^{2}*sàw a* ^{3}*cát*^{3}? The period represents gradual drop in pitch and slowing down of speech organs. The question mark represents a rise in pitch, a little upturn toward the level of the next higher phonemic pitch. These variations in pitch and tempo are terminal contours, occasionally represented as arrows aimed downward or upward. Compare ^{2}*I sàw a* ^{3}*cát*^{1}↓ and ^{3}*Í* ^{2}*sàw a* ^{3}*cat*^{3}↑. A third terminal contour is indicated by an arrow aimed to the right and represents a slowing down without much enfeeblement or fluctuation in pitch: ³*Í* ²→ ²*sàw a* ³*cát*³↑ is a representational improvement upon the conventionally indicated question, *I saw a cat?* The word *cat,* then, is not simply /kæt/ on the phonemic level and {*cat*} on the morphemic level. The word *cat* cannot be uttered without a meaningful intonation, an intonation which indicates that an assertion, for example, or a question is at issue. The assertion of *cat* as an item in a list of animals thus might involve the sequence /³¹↓/ with primary stress: /³kǽt¹↓/; and it is more realistic to see an intonational morpheme {ASSERTION} with a number of intonational allomorphs than to ignore it. Since conventional spelling often fools people by distracting them from living speech, it is not surprising that intonational or supra-segmental phonemes have not been as carefully studied in general as those which are segmental. The study of intonation comes under the heading of prosody or phrasing. In analyzing a sentence like *John ran* /²ǰàn ³rǽn¹↓/, part of the analysis demands phrasing and the rest parsing. Some linguists start with a convenient fiction and make an initial immediate constituent cut between the intonation and the remainder of the utterance, as it were, and then they identify the immediate constituents of the intonation as a phrasing operation, and then they identify the immediate constituents of the remainder as a parsing operation. Suppose again that I utter the word *cat:* I have on one level a stream of phonemes /³kǽt¹↓/ and on another level a couple of morphemes which can be analyzed as {*cat*} with {ASSERTION}.

Now let us come back to the meanings of the sign {*cat*}. A meaning, as we have seen, may be specified differently according to different definitions which focus upon different and often cross-cutting elements of the total context of the sign. We have used such terms as situational or designative, or referential or semantic meaning, behavioral or expressive or pragmatic meaning, sememic or differential meaning, implicative or syntactic or linguistic meaning, extraorganismic or intraorganismic or extralinguistic meaning, cognitive or affective, overt or covert meaning. The terminology is dizzying, but we have not yet exhausted all possibilities. An iconic diagram for some of the more important possibilities is useful at this point.

A scholar may confine his attention to situational stimuli (let us use symbols for some of these things, here *S*) or to behavioral responses (*R*).

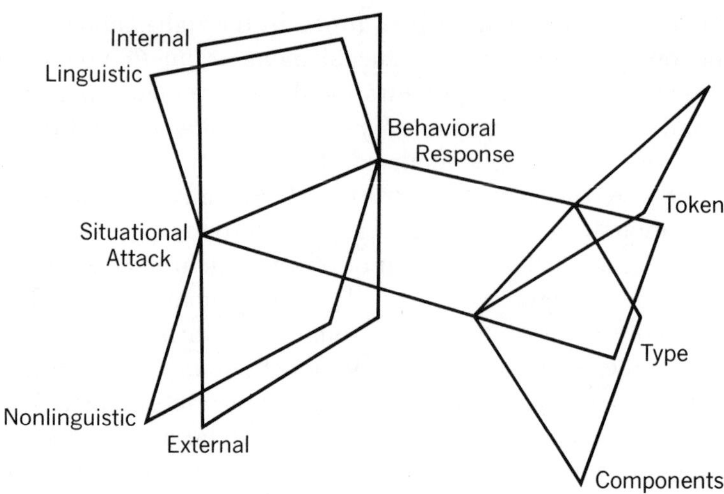

FIGURE 6 Meanings of meaning

On another line of thought, he may pay attention to external (E) or internal (I) events. Again, he may deal in nonlinguistic contexts (N) or linguistic contexts (L). And he may have in mind a particular item or token (T), a single case like a phone or a morph; or a set of tokens, a general class which has variants like a phoneme or a morpheme, called here a type (symbolized by sigma T, ΣT); or he may wish to confine his attention for the moment to components or distinctive features or criterial attributes (C). We have mentioned seven components for the situation and seven for the behavioral response. Using our inventory, we can now represent various definitions or meanings of meaning in algebraic fashion. Bloomfield, for example, concentrated upon the total immediate context of a given language sign, for which we use the symbol T. This restricts us to a single total immediate context. We need N but not L; and we need S, R, E, and I. We then express Bloomfield's 'meaning' (not his 'distinctive meaning') as follows: $(S + R) \cdot (E + I) \cdot N \cdot T$. This is a brief symbolic way of representing what Bloomfield has said in plain English. We cannot be as clear about his 'distinctive meaning'; our formula is $S \cdot (E + I) \cdot N \cdot C$ or perhaps $S \cdot (E + I) \cdot (N + L) \cdot C$.

The student has the right to ask any question he may think of, and he may want to know at this point why one should use symbols instead of plain English. The advantage in using these symbols, as logicians already know, is that there is no room for equivocation: either the formula is correct or it is not, and it faces the public in any event with bare but honorable simplicity. Moreover, we can compare definitions of meaning on essential points when they are written symbolically. We can even discover sometimes, as in the Bloomfield case just mentioned, that an author was not clear about certain crucial matters in his discussion of a particular or putative meaning of meaning. Nor should we confine our attention, one wants to add as an afterthought, to senses or definitions of the concept *meaning;* there are other concepts which invite this kind of Boolean assault that we have been explicating, for example, the concept *universal.* One might ask if any questions are begged when we speak of universals in grammar. But that would lead us astray, and it is preferable to give some more examples of definitions of meaning.

In his work on the theory of signs, Charles Morris introduces the terms denotatum, designatum, and significatum. Formulaic representation yields $S \cdot E \cdot N \cdot T$, $S \cdot E \cdot N \cdot \Sigma T$, and $S \cdot E \cdot N \cdot C$, respectively. The meaning of 'linguistic meaning' for some writers, to take a new definition, is symbolized as $(S + R) \cdot E \cdot L \cdot C$, i.e. the situational stimuli and behavioral responses, restricted to external phenomena, further restricted to linguistic contexts, and further restricted to the distinctive features which are abstracted as common to all contexts within the specified limits. Let us take another example. The psychologist (since he works in the psychology of language we can call him the psycholinguist) who asks a subject to rate a concept like CAT on such scales as *hot-cold, rich-poor, up-down,* or *tight-loose,* in using Charles Osgood's semantic differential as a measure of 'connotative meaning' or 'behavioral mediational meaning,' devotes special attention to those responses which are internal or mediational, restricted to nonlinguistic contexts, and further restricted to the distinctive features which are abstracted as common to all contexts within the specified limits: $R \cdot I \cdot N \cdot C$.

If we add to our inventory of variables, of course, our definition-making powers will be modified. The variable of frequency (F), for example, has been widely recognized and occasionally with explicitness as of fundamental importance in the study of language and culture. The importance of this variable in human sign-behavior has been recognized by psychologists, for example, those who work with word associations; and it has been recognized by anthropologists, not the least by those Victorian moderns who, like Tylor and Frazer, were academic pioneers in the collecting and assessing of ethnographic data.

It is helpful in discussing metaphors to identify another variable, which we might call infrequency. Our symbol is F bar, $\bar{F}$. When we call a woman a cat, we are indulging in metaphor. Metaphor is peculiarly human; it is perhaps beyond the capacity of all brains but the human brain to see similarities between associations or reflex chains and to identify different entities on the basis of shared criterial attributes. A crow, a bee, or an ape cannot see that a woman sometimes is feline and scratches, if only verbally with nasty gossip, much as a cat is feline and scratches. At any rate, somewhere in history someone called a woman a cat for the first time. From the criterial distinctive features of all situations in which the language-sign {*cat*} was operative, i.e. from what people had learned to associate in the everyday world with the sign {*cat*}, certain features criterial to other situations were abstracted and an equation was made as an act of identity. We engage in metaphor-making, this imaginative form of meaningful innovation, all the time; and willingly we honor literary men with special metaphorical skill. A Navaho once told me that he shivers with joy when he hears a good Navaho metaphor; we do the same sometimes in reading William Shakespeare or Vladimir Nabokov. Perhaps we can make this general observation: one observes the creation of a metaphoric sign from a sign with relatively high frequency in the speech community, such a sign as {*cat*}, defined as $S \cdot E \cdot N \cdot C \cdot F$. This formula gives us a substitution theory definition of meaning with the special restriction that the stimuli which are external and exist in nonlinguistic contexts and are criterially distinctive are also frequent. Now let us suppose that when someone saw that a woman in a given total context shared with cats the ability to scratch or to manifest feline appetites and called her a *cat,* he created a new sign. He created $\{cat\}_2$ beside $\{cat\}_1$. Before, he had two morphemes, $\{cat\} = S \cdot E \cdot N \cdot C_1 \cdot F$, and $\{woman\} = S \cdot E \cdot N \cdot C_2 \cdot F$. C represents a bundle of distinctive semantic components, an arrangement of components which one might represent formulaically and identify with the morphemic language-sign. The subscripts show that the bundles of components are not identical. But there is an intersection of bundles at one point at least, that is, at least with one identical component. This insight about identity is novel; its frequency in human intercourse is practically nil; and we must invoke our infrequency variable. Given the facts as presented above, $\{cat\}_2$ is $S \cdot E \cdot N \cdot (C_1 \cdot C_2) \cdot \bar{F}$.

For Wittgenstein, who aimed not at scientific analysis so much as at synthesis, the atomistic variables we have been discussing were not as interesting as generalizations across all data. The records kept in neural tissue, it seems probable to some imaginative scholars, poets, and philosophers, are made available as perceptions and cognitions of signs. Wittgenstein saw language as a kind of machine so cunningly wired that it could equate certain parts of human experience to certain other parts by rule. Our world, he said in his *Tractatus Logico-Philosophicus* (1922), is constructed of well-ordered experiences of signs. Experience gives each man a part only of that infinite universe which Stevens calls the supreme fiction. The part which is given cannot be examined or manipulated without language, so that the world exists only by virtue of nervous insights which are ordered experiences of signs. And so Wittgenstein would have agreed with Stevens that the gaiety of language is our Seigneur. Thought and the world are inseparably united by language. Language allows me to organize my world, in the sense in which words come to be peculiarly associated with things and events in my given cultural environment. Where language is limited, my world is too; the events or facts which I know, in a captivating tissue of grammatical signs and operations, in a tissue which Wittgenstein called his 'logical hold,' are the world.

III

Linguistics

They want all the labial letters; which is the reason why they all open their lips so ungracefully, and you can hardly understand their whistling or when they speak in a low tone.

—Translated from Jean de Brebeuf's account of the Hurons, dated 16 July 1636, in Paul Le Jeune's *Relation de ce qvi s'est passe' en la Novvelle France en l'anne'e 1636* (1637), by Albert Gallatin for *A Synopsis of the Indian Tribes within the United States East of the Rocky Mountains, and in the British and Russian Possessions in North America.* In *Archaeologia Americana, Transactions and Collections of the American Antiquarian Society,* Vol. II (1836).

11 «

The Taxonomic Approach to Phonemes

In anthropological history, there have been two major trends of linguistic influence. The first trend impressed anthropologists like Kroeber and Kluckhohn with the view that in the rigorous dedication to analysis demonstrated by Bloomfield and his students lay hope for similar activity, equally productive, in anthropology at large. It was admitted that contrastive units similar to the phoneme or morpheme in language probably would not be so easy to find in culture; but it was admitted also that it would be good to operate with such units. Phonemes and morphemes were found by discovery procedures applied to raw data. Out of a welter of phenomena of a phonetic nature emerged distinctive units or phonemes, abstractions emitted in a stream in a duality with abstractions of a different order, called morphemes. These abstractions existed by virtue of contrast, contrast identified by distributional analysis. For those not mindful of larger, more compelling theoretical problems of sign behavior, it was enough to consider the ways of the taxonomic or class-discovering linguist, to consider his ways and be wise.

More recently, a second major trend in linguistics, inimical on theoretical grounds to the first, has undermined the view that a taxonomic approach provides the best framework for a proper understanding of cultural events. Our task is to examine the older linguistics, to contrast it with the newer, and to see how each has had its impact upon the best of the anthropological theoreticians.

Both taxonomic and generative grammarians devote considerable attention to phonetics. The cultivated reader cannot confront some of the issues unless he devotes part of his attention, too, to the rudiments of phonetics. In this section, we will be concerned primarily with the stratificational approach to grammar. Our first job will be to learn the values of certain phonetic symbols. The phonetician uses them to record what he hears of human speech. He is not seduced by the spelling taught to children in school. He uses one particular symbol for a particular sound. If he hears someone say 'pill,' he writes [pIl] or something similar. The brackets show that the transcription is phonetic. Several phonetic alphabets are in use. The professional must learn several groups of symbols for advanced work.

It will be less tedious to begin with fifty words than with a dry list or table of symbols. Copy these words very carefully, and do not change anything. The student who copies [r] and writes [R], who substitutes capitals for lower case letters, that is, may actually indicate a sound he does not want to indicate. Here are the words to copy:

1. *pit* [pIt]
2. *pet* [pɛt]
3. *bit* [bIt]
4. *bet* [bɛt]
5. *bid* [bId]
6. *bed* [bɛd]
7. *pick* [pIk]
8. *pig* [pIg]
9. *brick* [brIk]
10. *big* [bIg]
11. *beg* [bɛg]
12. *help* [hɛlp]
13. *bag* [bæg]
14. *back* [bæk]
15. *bat* [bæt]
16. *bad* [bæd]
17. *pat* [pæt]
18. *pad* [pæd]
19. *book* [bUk]
20. *bull* [bUl]
21. *kiss* [kIs]
22. *kill* [kIl]
23. *yell* [yɛl]
24. *sell* [sɛl]
25. *shrill* [šrIl]
26. *chill* [čIl]
27. *chick* [čIk]
28. *check* [čɛk]
29. *Jeff* [ǰɛf]
30. *deaf* [dɛf]
31. *thin* [θIn]
32. *thing* [θIŋ]
33. *smash* [smæš]
34. *then* [ðɛn]
35. *win* [wIn]
36. *wing* [wIŋ]
37. *spring* [sprIŋ]
38. *nut* [nət]
39. *cut* [kət]
40. *cat* [kæt]
41. *gut* [gət]
42. *rut* [rət]
43. *jut* [ǰət]
44. *shut* [šət]
45. *vision* [vIžən]
46. *pigeon* [pIǰən]
47. *lump* [ləmp]
48. *lamp* [læmp]
49. *zing* [zIŋ]
50. *cramp* [kræmp]

Note that a particular symbol is used for a given sound. The sound is something we hear, not something we see. It originates in and emanates from a speaker's organs of speech, organs which in lower creatures are used mostly for respiration and digestion. The sound is not given infallibly by the spelling used in newspapers and magazines; it is given infallibly only by the organs of speech. Speech and writing are two cherries on the same twig, but we must be careful to distinguish between them. The kind of writing which we call phonetic transcription is much more sensitive to the realities of speech than the kind of writing which educated men and women use in preserving the best that has been thought and said in our culture. Much that is valuable and sublime in human experience has been preserved as an indirect consequence of the invention of our alphabet. It would be manifestly more nonsensical to argue that one can live the good life by the study of grammatical theory than to argue that the intelligent reading of great literature helps one to live the good life. In making a distinction between the conventional spelling which is used to preserve our cultural values and the best thought of the best thinkers, on the one hand, and the special phonetic transcription which is used to record actual sounds generated by actual speech organs, on the other hand, we are not dismissing the profound importance of great literature to human society. We are clearing the ground for a useful warning, a warning for the beginner: don't be fooled by conventional spelling. A phonetician uses a [k] for the first sound in 'kiss.' He uses the same [k] for the first sound in 'cramp.' Some beginners would prefer to use the letter *c* for the first sound in 'cramp,' because they have been fooled by conventional spelling. It is unsatisfactory, however, to have two symbols for one type of sound. The good phonetician is satisfied to write [k] whenever he hears that particular sound, and he does not care if it comes in 'kiss,' or in 'cat,' or in 'kick.'

Note also that a particular symbol has a fixed shape. Good phoneticians are quite neurotic about writing a symbol down in precise and exact fashion, without new slants, loops, curlicues, or other embellishments. If the student is supposed to copy a lower case letter, he must not copy it as a capital letter. A capital [L] might send a specialist in Chinookan languages off into daydreams; a capital [R] would invite some phoneticians to wiggle their uvulas. Similarly, the student who makes his [g] like the flag at the 18th hole may be directing the reader of his transcription to think of a sound which is quite useful to an Eskimo, but not the same thing as the [g] of English at all. Please do not use anything like [q] if you want to write [g]. The importance of an instructor with a blackboard, a piece of chalk, and a set of speech organs, in setting the beginner straight, cannot be underestimated. Finally, just as it is essential not to put down too many symbols (as in the case of the student who wrote [bUll] instead of [bUl]), it is essential not to put down too few. On the phonetic level of analysis, a cluster of consonants cannot be represented by just one of them. Thus the cluster [mp] in 'cramp' cannot be rendered by one letter alone.

We have had a taste of phonetic transcription. We will return to phonetic symbols in a little while, but it is necessary at this point to show what we are building up to. We do not want to neglect the forest by looking too closely at individual trees. What we are building up to is a comprehensive understanding of grammatical theory. We cannot come to such an understanding unless we learn about the various levels of grammatical analysis. There is the phonetic level. When a linguist operates on this level, he uses a supply of phonetic symbols. His supply is rich enough to enable him to capture subtleties of sound which will escape the beginner. There is the phonemic level. After the linguist has filled several notebooks with phonetic transcription, he can consolidate his data. He reduces the number of symbols that he has to use, and he starts to talk about phonemes, things like /p/ which are written between slash marks, rather than about phones, things like [p] which are written in brackets. We will see that the symbols that are used to represent phonemes are very much like those used for phones. Phonemic symbols, however, should not be confused with phonetic symbols and their phonetic values. A phonemic symbol represents a variety of phonetic types. It takes only an instant to read such a symbol, where it rests upon the page, but it takes a long time to determine just which phonetic types or allophones relate to it. A world of variation hides behind each phonemic symbol.

Studies of the phonetic and phonemic facts of life for a particular language come under the heading of 'phonology.' Phonological theory has captured the attention of many linguists in the past three or four decades. Not quite so popular or well-worked is the field of 'morphology.' Just as the phoneme is the star on the phonological stage, so the morpheme is the star on the morphological stage. Given the phonemic transcription of an utterance, we can chop it up into minimal meaningful segments called morphs. The identification of morphs, and their consolidation into elements called morphemes, the chief business of the linguist working on the morphemic level of analysis, permits one to define and classify certain parts of speech, called the morphological or inflectional parts of speech, in a rigorous and scientific way. So far our main preoccupation has been with the cataloguing of basic elements called phonemes and morphemes. The linguist is also concerned with how these elements are arranged, in the progress of human speech. Arrangements of words in constructions and transformations come under the heading of 'syntax' or grammar proper. The field of syntax has not been plowed very much; it is full of rocks, boulders, and scrub brush. Some doctoral studies of the grammar of a particular language go into impressive phonological detail, a fair amount of morphological detail, and peter out with a slim section on syntax. Much work remains to be done on syntactic and transformational problems, even where English is concerned. Transformational analysis in taxonomic perspective takes the construction as its basic unit, just as syntactic analysis on a lower level takes the word or lexeme as its basic unit. Structural analysis proceeds on all levels at once, as a linguist throws himself impetuously into the study of a new language. When he writes his grammar, however, he may pay special attention to one level at a time, each with its basic unit. He does not mix levels, in describing his discoveries, if he feels that such mixture would be confusing and unscientific; rather, he talks about one level at a time. He might, for example, talk first about Cherokee phones, then about Cherokee phonemes, then about Cherokee morphemes, then about Cherokee constructions, and finally about Cherokee transformations. We have not mentioned some of the things which he might talk about. It has been enough at this stage to anticipate that our study of what might otherwise seem to be a perverse welter of phonetic detail is essential to an understanding of the higher levels, that is, the more abstract levels, of linguistic structure.

We cannot talk about phonemes unless we know something about the production or articulation of phones, and methods of classifying phones. The definition of the phoneme, for our purposes, will be as follows: *A phoneme is a class of phonetically similar and noncontrastive allophones.* In this definition, the words 'phonetically similar' and 'noncontrastive' need to be explained in some detail. It takes a while for the beginner to understand what a phoneme is, and how to go about finding phonemes. There are a few terms that have to be learned first. One of these terms is 'environment.' Another is 'distribution.' Then we have to know what kinds of distribution there are. The term 'noncontrastive' will then be clear to us.

An understanding of what 'phonetically similar' means requires an understanding of phonetic details to be presented later. For the moment, it is enough to agree that English has three varieties of *p*-sound, which a sophisticated phonetician would write as [p^{h}], [p^{c}], and [p]. (The [p] of 'pit' and some other words in our fifty-word list was really a baby step for baby feet.) Say 'pit.' Note that there is a healthy puff of breath, called strong aspiration, after the initial consonant. A raised [ʰ] is used to record strong aspiration. When the aspiration is audible but not so strong, we use the curved mark [ʿ]. A consonant without appreciable aspiration, a so-called unaspirated consonant, needs no special aspirational companion. The various *p*-sounds of English are said to be 'phonetically similar.' They sound similar, and they are generated with similar configurations and motions of the organs of speech. They are candidates, therefore, for phonemehood, according to our definition. Can we group them together, as the allophones of a phoneme to be designated as /p/?

This question takes us back to the word 'noncontrastive,' which we mentioned a moment ago. Before we can group some phonetically similar phones together, and put them into a box marked PHONEME /p/ or PHONEME /X/ or whatever seems best, and call them allophones of that particular phoneme, we have to make certain that they are not in contrast with each other. They are in contrast with each other if they come in the same environment. Linguists enjoy breathtaking prerogatives, when it comes to specifying environments. An environment is the neighborhood of a form, and that neighborhood may be easy to specify in a few words, or it may not. Three very convenient environments for our purposes are (1) initial position in a word, (2) final position in a word, (3) medial position in a word. A phone is said to be medial if it is not in initial or final position. Thus in word 45 above, *vision,* each of the phones [I], [ž], and [ə] is medial or in medial position, and [v] is initial and [n] is final in the word. The phone which we have written as [p] in our list can therefore be said to occur word initially, as in *pit,* word finally, as in *cramp,* and word medially, as in *spring.* But now that we have gone past our first baby steps, we must be on guard about varieties of [p]. We know that there is a strongly aspirated variety of [p], written [pʰ]. We can expect this phone in a certain environment, namely in word initial position, before strong stress. Examples: *pit, pet, pick, pig, pigeon.* We know that there is a variety of [p] with medium aspiration, transcribed by [pʿ]. We can expect this phone sometimes in word final position: *lip, help, buttercup.* We can expect the phone that has no appreciable aspiration, transcribed by the symbol [p] alone, to occur medially, after [s] and before stress: *spit, spin, Spain.* Let us suppose, to make things easy by means of simplification, that the [pʰ] with strong aspiration comes only word initially before strong stress, that the [pʿ] with medium aspiration comes only word finally, and that the unaspirated [p] comes only word medially, after [s] and just before strong stress. We know that these phones have other environments too, but let us suppose that the ones we have just stated are the only ones. Then we would have what is called 'complementary' distribution or mutual exclusiveness. If a certain phone has the deed and title to a given set of environments, and another phone has the deed and title to an entirely different set of environments, so that when one shows up it is a foregone conclusion that the other cannot show up in that place, then we say that the two phones are in mutually exclusive or complementary distribution. In terms of the three numbered environments above, if the first phone occurs only word initially and the second phone occurs never word initially and only word medially or finally, then the two phones are in complementary distribution. Complementary distribution is one kind of noncontrastive distribution. Another kind has the label 'free variation.' A careful study of the distribution of English phones reveals that our two types of aspirated [p] are not always in complementary distribution: one can get away with saying [pʿIk] *or* [p^{h}Ik] for *pick.* The slight variation in aspiration is innocuous. A speaker or hearer would not ordinarily pay any attention to the variation. Change the initial phone of *pit,* however, from [p] to [b], and one no longer can satisfy one's hearer that both forms are the same. *Pit* is [pIt] and [bIt] is *bit.* The initial phones are said to be in contrast in the environment made up of the rest of the word, namely [It]. We say we have a 'minimal pair' and that by virtue of contrast we can isolate three important segments: [p], [b], and [It]. If we compare *pit* and *bit* with *pig,* the minimal pair *pit* and *pig* points up the value of [t] and [g] in telling words apart. This leads to segmentation of [I] away from [t] and [g]. The impetuous linguist, working with a new language in a strange place, usually looks for minimal pairs of words. He does not worry at the start about complementary distribution or free variation of phones as much as he worries about working up an initial inventory of phonemes on the basis of the segmentation which minimal sets of words make possible. He is alert, however, to the fact that eventually he will have to specify the environments of each phone type that he is able to record. The environments of an element, be it a phone, a phoneme, a morpheme, or a construction, comprise the element's distribution. We have discussed three kinds of distribution above. A knowledge of what contrastive distribution is helps us to identify distinctive units. A knowledge of what complementary distribution is, and what free variation is, both of these adding up to noncontrastive distribution, helps us to group subsidiary members into the categories which we have and hold as distinctive units.

The most important of these distinctive units, for present purposes, are the phoneme and the morpheme. The subsidiary members of phonemes are called allophones. The subsidiary members of morphemes are called allomorphs. Our definition of the morpheme runs parallel to that of the phoneme. *A morpheme is a class of semantically similar and noncontrastive allomorphs.* Our attention has moved from phonetic to semantic similarity, but reliance upon contrastive distribution in finding basic units and upon noncontrastive distribution in grouping subsidiary members of these basic units remains. Elements, one assumes, exist through contrast, on a given level of analysis.

12«

Phonetic Articulation

Each phonetic symbol implies certain physical activities. It is possible to scrutinize these activities and the organs involved so finely and closely that the scrutiny captures the imagination, and furniture becomes landscape. The phonetician lives in awareness of his lungs, and knows how they are compressed by certain muscles such as the diaphragm and intercostals. He knows that chest pulses move breath out of the lungs in more or less syllabic units.

He knows that the vocal folds lie within the larynx, and look from above vaguely like the top of a drum slit down the center. The slit can be widened or its edges can be vibrated. The opening is called the glottis. When the glottis is opened abruptly a sound called a glottal stop, something like a pop or little cough, is produced. A sound made with wide glottal opening and lack of vibration of the folds is said to be voiceless. A sound made with vibration of the folds (popularly, the vocal cords) is said to be voiced. The quality of pitch is heard just when the vocal folds vibrate.

Phones, then, are voiced or voiceless. The glottal stop, symbol [ʔ], is neither voiced nor voiceless, and not so much a stop as a catch. Slighted as a consonant in English phonemic analyses, perhaps because of orthographically biased analysts, the glottal consonant figures importantly in a variety of languages from Navaho to Cambodian.

Above the vocal folds lie the throat, tongue, mouth or oral cavity, and nasal passages or nasal cavity. A great fluidity of motions and contacts, susceptible of co-ordination with the qualities of voice and voicelessness, are possible in this area. The description of this area involves competing terminologies. A speaker can be expected to have lips, a tongue, teeth, and a palate. These may be expected to be shown facing to the reader's left, in the saggital axis, in the ordinary phonetics textbook. But labels for articulatory parts show diversity rather than agreement. The articulators, parts which move around and make contact here and there, are the lower lip and various sections of the tongue. Everybody, so far as I know, calls the lip a lip. Some phoneticians, however, like to call the back of the tongue the back, and some like to call it the dorsum. Some call the central part of the tongue the center and some call it the front. The part of the tongue which is used to crush soft food against the palate may be called the blade, though some saggital diagrams have only a front and no blade. The pointed part often is labeled tip or apex. The target areas of the mobile articulators are called the points of articulation. Working back from the front, these points are the upper lip, upper teeth at cutting edge, upper teeth at gum edge, the gum ridge just behind the upper teeth, somtimes called the alveolar ridge, the palate behind this ridge, sometimes called the dome, and the softer, tail-end of the palate, often called the velum. The velum can be used to block off the nasal cavity. When it presses against the pharynx, breath cannot go through the nose from the lungs. Sounds made with the velum raised and pressed against the pharynx are said to be oral; sounds made with the velum relaxed so that breath moves out at least through the nose and sometimes through the nose and mouth are said to be nasal. At the end of the velum is an appendage called the uvula. Some speakers are very good at making the uvula vibrate in a kind of sound known as a trill; the uvular trill reminds one of a little gargle, and it is represented often by [R]. The apex of the tongue is also used to make a trill, which may be long or just a short tap. The tap is heard sometimes in the word *very,* or between vowels, intervocalically that is, where *tt* is in *butter* or *Betty*. A phonetician would prefer not to say 'where *tt* is.' He would prefer to say 'where some speakers have a voiceless alveolar stop.' Such labels are quite useful. We do not have to use the symbol [t]; we can say the voiceless alveolar stop. Some phoneticians might refer to our symbol [t], depending upon circumstances, as the voiceless dental stop, or the voiceless apico-dental stop, or the voiceless apico-alveolar stop. Because they are using different frames of reference or are trying to shield the reader from cathartic detail, different phoneticians sometimes prefer different labels.

The student's confusion is regularly compounded by the fact that while phones exist on one level of linguistic analysis and phonemes exist on the next higher level, the same phonetically based labels generally are used for both. The linguist may refer to [p] as a voiceless bilabial stop, or he may refer to /p/ as a voiceless bilabial stop. In some languages, the phoneme /p/ may include an allophone, say [b], which is not voiceless. Our definition of the phoneme permits such inclusion, if phonetic and distributional conditions are just right, but our label of the phoneme may in some cases tempt us to forget what a diversity of allophonic material we have in hand.

The word stop refers to stoppage or blocking of breath, as it moves toward release from the body. In articulation of a bilabial stop, the lips stop the breath momentarily. In articulation of an alveolar stop, the apex of the tongue presses against the alveolar ridge. In articulation of a velar stop, the back of the tongue presses against the velum. The windy or hissing type of sound made by the friction of breath as room for escape lessens and pressure increases is called a spirant. Some phoneticians like the word fricative instead of spirant. An utterance fraction with rapid progress from stop to spirant sometimes is called an affricate. Other categories of sound, which the advanced student will want to study in detail, are the nasals, the laterals, and the semivowels. All the types which we have just mentioned sometimes are called contoids, as opposed to the vowels or vocoids.

Our limited objective, a cursory view of the means for determining when two phones are phonetically similar, permits us to cut corners in reviewing popular labels. The symbols given with these labels are phonemic. In purely phonetic contexts, the same symbols are placed in brackets. They are augmented by marks or diacritics which indicate subtle phonetic variations. Some students find it helpful, in learning the symbols presented below, to observe motions which accompany the sounds. Such observation should be done with a small mirror, and in strict privacy.

The consonants mentioned here all belong to the list of English phonemes. The bilabial consonants are /p/, /b/, /m/, and /w/. Both /p/ and /b/ are stops, /m/ is usually called a nasal, and /w/ is usually called a semivowel. All are voiced except /p/, which is voiceless. The labiodental consonants are /f/ and /v/, voiceless and voiced, respectively. The consonants /θ/ and /ð/ are usually called interdental spirants or fricatives, voiceless and voiced, respectively. When the tongue does not protrude between the teeth, these consonants may be called dental rather than interdental. A sound made by pressing the tongue against the upper teeth is said to be dental. If the gum ridge rather than the teeth is pressed, the sound is alveolar. Some speakers favor alveolar sounds; others prefer dentals. Hence one speaker, in his own proper usage or idiolect, may use a voiceless dental stop where another man, in *his* idiolect, uses a voiceless alveolar stop. In both instances, a distinctive phonemic unit is at issue, and it is written as /t/. The consonants which serve many speakers as alveolar stops are /t/ and /d/, voiceless and voiced partners. The alveolar spirants are /s/ and /z/, voiceless and voiced partners. English has a voiced alveolar nasal /n/, a voiced alveolar lateral /l/, and in some interpretations a voiced alveolar semivowel /r/. Some linguists count two alveopalatal consonants as members of the stop series; others prefer to see them as affricates. They are /č/ and /ǰ/, voiceless and voiced partners. The voiceless alveopalatal spirant is /š/ and its voiced partner is /ž/. Other popular symbols for these two are /ʃ/ and /ʒ/, respectively. In some interpretations, /č/ and /ǰ/ are taken as the consonant clusters /tš/, also written /tʃ/, and /dž/, also written /dʒ/. The voiced alveopalatal semivowel is /y/. The velar consonants include the voiceless and voiced partners /k/ and /g/, both stops, and the voiced nasal /ŋ/. Spelling leads the beginner to suppose that /h/ is a consonant pure and simple. But many linguists, because of phonetic and distributional considerations, consolidate vocoid as well as contoid phenomena in dealing with /h/. Their /h/ then covers a variety of phonetic variations. Some of these variations are glottal spirantic or velar spirantic in nature, and some are vocalic, and involve voiceless and voiced vowels alike.

A table with elements strung out along a horizontal and a vertical axis is called a matrix; the boxes of the matrix are its cells. Phonetic matrices are common in elementary phonetic texts. Sometimes an inventory of the phonemes of a language is presented mainly by means of matrices; such devices, of course, mislead the beginner who forgets that a phonemic symbol may stand for several different phonetic symbols. But the phonemic matrix is useful for typological purposes, when one wants to compare the inventories of different languages. And it helps to show relationships of phonetic similarity. We know that

[p] and [b] are phonetically similar because of what our ears tell us. But it helps to note the similar procedures which we use in articulating [p] and [b]; they are articulated in the same way, except that the vocal folds produce voice for [b] and do not produce voice for [p]. A judgment of phonetic similarity often follows due recognition of articulatory similarity, similarity in which only one or two, or at least relatively few, contrastive articulatory motions inhere. In specifying that [p] and [b] are phonetically similar, to take a specific case, we recognize that they would be the same except for glottal motion. In specifying that [m] and [b] are phonetically similar, we recognize that they would be the same except for motion of the velum.

A consonantal matrix which shows relationships of similarity is presented below.

		Bilabial	Labio-Dental	Alveolar or Dental	Alveo-Palatal	Velar
Stop	voiceless voiced	p b		t d		k g
Affricate	voiceless voiced				č ǰ	
Spirant	voiceless voiced		f v	θ ð		
	voiceless voiced			s z	š ž	
Nasal	voiced	m		n		ŋ
Lateral	voiced			l		
Semivowel	voiced	w		r	y	

A matrix can be constructed for vowels as well as for consonants. The height of the tongue and the way the tongue bulges affect vowel quality. So do other factors, such as the position of the velum: a vowel articulated with a relaxed velum that permits passage of breath out through the nose as well as out through the mouth is said to have nasal quality or to be nasalized. In certain technical, matrix-oriented descriptions, the height of the tongue is labeled on a vertical axis as high, mid, or low; the bulge of the tongue is labeled on a horizontal axis as front, central, or back. Refinements of level are possible. Some phoneticians speak of vowels as higher high or lower high, as higher mid, mean mid, or lower mid, and as higher low or lower low. A phonetician might be motivated to refer to a 'higher high front vowel [i]' or to a 'higher mid back vowel [o].' In contexts of phonemic description, however, such cumbersome labels often turn out to be otiose. Variants or allophones of the English phoneme /i/ are represented by the symbols [i] and [I], both of which belong in the high front area. Their individuality on the phonetic level, as higher high and lower high, has no point on the phonemic level of analysis. The same is true of the allophones of other vowel phonemes. Such allophones are phonetically similar and noncontrastive. It is enough, when discussing /i/ or /o/ as phonemes, to refer to distinctive features, features which are crucial to phonemic contrasts. It is enough to call /i/ the 'high front vowel,' and /o/ the 'mid back vowel.'

Experts are fairly consistent in their own use of vowel symbols. They may differ with others, however, about the best way to transcribe vowel sounds. Different lineages of scholarship sometimes seem to work at cross-purposes. One man may prefer the symbol [E] for a mean mid front vowel, just as his teacher did, and another man, who had a different teacher, may prefer the symbol [ɛ] for the same vowel, perhaps with a mark to show that the sound has been raised from a lower position, as in *bed* transcribed [bɛ^d]. The next matrix, just below, shows some of the symbols which phoneticians use in transcribing the vowels that they hear in English speech. The student will require special training before he can use these symbols with the skill of a professional. Even as a professional, he will not be immune to the embarrassments of impressionism. How can we avoid impressionism? Would a tape recorder help? Somewhat, perhaps. But tape recordings, though valuable in field work, do not remove the pencil from the phonetician's hand. His pencil is not under control of a machine, no matter what he is listening to. And if he is listening to a recording rather than to a human voice, he has lost some of the sound waves which give the human voice its living fidelity. What is needed is a machine which listens and transcribes. For the time being, then, there is no absolute concurrence and certitude in transcriptional matters. This fact should not depress us unduly. An elementary knowledge of phonetics, in spite of lack of agreement on particular points, is indispensable for a deep and satisfying understanding of the structure of language.

	Front	Central	Back
High	i I	ɨ	u ɣ U
Mid	e ɛ	ɜ ə ʙ	o ɵ ʌ
Low	æ a	ɐ ɑ	ɔ ɑ ɒ

The vocalic inventory of one idiolect sometimes is not the same as that of another idiolect. In examining the following matrix, which represents the vowel phonemes of a particular idiolect of English, the student should remember that other matrices are possible for other idiolects. He should note, too, that the phonemic symbols have been assigned in a way which facilitates typing and printing. Finally, he should consider the aptness of a metaphor. Can one properly say that the phoneme /i/ and the phone [i] differ as a dollar does from a dime?

	Front	Central	Back
High	i	ɨ	u
Mid	e	ə	o
Low	æ	a	ɔ

13«

How Primitive is the Phonology of a Primitive Tribe?

Our object is to consider a list of words that have been transcribed with phonetic symbols. Then we must consolidate our data by assigning allophones to phonemes. Then we must transcribe the list, using phonemic symbols. In the process, we will find a basis for generalizing about the phonological equipment of supposedly primitive tribes.

Some 1500 American Indians preserve and support their culture as they use the words behind the phonetic transcriptions. These Indians, of the Jebero tribe, live in South America. They have descended from a migrant group which settled in northeastern Peru in ancient times.

Where do these Jebero live? There is, if one remembers a map of South America, a westward bulge of the continent, a huge curving headland. A line due north from Lima describes the string of a gigantic bow facing the Pacific. The bowstring crosses the Marañón river twice. Lima is on the coast. About 100 miles inland, the Marañón starts its northwesterly course, curving not quite at the midpoint of the bowstring into the dome of an elephant's head. The Marañón runs for hundreds of miles from the Lima area northwestward, about 100 miles from the coast. Roughly parallel to the Marañón is a second great river, the Huallaga. Both rivers describe an elephant's trunk. Then the Huallaga veers to the northeast, where it joins the Marañón, coming down along the top of the elephant's head. The Marañón continues along into the curve of a spine, perhaps for 200 miles: and then the spine opens into the majestic Amazon river. The Amazon flows through lush and perilous jungles some 1500 miles to the east, where, by various mouths, it empties into the Atlantic Ocean. The Jebero people live between the Marañón and the Huallaga rivers, mostly at the place of confluence. Our knowledge of the language of these people of the far western heartland of Amazonia reflects a pilgrimage and field work by John Bendor-Samuel.

The location of the Jebero in the tropics, far from the advantages of civilization, would have been enough, in past centuries, to guarantee a claim by some self-appointed experts that the Jebero mentality was defective. How easy it has been for such experts to deny ancient and medieval populations, no less than so-called primitive groups, credit for native intelligence and intellectual capacity on a par with their own! The fact of the matter is, of course, that such experts are too free with dichotomies.

There is no primitive mind, rich in archetypal images and stupid superstitions, and manifestly inferior to the civilized, scientific, abstractionistic mind. Nor is there any valid dichotomy between a primitive, concrete, handicapped language used by benighted savages, and any of the rich, subtle, expressive, artistic, and technical languages used by people who have been educated in big cities. Such a dichotomy begs the question—it assumes as proved something which, when one bothers to examine the evidence, cannot be proved. Any language does its business with the aid of structural elements which are associated with meanings. Two of these structural elements are the phoneme and the morpheme. All languages have phonemes and morphemes, by definition; and all speakers of languages, regardless of their surroundings and past history, make use of such structural elements. If the vocabulary of Julius Caesar had more words in it than the vocabulary of Carlos Talexio, a Jebero Indian, we are closer to the truth in admitting that Roman culture was more complex than in arguing fatuously that there is something defective about the Jebero language. The Jebero words that will consume our interest, we want to emphasize, are as proud as any other words in any other language and are worthy of respect. The student, for best results in completion of this exercise, should scrutinize them with care and love, and without the devaluation reserved by some for exotic museum exhibits.

The chief purpose of this exercise is to consolidate and vivify the student's apprehension of what has come to be called a discovery procedure in linguistic analysis. The procedure as it relates to phonemes is developed at length in three books which the student will want to study as a means toward deepening his understanding of language. In ascending order of difficulty, they are: H. A. Gleason, Jr., *An Introduction to Descriptive Linguistics* (1961), C. F. Hockett, *A Course in Modern Linguistics* (1958), and Z. S. Harris, *Structural Linguistics* (1960).

The student may profitably pretend that he has penetrated to the confluence of the Marañón and Huallaga rivers, equipped with certain phonetic symbols. He cannot be certain in advance that the symbols in his possession will be entirely adequate, if his phonetic training has been sketchy, or has been oriented toward a small group of languages such as German, French, and Spanish. A field worker must be prepared for confusion and embarrassment, if he is going to live with people whose culture is quite different from his own. Each culture has its own structure of expectations, and an outsider's expectations may not be in congruence with those of the people who consider him a stranger. A useful term for the discovery of misplaced expectations is 'culture shock.' The linguistic anthropologist knows that his first work will be 'etic,' based as it is upon his usual expectations. Later on, he will learn to recognize a network of relationships which involve distinctive elements of the new culture. To the extent that he can show which elements are distinctive, and how they relate to each other, his work will be 'emic.' It may take ten years or longer to do emic justice to the new culture. One's early work has to be tentative to be sophisticated. But we will pretend that the student's stock of phonetic symbols is entirely adequate. His symbols are as follows:

[i] A high front vowel.
[a] A low central vowel.
[u] A high back vowel.
[ə] A mid back vowel.
[p] A voiceless bilabial stop.
[b] A voiced bilabial stop.
[t] A voiceless dental stop.
[d] A voiced dental stop.
[č] A voiceless blade-palatal stop. The blade of the tongue strikes the palate while the tip of the tongue rests behind the lower teeth.
[ǰ] A voiced blade-palatal stop, made as above, but with voicing.
[k^y] A voiceless velar stop with palatal quality.

[k^{w}] A voiceless velar stop with labial quality.
[g] A voiced velar stop.
[ʔ] A glottal catch or stop.
[k^{ʔ}] A glottalized [k]. The glottis closes an instant before the [k] is exploded, and then pops open.
[r] A voiced alveolar flap.
[r^{ʔ}] A glottalized [r].
[s] A voiceless alveolar spirant.
[š] A voiceless alveopalatal spirant.
[l] A voiced alveolar lateral.
[l^{y}] A voiced blade-palatal lateral. The blade of the tongue strikes the palate while the tip of the tongue rests behind the lower teeth.
[m] A bilabial nasal. This and the next six phones are voiced.
[n] A dental nasal.
[n^{y}] A blade-palatal nasal. The blade of the tongue strikes the palate while the tip of the tongue rests behind the lower teeth.
[ŋ] A velar nasal.
[w] A bilabial continuant without friction.
[y] A blade-palatal continuant without friction.
[Y] A blade-alveolar continuant generally without friction. The blade of the tongue approaches the alveolar ridge while the tip of the tongue rests behind the lower teeth.

Specimen utterances of Jebero, transcribed with the symbols given above, are:

1. [amanaʔkaʔl^{y}i] the tiger ate
2. [amanaʔluk^{ʔ}] with a tiger
3. [asuiʔn^{y}i] he did not tie
4. [asumbalaʔnǰa] have you tied up
5. [asumbaYi] he is fastening
6. [aytək] jungle bird
7. [il^{y}ambasik] when he is making a noise
8. [insək^{y}itulək] I hid myself
9. [inYək^{ʔ}aŋima] and jumping
10. [in^{y}ər^{ʔ}] every
11. [iŋgatuʔYapərima] four of them
12. [itaŋniʔma] saying
13. [itək^{ʔ}] root
14. [ituk^{w}un^{y}i] he went and said
15. [iyal^{y}i] fellow
16. [iyal^{y}iʔ] man

17.	[uta]	evening
18.	[uteri]	sister of a man
19.	[uʔay]	large
20.	[uʔlanša]	a little rain
21.	[uʔlaŋ]	rain
22.	[əkl^{y}i]	tomorrow
23.	[ək^{y}ilala]	summer
24.	[ənǰuinləčək]	I will go and cut
25.	[ənǰək]	hair
26.	[əŋgaʔla]	you gave
27.	[ərwasik^{y}ima]	when it is late
28.	[ər^{ʔ}wa]	afternoon
29.	[čimin^{y}i]	he died
30.	[čimipi]	dead
31.	[čipəča]	little mosquito net
32.	[kala]	three
33.	[kapər^{ʔ}]	poison
34.	[kəl^{y}ulun^{y}in^{y}iʔ]	a black tiger
35.	[kəŋmiʔna]	but you
36.	[kər^{ʔ}]	manioc
37.	[kəʔča]	a little manioc
38.	[kwa]	I
39.	[k^{w}uYa]	we
40.	[k^{w}uʔwapən^{y}əŋ]	his wife
41.	[kwəʔl^{y}a]	you are heavy
42.	[laYək^{ʔ}]	face
43.	[l^{y}iʔlaʔnǰa]	did you see?
44.	[l^{y}iʔl^{y}ipəŋ]	he saw the fire
45.	[l^{y}iʔpəriʔl^{y}i]	he struck and pinned down
46.	[mandər^{ʔ}]	fetch
47.	[maʔi]	er
48.	[milalək]	I went and gathered
49.	[musəngək]	on high
50.	[məʔčapal^{y}i]	it is ripening
51.	[nalaima]	tree
52.	[nambipala]	you are living
53.	[nana]	the
54.	[nana]	he
55.	[nawaʔk^{y}i]	belonging to them
56.	[n^{y}apala]	are you there
57.	[nunša]	a little canoe

No.	Form	Gloss
58.	[nuŋgək]	in the canoe
59.	[pawimbal^{y}i]	it is lacking
60.	[paɂkərˀ]	go
61.	[pinəŋ]	his body
62.	[piYəkˀ]	house
63.	[pəkˀkwəɂnǰaɂl^{y}i]	stretched out
64.	[pəŋ]	fire
65.	[pwin^{y}u]	water pot
66.	[sakaɂtul^{y}i]	he worked
67.	[supay]	demon
68.	[suYambəŋ]	your husband
69.	[sək^{y}ituYəklək]	I hid them
70.	[šayaɂ]	woman
71.	[šiwiluk]	at Jeberos
72.	[tambaɂ]	arm, branch
73.	[tambuɂYunsanəŋnakˀ]	at the side of their shelter
74.	[tamutuɂ]	noon
75.	[tanYikˀ]	on the Marañón
76.	[taŋgumərˀkun^{y}ima]	it went under the water
77.	[tasərpik^{w}u]	the old man
78.	[təkˀkaiɂmbuɂYi]	he did not run
79.	[təkˀkaɂl^{y}i]	he ran
80.	[təkˀkwaɂl^{y}i]	he fears
81.	[təŋdaŋnaɂ]	smoothing their beds
82.	[wan^{y}iyəkˀl^{y}i]	he stood in the water
83.	[wapuk]	many
84.	[wapur]	boat
85.	[wičiɂl^{y}inaɂ]	they slept
86.	[wila]	boy
87.	[wəklaYəkˀnəŋ]	his blood
88.	[wənǰaɂl^{y}i]	he came back
89.	[wəraŋ]	food
90.	[wəy]	far off
91.	[yaɂ]	yesterday
92.	[Yasuɂla]	morning
93.	[Yukər]	month
94.	[Yukˀtaɂla]	even water
95.	[Yəkpil^{y}i]	in the night
96.	[Yəkˀ]	water
97.	[YəkˀkəɂčuYəkl^{y}i]	he killed them all
98.	[Yəkˀuk^{w}učik]	to the shore

In undertaking this exercise, as in the initiation of any analytic inspection of a small corpus just acquired, one profitably begins by looking for minimal pairs, sets of words or utterance fractions like English [lIt] and [bIt]. A set like [lIt] and [bIt] forces us to recognize two phonemes right away, /l/ (with an allophone [l]) and /b/ (with an allophone [b]). Items 15 and 16, [iyal^{y}i] and [iyal^{y}iʔ], come close to being a minimal pair. We might suppose that [#] (silence, absence of any qualities of sound) contrasts with [ʔ], the glottal catch. On the other hand, the meanings 'fellow' and 'man' are strangely close, and it might be well to reserve judgment. Since informants can be confused, malicious, or mischievous, caution is useful. A native of a South Pacific island, questioned by a French investigator about the number system of his language, ran out of numbers before the Frenchman did. He then supplied a complete list of curse words. Then he supplied some nonsense syllables. The Frenchman's betrayal was not discovered until a generation after his published report of the astronomical number system of South Sea natives had appeared. In the early stages of analysis, then, we must cherish the axiom: 'Never trust your informant.' Record what he gives you, pleasantly, but keep an open mind. So it is with items 15 and 16. We must reserve judgment until our axiomatic mistrust of the data has been overcome. Items 15 and 16 may or may not turn out to be important. It is also helpful to wonder about one's own early transcriptions. These should be checked repeatedly, if there is any doubt about their accuracy. 'How do you say "fellow"?'—'[iyal^{y}i].' 'Could I say [iyal^{y}iʔ] for "fellow"?'—'No, [iyal^{y}iʔ] means "man." ' And so on. In such questioning lies the superiority of direct contact with informants, as opposed to the collection of tape recordings of texts and lists of words. One's ability to question a tape recording, no matter how nicely transistorized or expensive the tape recorder, is limited. A healthy dead-file requires a live informant.

In the pair of utterance-fractions 29–30, we encounter what seems to be a case of contrast. (It is convenient, if less accurate, to speak of utterance-fractions as though they were single words. What is meant by 'word' may vary from language to language, once terms are defined with rigor. But here we will avoid the cumbersome term 'utterance-fraction' and will use 'word.') Word 29 means 'he died,' and word 30 means 'dead.' In the environment [čimi_i] we have [n^{y}]

versus [p], the difference between 'he died' and 'dead.' Tentatively, then, we can recognize two phonemes, /n^{y}/ (with an allophone [n^{y}]) and /p/ (with an allophone [p]). Another minimal pair, 83-84, contrasts [k] and [r] in the environment [wapu_]. Here the difference is between 'many' and 'boat.' Does a Spanish word for 'boat,' *vapor,* invalidate word 84, and disqualify it as part of the Jebero vocabulary? No scholar has yet certified a method for identifying alien words. Is [wapur] Spanish or Jebero?

It seems best to postpone questions of linguistic borrowing or the naturalization of alien words until a rough notion of the phonemic inventory has been worked up. Some linguists wish to rid their data of supposed alien words right away. It does little harm, however, to 'play dumb' about such words. They might not be loan words, despite fortuitous resemblances. We do not want to lose valuable data because of linguistic hubris. Such hubris, or criminal bumptiousness, occasionally manifests itself in admixture of description and past history, two aspects of analysis best kept separate, if one's policy is, 'Describe the blossom, not the genes.' Descriptive or synchronic techniques do not presuppose or require historical or diachronic knowledge. Such knowledge has its place, as the full story of a language is presented. Sometimes, however, it gets in the way of elegant description.

After a corpus has been studied for minimal pairs, for a rapid listing of unquestionably distinctive phonemes, the corpus may be studied for recurring segments, items represented, that is, by the same graphic sign or signs. We search for phonetically similar segments which are in complementary distribution in easily identified environments. 'Initially in a word,' 'medially in a word,' and 'finally in a word' are three such environments. They are convenient starting points, and other environments may appear as useful once we have undertaken the identification of phonetically similar elements.

Suppose that we start with elements that involve [k]. Does [k] occur initially in a word? Yes, for example in 32 [kala] 'three.' Does it occur medially? Yes, for example in 60 [paʔkər^{ʔ}] 'go.' Does it occur finally? Yes, for example in 6 [aytək] 'jungle bird.' We may become concerned, in the process of finding such specimens of [k], by the elements [k^{w}], [k^{y}], and [k^{ʔ}]. A discovery that it is possible to predict the occurrence of [k^{w}] and [k^{y}] will enable us to regard these as two allophones of a phoneme tentatively to be identified as /k/. Can we say that [k^w] is the allophone of /k/ which occurs only before [u]? And that [k^y] is the allophone of /k/ which occurs only before [i]? And that [k] is the allophone of /k/ which occurs before vowels other than [u] or [i] and before consonants, including the consonant-like component of glottalization [^{ʔ}] and the semivowel [w]? There are some troublesome problems hidden in this last question.

It appears that [k^w] occurs normally before [u], witness words 39, 40, and 98. Also, [k^y] occurs before [i], witness words 23, 27, and 69. And [k] occurs before [ə] and [a], witness words 32, 33, 34, and 37. Word 38 [kwa] 'I' has [w], not [^{w}]; words 41 and 63 have a sequence [kwə], not [k^wə]. Should careful checking with one or more informants prove that the transcriptions are valid, it would be natural, on the basis of the limited evidence in hand, to consider [k^w], [k^y], and [k] as noncontrastive allophones of /k/. If we were to discover at a later time that Jebero has a word [k^wa] (let us say with the meaning 'grape,' just to be concrete), we would have to think about a new phoneme, /k^w/. Some languages have labialized phonemes such as /k^w/. Some languages have glottalized phonemes, too. We have to decide sometimes, given [$k^ʔ$] in phonetic transcription, whether this represents a glottalized /k'/ or a sequence of two phonemes, /k/ followed (in terms of abstraction) by /ʔ/. Some linguists prefer to regard the intimate articulation of velar stop and glottal catch at practically the same moment, in this case, as proof of a phonetic unity which compels one to set up a single phoneme, a so-called checked or glottalized phoneme, /k'/. Others, having established a glottal catch phoneme /ʔ/ for the language in question, see economy and elegance in counting the glottalization component of a checked consonant as an allophone of the /ʔ/phoneme. Is there evidence in our Jebero corpus for a glottal catch phoneme? Compare words 6 [aytək] 'jungle bird' and 13 [itə$k^ʔ$] 'root.' Compare also words 37 [kəʔča] 'a little manioc' and 72 [tambaʔ] 'branch.' There is enough evidence in our corpus to justify our setting up a glottal catch phoneme /ʔ/, and not enough evidence, as yet, for the brief that /k'/ is a distinctive unit in contrast with /k/. Words 6 and 13 are not a minimal pair, and cannot justify, by themselves, the supposition that /k'/ is in contrast with /k/. Habit, faith, or lineage will settle the problem at a given point in time for a given scholar. For me, the tentative solution is to take

[$k^ʔ$] as /kʔ/ on the phonemic level. Such a solution is said to be 'componential' rather than 'rooted in phonetic unity.'

Our definition of the phoneme requires us to group noncontrastive allophones together into a given phonemic class, provided that these allophones are phonetically similar. Homorganic consonants, articulated with similar configurations of the speech organs but differing in one or several articulatory and hence acoustic respects, are safely taken as phonetically similar. Our Jebero /k/, then, is not properly or correctly described if we say that its allophones are [k^w], whose environment is 'before [u],' and [k^y], whose environment is 'before [i],' and [k], whose environments are neatly designated by the word 'elsewhere.' The fact that [k] occurs medially in a word and that its voiced partner, homorganic [g] also occurs medially in a word should not obscure the fact that medial [k] and medial [g] are in complementary distribution. For while medial [k] never occurs after a nasal consonant, [g] occurs only after a nasal consonant. Compare, for example, 49 [musəngək] 'on high,' 58 [nuŋgək] 'in the canoe,' 60 [paʔkər^ʔ] 'go,' and 76 [taŋgumər^{ʔ}kun^{y}ima] 'it went under the water.' Tentatively, then, we have four allophones for /k/, [k^w] before [u], [k^y] before [i], [g] after a nasal consonant, and [k] elsewhere.

Continue the analysis of Jebero phonemes, listing phonemes and their allophones; and then respell the words of our list phonemically.

14 «

The Taxonomic Approach to Morphemes

Just as allophones belong to phonemes, allomorphs belong to morphemes. A morpheme is a class of semantically similar and noncontrastive allomorphs. How does an investigator find these allomorphs?

Let us take a phonemic transcription, simplified by omission of prosodic or phrase marking phonemes, and cut it into minimal meaningful segments which for the moment will be called morphs. The utterance is as follows: 'Early students of the sociology of knowledge wrongly ignored the general cross-cultural relations of thought to society, and took as essential a harmony between thought and society within cultural limits. These men claimed that different types of thought stem from different types of society.' The transcription: /ərliy styuwdᵻnts əv ðə sowsiyaləǰiy əv naliǰ rɔŋliy ignɔhd ðə ǰenərəl krɔskəlčərəl rəleyšənz əv θɔht tuw səsayətiy ænd tuk æz ᵻsenšəl ə hahməniy bᵻtwiyn θɔht ænd səsayətiy wiðin kəlčərəl limits ðiyz men kleymd ðæt difrənt tayps əv θɔht stem frəm difrənt tayps əv səsayətiy/.

The words of this passage, on the allomorphic level of abstraction, break into minimal meaningful units, on comparison with such units in other words. These other words do not need to be part of the transcribed passage. We break *limits,* for example, into *limit* and *-s* because we can think of *cat: cats, cup: cups, pack: packs* (but not where verbs are implicated—the /s/ here is the plural suffix of nouns). We break *comical* into *comic* and *-al,* remembering *topic: topical, tropic: tropical, clinic: clinical.* What do we do with *journal?* This word ends with the same /əl/ as *comical* /kamikəl/, from a formal point of view. But from a semantic point of view, the /əl/ of *comical* means something like 'of or pertaining to,' and it is difficult if not impossible to cut off the /əl/ of *journal* /ǰərnəl/ and assign a meaning to it. Etymological reflections, concerning morphemes in past history and other languages, are profitless in the isolation of morphs. Description of the here and now concerns itself ideally only with the here and now.

This remark is easier to make than to live by. Take *sociology*. Comparisons such as *morph: morphology, phone: phonology, graph: graphology, cosmic: cosmology* suggest the isolation of *-ology* /aləǰiy/ as a derivational element. A student of Latin would think perhaps of the word *socius* 'companion,' in contemplating the /sowsiy/ of *sociology*. A student of Greek would think perhaps of the word *lógos* 'word, organization.' He might even think of English *logic* /laǰik/ and Greek *logikḗ* or *logikós* 'pertaining to rational organization.' He might then wish to isolate the *-log-* of *-ology*. Should he regard *-ology* as made of three morphs, a relatively meaningless or empty morph *-o*, announcing that another morph will follow, and then *-log-* /ləǰ/ of ancient dignity, and then *-y*, a derivational suffix that can be isolated from such words as *juicy, dreamy, chilly* and perhaps *robbery* with the meaning 'characterized by or inclined to'? Truly, *sociology* is characterized by organized discourse about groups of companions, if we wish to suck etymological juices from the word. But classification of morphs, especially in languages for which extensive written records do not exist, such as Jebero or Chipewyan, need not require knowledge of past history. It is useful, at least at the start of an investigation of morphology, to hold one's knowledge of past history in abeyance, while at the same time dividing words into segments whose meaning is readily identified as palpable on the basis of comparisons within one's immediate range of experience. The student will discover, if he reads extensively, that scholars who frame morphological statements sometimes operate on both sides of the etymological fence.

Part of the trouble which beginners experience with linguistic science comes from the casual disregard of definitions. Beginners sometimes fail to see the need to memorize definitions. But definitions need to be memorized and applied with relentless determination. A definition may turn out, after considered examination, to be inefficient or useless in terms of a comprehensive or general theory. It may be a leaky boat, bound to sink despite much bailing out. Time will tell, as it does with all statements which are vulnerable and so respectable in the society of scientists. Definitions, no matter how faulty in temporal perspective, however, must be honored. Our definition of the morpheme may turn out to be a leaky boat. We must pay careful attention, nevertheless, to all of its details and requirements.

Our definition of the morpheme requires us to classify morphs into one morpheme if those morphs are semantically similar and noncontrastive. Semantic similarity does not mean semantic concreteness and similarity. Some morphs lack concreteness of meaning: what does *-nik* mean in *sputnik, lunik, beatnik?* The palpability of meaning in any language runs on an impressionistic scale from a concrete pole (*brick, stone, dog, cat, hand*) to a vague or opaque pole (the *-nik* of *beatnik,* the *cran-* of *cranberry*). A second polarity, which obtains for derivational elements, involves productivity, the freedom with which an element is used. A freely used element is said to be productive; one used rarely is unproductive. Thus *-ness* as in *kindness, richness, madness,* is relatively productive; *-nik,* on the other hand, after a flurry of attention and such coinages as *muttnik* (a sputnik or Soviet space satellite with a dog passenger) and *sexnik,* is relatively unproductive. Productivity and semantic palpability, in English at least, correlate neither directly nor inversely.

Our definition of the morpheme has been challenged because in some cases we cannot deal crisply with meaning, even on an impressionistic basis. A purely formal definition of the morpheme is an alternative, a definition which does not require us to determine the semantic implications of a stream of phonemes. For a beginner, however, semantic short-cuts to the formal entities which function as basic units above the level of the phoneme are not out of place. Linguistics may be a form of discrete mathematics, but beginners traditionally start out as something less than mathematicians.

Despite a number of shaky or uncertain segmentations, reflecting etymological static or semantic indigestion, the grouping of morphs into classes called morphemes, once the morphs have been identified, generally poses no insurmountable problems. Students sometimes are troubled by derivational and other elements whose meaning cannot be stated or felt. They reject the notion that such elements have any meaning at all. Others find meanings where they do not exist. Thus some will say that *-ness* is 'meaningless,' and others will cut *shrimp* /šrimp/ 'decapod crustacean' into /šr/ and /imp/, on the grounds, perhaps, that a shrimp is small and, so is an imp. Insistence on the one hand that not all meaning is concrete and on the other hand that one should use common sense and not play games seems useful in these cases.

Morphs occur or are distributed in environments or neighborhoods. Two morphs are said to be in contrast or in contrastive distribution when they occur in the same environment. In the forms *manly* and *friendly, man* and *friend* are in contrast in the environment *-ly*. Morphs in contrast belong to different morphemes; they cannot belong to the same morpheme.

Braces are used by many linguists to indicate morphemes; thus *man* might be represented by {*man*} or by {*A*}. Or, with recourse to phonemic transcription, by {mæn}. The choice is up to the linguist. For pedagogical reasons, I prefer to use regular spelling and some easily identified tag; as: {*man*}, {*dog*}, {*cat*}, {*-ness*}, {*plural*}, meaning, respectively, 'man,' 'dog,' 'cat,' 'with the quality, condition, or state of being . . . ,' and 'plural.' The glosses within quotation marks are, of course, mere tokens of meanings, tokens which facilitate linguistic investigations but which cannot by themselves be more than stabs at profound and intricate sociocultural realities.

Some morphemes have just one morph which, when it joins the morpheme, can be called an allomorph. An example is {*stone*} 'stone,' with one allomorph, /stown/. Some morphemes have more than one allomorph. Ordinarily the allomorphs are in complementary distribution; that is, the allomorphs, semantically similar though they are, do not share any environments. An example of a morpheme with two allomorphs is the noun {*house*}. The allomorph /haws/ 'structure people live in' occurs in various environments, but not in the environment 'before {*plural*}.' In this environment, which can be represented as '_____ + {*plural*},' we have a second allomorph, /hawz/. If we see {*house*}, we know that the phonemic representation at issue is /haws/, unless the {*house*} is followed by {*plural*}. That is, given {*a*} + {*big*} + {*house*}, the morpheme {*house*}, a noun, is represented by the allomorph /haws/. But given {*big*} + {*house*} + {*plural*}, the morpheme {*house*} is represented by the allomorph /hawz/. Regular English spelling is cruelly misleading. So powerful are the spelling habits of a lifetime that students sometimes are deceived into supposing that one rather than two pronunciations are involved in the spelling *house*. Reflection will help to establish, however, that many English nouns, verbs, adjectives, and other forms have multiple allomorphs or, to introduce another term, morphophonemic alternants. Part of the job of a linguist, as he writes a grammar, is to offer a list of morphemes and their allomorphs. A statement about the distribution or environments of the allomorphs of a morpheme is, in technical parlance, a morphophonemic statement. To say, for example, that English has a noun {*house*} with an allomorph /hawz/ before the plural suffix and an allomorph /haws/ elsewhere, is to make a morphophonemic statement.

15 «

Morphophonemic Exercises

1. *Eskimo.* An ethnologist in South Greenland sits down with an informant and elicits three Eskimo words: /iγlu/ 'house,' /iγlut/ 'houses,' and /iγluk/ 'two houses.' How many morphemes does he have here? Limited in his data, he must not be alarmed by morphological surprises later in his study of the language. But for the moment, tentatively, he has {*iγlu*} 'house,' with one allomorph, /iγlu/; a morpheme with an allomorph /t/ 'plural'; and a morpheme with an allomorph /k/ 'two' or 'dual.' The suffix /k/ seems to restrict plurality to two objects. The morpheme with /t/ might best be represented, then, by {*plural, but not two*} or simply {*-t*} 'plural, but not two.' The morpheme with /k/ could be represented by {*dual*} or {*-k*} 'dual.' These inferences must be tested by direct questioning of the present informant and other informants, and, ideally, after a few months of study, by indirect eliciting, alert listening to unguarded conversation or speech. In that way, he can satisfy professional mistrustfulness of the casual or even deliberate observations of informants, and professional modesty about his own preliminary inferences. For the moment, however, he must suppose that the morphemes at hand have one allomorph each. In the next hour, the ethnologist runs into these forms: /iγlua/ 'his house,' /iγlui/ 'his houses,' /iγluk/ 'his two houses,' /iγluat/ 'their house,' and /iγluak/ 'the house of both of them.' Do any of the inferences that he made in connection with his first three words require revision? Be specific in your answer.

2. *Zapotec.* An ethnologist in Oaxaca, Mexico, discovers what he wants to call a morpheme {*second person plural possessor*} with a suffixal allomorph /le/ 'your.' He also finds a morpheme {*third person singular animate possessor*} with a suffixal allomorph /ïb/ 'a living thing's: his,

her, its.' The ethnologist's corpus includes these forms: /yišïʔ/ 'weed,' /lišïʔïb/ 'its weed,' /ližïb/ 'its house,' /ližle/ 'your house,' /yoʔo/ 'house.' Analyzing these forms, he recognizes the suffixes which are represented by /ïb/ and /le/. He is left with /yišïʔ/ 'weed,' which seems to have a possessed variation /lišïʔ/, as in /lišïʔ-ïb/ 'its weed.' He also has /yoʔo/ 'house' and a possessed variant /liž/, as in /liž-ïb/ 'its house,' /liž-le/ 'your house.' On grounds of complementary distribution and semantic similarity of allomorphs, he sets up a morpheme {*yoʔo*} 'house' with an allomorph /liž/ before a possessor suffix and an allomorph /yoʔo/ elsewhere. In doing so, does he violate our definition of the morpheme? Should one also postulate a morpheme {*yišïʔ*} 'weed' with two allomorphs?

3. *Rumanian.* An American college student vacationing in the Macedonian port of Salonica meets a Transylvanian ballet dancer, who offers to tutor him in Rumanian. Mistrustful of her ingenuous conventions, he insists on using his own phonemic transcription and devising his own morphological rules. He collects these forms during his first few lessons.

/vakə/	cow	/ursu/	bear
/vač/	cows	/urš/	bears
/vačile/	the cows	/uršiy/	the bears
/fiykə/	daughter	/čeapə/	onion
/fiyče/	daughters	/čepe/	onions
/fiyčele/	the daughters	/čepele/	the onions
/slugə/	servant	/bəyə/	bath
/sluǰ/	servants	/bəy/	baths
/sluǰile/	the servants	/bəyile/	the baths
/fragə/	strawberry	/kalu/	horse
/fraǰe/	strawberries	/kay/	horses
/fraǰele/	the strawberries	/kayiy/	the horses
/rusu/	Russian	/zilə/	day
/ruš/	Russians	/zile/	days
/rušiy/	the Russians	/zilele/	the days

His earliest morphological notes, based on these forms, are as follows.

1. {*singular*} 'singular' or perhaps, better, 'nonplural.'

a) An allomorph /ə/ appears in

/vak-ə/	cow
/fiyk-ə/	daughter
/slug-ə/	servant
/frag-ə/	strawberry
/čeap-ə/	onion
/bay-ə/	bath
/zil-ə/	day

b) A second allomorph, /u/, appears in

/rus-u/	Russian
/urs-u/	bear
/kal-u/	horse

The /u/-allomorph is in complementary distribution with the /ə/-allomorph, and each is semantically similar to the other, so these allomorphs belong to the same morpheme.

2. {*plural*} 'plural.'

a) An allomorph /e/ appears in

/fiyč-e/	daughters
/frǰ-e/	strawberries
/čep-e/	onions
/zil-e/	days

b) In some words, I would expect to find /e/ 'plural' but I find nothing. For example, I would expect /vač-e/ 'cows' but I find /vač/; I would expect /sluǰ-e/ 'servants' but I find /sluǰ/. I find /vač/ 'cows' beside forms like /fiyč-e/ 'daughters' and /sluǰ/ 'servants' beside forms like /fraǰ-e/ 'strawberries.' Absence of any phoneme exists, then, at a point in some words where one would expect something to indicate the plural. The absence is informative: it conveys the same semantic information that /e/ does. I will call this absence a 'zero' allomorph and represent it by 0. The zero allomorph is in complementary distribution with the /e/-allomorph, and each is semantically similar to the other, so these allomorphs belong to the same morpheme.

Words with the zero allomorph of {*plural*} are

/vač-0/	cows
/sluǰ-0/	servants
/ruš-0/	Russians
/urš-0/	bears
/bəy-0/	baths
/kay-0/	horses

c) A third allomorph, /i/, appears sometimes before a suffix which means 'the' and has the form /le/ or /y/. This /i/-allomorph is in complementary distribution with the zero allomorph and with the /e/-allomorph, and each of the three is semantically similar to the other two, so these three allomorphs all belong to the same morpheme.

Words with the /i/-allomorph of {*plural*} are

/vač-i-le/	the cows
/sluǰ-i-le/	the servants
/ruš-i-y/	the Russians
/urš-i-y/	the bears
/bəy-i-le/	the baths
/kay-i-y/	the horses

3. {*the*} 'the.'

a) An allomorph /le/ appears in

/vač-i-le/	the cows
/fiyč-e-le/	the daughters
/sluǰ-i-le/	the servants
/fraǰ-e-le/	the strawberries
/čep-e-le/	the onions
/bəy-i-le/	the baths
/zil-e-le/	the days

b) A second allomorph, /y/, appears in

/ruš-i-y/	the Russians
/urš-i-y/	the bears
/kay-i-y/	the horses

4. Some nouns have one root allomorph. Others have more than one. Nouns with one root allomorph are:

{*bath*} bath
/bəy/

{*day*} day
/zil/

Nouns with more than one root allomorph are:

{*cow*} cow
/vak/ before {*singular*}
/vač/ before {*plural*}

(This pattern is followed in the rest of the list—the first allomorph before {*singular*}, the second before {*plural*}.)

{*daughter*} daughter /fiyk/ ~ /fiyč/ (with the sign ~ used to show complementary distribution)
{*servant*} servant /slug/ ~ /sluǰ/
{*strawberry*} strawberry /frag/ ~ /fraǰ/
{*Russian*} Russian /rus/ ~ /ruš/
{*bear*} bear /urs/ ~ /urš/
{*onion*} onion /čeap/ ~ /čep/
{*horse*} horse /kal/ ~ /kay/

Identify and revise any objectionable material or inferences in the foregoing notes. Is your revision, if you have decided that one is needed, based only on the data and orientation of this book?

Once one accepts the Salonica formulation, how would one represent the following Rumanian sequences phonemically?

1. {*bear*} + {*plural*}
2. {*strawberry*} + {*singular*}
3. {*strawberry*} + {*plural*}
4. {*strawberry*} + {*plural*} + {*the*}
5. {*onion*} + {*plural*}
6. {*horse*} + {*singular*}
7. {*horse*} + {*plural*}
8. {*day*} + {*plural*} + {*the*}
9. {*daughter*} + {*singular*}
10. {*cow*} + {*singular*}

The student discovers that he has been in error about some of his transcriptions. His Transylvanian informant insists that she has not changed her pronunciations. He reviews his notes and determines that he must make these changes in his transcriptions:

CHANGE		TO
/rusu/	Russian	/rus/
/ursu/	bear	/urs/
/čeapə/	onion	/čapə/
/bəyə/	bath	/baye/
/kalu/	horse	/kal/
/zilə/	day	/zi/

Revise the student's earliest morphological notes (*1–4* above) in view of these changes.

The student discovers these forms:

/vaka/	the cow
/fiyka/	the daughter
/sluga	the servant
/fraga/	the strawberry
/rusul/	the Russian
/ursul/	the bear
/čapa/	the onion
/baya/	the bath
/kalul/	the horse
/ziwa/	the day

Revise your revision of *1–4* above, in order to include the new data.

This exercise demonstrates graphically the fact that constant revision and checking are necessary concomitants of preliminary linguistic research.

4. *English.* The Sanskrit word *mukta* means 'let loose, emancipated.' The word may be applied to a person, one freed from the entanglements of matter or custom. Thus Seymour Glass, a brother of Zooey in Salinger's *Franny and Zooey,* has been called a *mukta* by one critic. One does not become a *mukta* in matters of language without practice. Freedom from enslavement to conventions of spelling, particularly by members of a literate society, entails much practice and not a little suffering. Defensive hostility, marshaled against the pain, is no substitute for practice.

This observation is necessary as we move from languages which are novel, like Jebero or Rumanian, to the language that is home base for most readers of this book. More bias, more prejudice, more willful commitment to unthinking entanglement in grammatical custom, some of it going back to ancient times, can be expected from a literate reader whose native language is English when he has to make grammatical statements about English, than when he deals with exotic languages. The authority of science is melted in the hot blood of customary opinion. In moving toward the state of *mukta,* the student will have to set the method of science above its content. There are many scholars, each with his own view of English phonemes, English morphemes, English syntax. The student who probes deeply into English grammar will reconcile himself to the fact of scientific pluralism soon enough. The question, 'Whose view is best?' then leads to other questions of the broadest and most comprehensive sort, questions of prime philosophical importance, to be broached later on. For the moment, however, agreeing with Aristotle in his *Metaphysics* that what is most universal is the hardest to know, let us turn to some interesting if not simple problems of English morphology, with constant alertness, if possible, against the distractions of customary opinion.

The American student, back from his adventure in Salonica, decides to analyze English as if it were an exotic language. His corpus, he feels, is already in his head. He begins his study with the paradigm of *girl.* The forms that he works with, and his analysis, are shown below.

1. 'young female'			
1 Routine Spelling	2 Phonemic Spelling	3 Allomorphs (hyphenated)	4 Morphemes (represented by allomorphs in col. 3)
girl	gərl	gərl	{*girl*}, the *base*
girl's	gərlz	gərl-z	{*girl*} + {*possessor*}
girls	gərlz	gərl-z	{*girl*} + {*plural*}
girls'	gərlz	gərl-0-z	{*girl*} + {*plural*} + {*possessor*}

2. 'mature female'			
1	2	3	4
woman	wumən	wumən	{*woman*}
woman's	wumənz	wumən-z	{*woman*} + {*possessor*}
women	wimən	wimən-0	{*woman*} + {*plural*}
women's	wimənz	wimən-0-z	{*woman*} + {*plural*} + {*possessor*}

3. 'working quadruped'			
1	2	3	4
horse	hɔrs	hɔrs	{*horse*}
horse's	hɔrsɨz	hɔrs-ɨz	{*horse*} + {*possessor*}
horses	hɔrsɨz	hɔrs-ɨz	{*horse*} + {*plural*}
horses'	hɔrsɨz	hɔrs-0-ɨz	{*horse*} + {*plural*} + {*possessor*}

4. 'omnivorous quadruped, source of pork'			
1	2	3	4
pig	pig	pig	{*pig*}
pig's	pigz	pig-z	{*pig*} + {*possessor*}
pigs	pigz	pig-z	{*pig*} + {*plural*}
pigs'	pigz	pig-0-z	{*pig*} + {*plural*} + {*possessor*}

5. 'herbivorous quadruped'			
1	2	3	4
sheep	šiyp	šiyp	{*sheep*}
sheep's	šiyps	šiyp-s	{*sheep*} + {*possessor*}
sheep	šiyp	šiyp-0	{*sheep*} + {*plural*}
sheep's	šiyps	šiyp-0-s	{*sheep*} + {*plural*} + {*possessor*}

6. 'working steer'			
1	2	3	4
ox	aks	aks	{*ox*}
ox's	aksɨz	aks-ɨz	{*ox*} + {*possessor*}
oxen	aksən	aks-ən	{*ox*} + {*plural*}
oxen's	aksənz	aks-ən-z	{*ox*} + {*plural*} + {*possessor*}

7. 'immature human being'			
1	2	3	4
child	čayld	čayld	{*child*}
child's	čayldz	čayld-z	{*child*} + {*possessor*}
children	čildrən	čild-rən	{*child*} + {*plural*}
children's	čildrənz	čild-rən-z	{*child*} + {*plural*} + {*possessor*}

8. 'one who farms'			
1	2	3	4
farmer	farmər	farm-ər	{*farm*} + {*-er*}
farmer's	farmərz	farm-ər-z	{*farm*} + {*-er*} + {*possessor*}
farmers	farmərz	farm-ər-z	{*farm*} + {*-er*} + {*plural*}
farmers'	farmərz	farm-ər-0-z	{*farm*} + {*-er*} + {*plural*} + {*poss.*}

9. 'spiny plant' (casual speech)			
1	2	3	4
cactus	kæktəs	kæktəs	{*cactus*}
cactus's	kæktəsɨz	kæktəs-ɨz	{*cactus*} + {*possessor*}
cactuses	kæktəsɨz	kæktəs-ɨz	{*cactus*} + {*plural*}
cactuses'	kæktəsɨz	kæktəs-0-ɨz	{*cactus*} + {*plural*} + {*possessor*}

10. 'spiny plant' (formal speech)			
1	2	3	4
cactus	kæktəs	kæktəs	{*cactus*}
cactus's	kæktəsɪz	kæktəs-ɪz	{*cactus*} + {*possessor*}
cacti	kæktay	kækt-ay	{*cactus*} + {*plural*}
cacti's	kæktayz	kækt-ay-z	{*cactus*} + {*plural*} + {*possessor*}

The student reaches the following conclusion:

any word which has one base only, and sometimes has {*plural*} or {*possessor*} arranged with the base, is by convenient definition a *noun.* (If there are two bases, as with *blueberry,* we have a nominal phrase, not a noun.) A noun consists of a base by itself, or a base followed in the same word by an inflectional suffix {*plural*} or {*possessor*}, or a base followed in the same word by {*plural*} *and* {*possessor*}. The base sometimes is followed by one or more derivational suffixes too, as in *farmer,* {*farm*} + {*-er*}, where {*-er*} is an agentive suffix that means 'one who . . .' (a *farmer* is 'one who farms'), or in *beautifiers,* {*beauty*} + {*-fy*} + {*-er*} + {*plural*}. But the essential mark of a noun is that a single base occurs with a suffix {*plural*} or {*possessor*} as part of the paradigm.

In what way, if any, is the student's description of the noun scientific?

Do any of his inferences invite revision?

16«

Syntax

The experiments of linguists with phonological and morphological data, and their extensions of classificational procedures into syntax, considered as the analysis of the immediate constituents of phrases, clauses, and other sentence units, had an impact upon anthropology. Anthropologists acquired heightened awareness of the significance of distribution and contrast. The etic function of listing things to be searched out, a function with roots in natural historical research, gave way in popularity to the emic function of taking things, once they have been listed, and subjecting them to a distributionally and componentially sophisticated process of analysis. The anthropologist was exhorted to be emic, not simply etic; Pike in the mid-'fifties, when his tagmemic-behavioremic approach was moving toward its ultimate form, suggested that anthropological research has as its end the description of the relations of distinctive units of behavior, 'behavioremes.' Just as a sentence has slots for forms that fill the slots, so a cultural event may be studied to see which slots and fillers are significant for a particular society.

Chomsky's work in syntax was popularized in the late 'fifties; after a decade of development, serious flaws in the slot and filler approach have been identified and rejected; and the importance of axiomatization in linguistic and anthropological research has been established. While generative grammarians quite properly minimize the role of mathematics in their work, and emphasize the importance of characterizing a speaker's competence (as opposed to performance) and the rules for competence which must be provided, it is the mathematical basis which gives their theory its intellectual dignity. A scientist tries to expose himself to criticism and correction. He tries to frame impeachable statements. His aim is to propound a doctrine, but not to be doctrinaire. And the best means for making a statement impeachable is to use language free of ambiguity, language of mathematical purity. Only a few theorists are at work in axiomatizing languages; of these, the most important include Chomsky and his associates. The axiomatization is proceeding along Carnapian and set theoretic lines, the latter approach having been developed by Chomsky to the point where an impact upon anthropology and other social sciences can be discerned. For this reason, a brief statement about the nature and dangers of set theory as applied to language and culture may be entertained.

A mapping of any subset of the integers into an alphabet is a sequence. A sequence, in other words, is a set of ordered couples with every integer of the subset of integers appearing in one couple, along with a so-called primitive generator, i.e. an element of the alphabet. (The alphabet is a set of letters which are to be tied by co-ordinating definitions to facts in the real world; the size of the alphabet is not limited by the size of any popular alphabet. The term vocabulary is used sometimes instead of alphabet; in any event, one must have these primitives as well as rules that operate upon them. The investigator, using these primitives and rules, tries parsimoniously to predict 'true' from his data.)

Mappings are of two sorts, 'into' and 'onto.' Suppose we map set X, with three elements, x_1, x_2 and x_3 ($X = \{x_1, x_2, x_3\}$), into set Y, with four elements, y_1, y_2, y_3, y_4 ($Y = \{y_1, y_2, y_3, y_4\}$). We need three ordered couples, one with x_1, one with x_2, and one with x_3. One possible mapping of X **into** Y, then, is

$$M = (x_1, y_2), (x_2, y_3), (x_3, y_2),$$

also written

$$M(x_1) = y_2, M(x_2) = y_3, M(x_3) = y_2.$$

(A mapping of X **onto** Y brings every element of Y into some couple. The mapping is biunique when X is mapped onto Y and every element of Y appears just once.)

Take a set of sequences. If these sequences meet certain conditions, over a given alphabet, we speak of a similarity class of sequences. Each sequence—that is, each set of ordered couples—is of the same length, for a given similarity class. And for that class, each sequence has the same generator in its i-th position, for each i. But each sequence in the similarity class has a different index set.

Each particular similarity class of sequences is a string. (Note that a string is not a sequence.) Facts of experience are co-ordinated with strings in applications. Texts in experience are co-ordinated with ordered collections of occurrences of primitive generators.

There is a set E of all finite nonempty sequences over a given alphabet A. E is constructed by taking every finite subset of the integers as an index set. Using these index sets, we take all possible different mappings of index sets into A. This means that we have an infinity of similarity classes in E. The whole set of them we call L. Take any one of these similarity classes of sequences, and we have a string. (Since there is an infinity of integers, there is an infinity of index sets and an infinity of members in any string.)

To characterize the arrangements of strings, we need to apply the noncommutative, associative law of composition called the law of concatenation to sequences and strings. The concatenation of any sequence in one similarity class with any sequence in another is characterized by a class determined by the two similarity classes, not by any representative sequences of these two classes.

It can be proved (seeing that our law of composition is associative) that the letters or shortest strings of the set L of similarity classes in E—E being the set of all sequences over A—that these minimal generators are the basic elements from which, by concatenation, every string in L can be produced. The proof is a theorem of decomposition.

When we define the law of concatenation over the set L (of similarity classes in E), we have a semigroup or monoid, since for that we need an associative law of composition; and we have a free monoid, since for that we need our noncommutative law of concatenation.

In our free monoid we have the set of all possible finite strings over our alphabet. The empirical collection of analogues of strings is the basis for the description of a subset of a free monoid, the logician's 'language.'

Primarily out of the work of Chomsky and the mathematician Schützenberger, it can be seen, the Peircean vision of the universe of that which is cognizable, the universe of signs, has come to be supplemented with an entirely adequate mathematical characterization. In his early work, Chomsky developed what in Morris's terms would be called the syntactic part of semiotic theory. This co-ordinates formal signs, as facts in the real world, with strings, which are logical entities. As the scientist readily agrees, facts have priority, not the formalism. If the specifications of the formalism turn out to be inadequate, the specifications must be modified, not the facts. To deny the facts so as to preserve illogical applications of the formalism is to pour new mathematical wine into old prescriptive bottles. To deny the importance of formalization, on the other hand, is to retard the progress of science.

The dangers of being too rigid in specification of rules are real, and generative grammarians have been criticized for such rigidity. Such criticism, however, diverts attention from the fact that generative grammatical theory is truly scientific, whereas other approaches may only seem to be so, through a clutter of jargon and data. The basis for this statement of scientific respectability lies in the formalism and attendant impeachability just described. There is no exclusiveness about the theory so far developed; other truly scientific approaches, equally impeachable, are conceivable and under construction; but this word of caution is needed before we turn to various views and methods of contemporary syntax.

Relations, in the formalism just mentioned, are characterized by couples of a Cartesian product. In each ordered couple there appears a symbol of a primitive alphabet which is co-ordinated with some fact in experience. Some relations of elements, say of morphemes with other morphemes, in sentences, are apparent from the inspection of the constituents, and from the assessment of transition probabilities between elements. Consider:

Joe was kissing all the girls.

This—intonation aside—reduces maximally to

{Joe} *1* {be} *4* {-D_1} *3* {kiss} *4* {-ing} *2* {all} *4* {ð-} *6* {-e} *5* {girl} *6* {-Z_1}

or, using letters A, B, and so on respectively for morphemes,

{A} *1* {B} *4* {C} *3* {D} *4* {E} *2* {F} *4* {G} *6* {H} *5* {I} *6* {J}.

The sequence of relations of morphological elements, mapping the index set $I = \{1, 2, \ldots, 10\}$ into the primitive set $A = \{A, B, \ldots, J\}$, is a set of ordered couples: {(1,A), (2,B), (3,C), (4,D), (5,E), (6,F), (7,G), (8,H), (9,I), (10,J)}.

This sequence concerns morphemes represented by phonemes. Other sequences, however, concerning transitional expectations, must be constructed in characterizing constituent structure. The assignment of cut numbers ranking ICs hierarchically may be geared to such expectations. More elements, that is, precede and follow cut number *1* than cut *2*, and so on down the line: 'more' or 'less' here reflecting the speaker's practical experience, not the infinite possibilities of sign behavior.

Generative grammarians have pointed out that an insufficient range of phenomena is covered by the usual phrase or constituent structural syntactic analysis; the linguist must worry about the speaker's competence with language, not just his competence over a limited range of language. And the construction of a theory to account for the data of language therefore must extend in two directions away from cut-up sentences, into transformations, rules for manipulating constituent structures, and into morphophonemics, rules for arriving at the ultimate articulations. More recently, semantic information has come to figure in the best of generative theory. What marks the bulk of this theory from the very beginning is an anti-taxonomic bent, a rejection on very sound theoretical grounds, grounds of parsimony, of discovery procedures unrelated to the description of competence.

The central problem in theoretical anthropology is how to make predictions about the interlocking systematic expectations within a culture. In their rejection of taxonomic linguistics, generative grammarians have emphasized the importance of studying data in relation to systems. The term 'systematic linguistics' has been proposed as a counter to 'taxonomic linguistics.' In generative phonology, the systematic relations of distinctive features of phonemes (as determined largely by Jakobson and Halle) to grammatical classes is given importance. Statements about the history of sounds, the sound-laws of historical phonology, also are framed with systems in mind. As Jakobson put it, in anticipation of generative developments, 'The idea of a sound law operating without exceptions in a given language must be limited to a linguistic system characterized by one and the same function, i.e., to linguistic entities which are functionally equivalent.' (*Selected Writings* I.l.) One of the weaknesses of systemic analysis, a fault of technique rather than theory, is a too-great dependency upon too-simple theorems of decomposition. As greater care is taken to avoid this weakness, which we shall examine below, anthropology will come closer to its major theoretical goal.

Let us begin with some simple decompositions, also called partitions, and their refinements. In general,

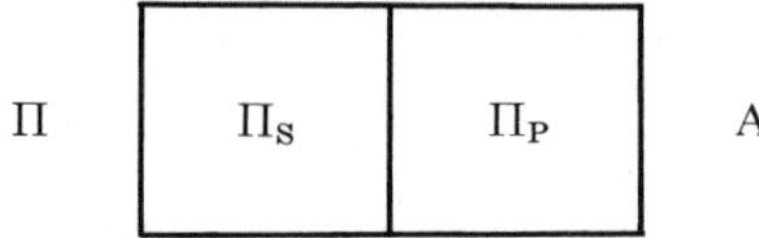

Π is a partition of A $\leftrightarrow U\Pi = A$ & $(\forall \Pi_S)(\forall \Pi_P)$
$(\Pi_S \in \Pi$ & $\Pi_P \in \Pi$ & $\Pi_S \neq \Pi_P \rightarrow \Pi_S \cap \Pi_P = 0)$
& $(\forall x)(x \in \Pi \rightarrow (\exists y)(y \in x))$.

This amounts to our saying that we have a collection of sets of A (Π_S and Π_P) labeled Π, such that Π is a partition or decomposition of A. Roughly speaking, we have a family of mutually exclusive non-empty subsets of A whose union equals A. The disconnected sets Π_S and Π_P are finer than Π as shown here. If we co-ordinate elements of the S class with singular nouns and those of the P class with plural nouns, a further refinement would be to co-ordinate elements of $\{m_1\}$ and $\{f_1\}$ in the S class with (singular) masculine and feminine nouns, and of $\{m_2\}$ and $\{f_2\}$ in the P class with (plural) masculine and feminine nouns.

In a theory propounded by Kulagina, partitional logic is used in such a way that in a partition *gamma,* defined on a primitive vocabulary *xi*, there are finer partitions called neighborhoods. The neighborhood of a form *gamma* (x) can be shown as follows: Γ (*fille*) = {*fille, filles*}, Γ (*grande*) = {*grande, grandes, grand, grands*}. The formalism is so constructed that a phrase is grammatical or not depending on various rules, despite substitutions. The model permits the following constructions:

	ATTRIBUTE	HEAD	
f	grande grandes	fille filles	sg pl
m	grand grands	fils fils	sg pl

But the model does not reckon well with the possibility that rules may be broken. Marot has *grandes choses,* and perhaps had *grande chose;* he has *grand bonté,* and perhaps had *grands bontés.*

Similarly, Navaho has a large number of object classes and general rules for assigning particular verbs to objects of particular classes. To say 'it's there' of a round object class member, one uses the verb *siʔą́;* of a long object class member, *sithą́;* of a living being class member, *sithį́;* and so on for classes designated as follows: set of objects, *sinil;* rigid container with contents, *sikhą́;* fabric-like object, *siłtsooz;* bulky object, *šižóót;* set of parallel objects, *šižoož;* a mass, *šitžaaʔ;* wool-like mass, *sitžool;* rope-like object, *silá;* and mud-like mass, *sitłééʔ.* When a partitional schematism is too rigid, rules are used that deny the flexibility of real life. If we designate subsets of verbals by *A* through *L* and use subscripted *Ns* to designate subsets of nominals (units functioning respectively as verbs and nouns), we can represent topic-comment sentences by symbol, e.g. *tsin sithą́* by N_b *B*. Here *tsin* 'stick' requires the long object verbal stem. In a rigid partitional schematism we would have:

Topic	N_a	N_b	N_c	N_d	N_e	N_f	N_g	N_h	N_i	N_j	N_k	N_l
Comment	A	B	C	D	E	F	G	H	I	J	K	L

A generative rule uses an arrow as an instruction to replace one symbol with another or others. Thus an expansion is indicated by

$$S \rightarrow NP + VP,$$

to be read, sentence goes to noun phrase plus verb phrase. The expansion rule can be expressed as a reduction rule by reversing the arrow's direction: $S \leftarrow NP + VP$. The grammarian's problem is to specify those rules, operating over properly selected generators, which will, in a completely satisfactory fashion, characterize all and only the grammatical sentences of a language. (For 'characterize' some prefer 'generate,' whence the expression 'generative grammar.')

It is obviously too simple to use the following rules for Navaho:

$N_a \rightarrow$ *tsé* rock
$N_b \rightarrow$ *tsin* stick, log
$N_c \rightarrow$ *ʔawééʔ* baby
$N_d \rightarrow$ *ʔatʔaʔ* feathers
$N_e \rightarrow$ *thó* (pool of) water
$N_f \rightarrow$ *peeltléí* blanket
$N_g \rightarrow$ *tsʔaaʔ* basket
$N_h \rightarrow$ *tsin* logs
$N_i \rightarrow$ *pəkʔaʔ* his arrows
$N_j \rightarrow$ *ʔaγaaʔ* wool
$N_k \rightarrow$ *tłʔóół* rope
$N_l \rightarrow$ *haštłʔiš* mud

Given that classes must co-occur as shown in the topic-comment partitioning, and that C → *sithį́* 'it's there (as a live object),' *tsé* 'rock' would be prevented from co-occurring with *sithį́*, according to generative rule. This seems like a rational restriction, since it is absurd to say that a lifeless rock is alive. Yet absurdity enters experience through metaphor.

One of the fruits of developing generative theory is the discovery of systems for breaking rules. Just as competence has to be learned by discarding, at the behest of parents and other teachers, ungrammatical sentences, so other kinds of competence, all of them normative, have to be learned. There are rules for breaking rules. Such iconoclastic rules are based on cultural competencies whose study has barely begun. Staging of 'mistakes,' disintegration, error, teasing, naughtiness, humor—such bases for the production of ungrammatical utterances exist as a temporary embarrassment to the framers of general rules. There is no reason, however, for rejection of the hope that the problems inherent in co-ordinating strings of symbols with facts of experience are not insoluble. And, while this hope prospers, anthropologists have at hand the means for limited studies, marked by formal dignity, in cultural systems.

17«

Phonological Horizons

The popularization of sound spectrographic equipment since the mid-'forties has accelerated research into the physical nature of speech sounds. In the late nineteenth century, phonetic research explored the relation of sounds to articulatory motions. With new equipment, emphasis has shifted to the analysis of spectrographic pictures of the sound waves of speech. Along with some controversy, this shift has produced interesting experimentation and a basis for the development of systematic phonology.

One hesitates to say 'a new' systematic phonology, because the notion of the insufficiency of a mere phonemic inventory has been propounded almost as long as the term phoneme itself. Phonemicists who simply list graphemes for distinct phonemes, or who use phonetic definitions (e.g. saying that French /g/ is a 'postpalatal stop'), have long been criticized for divorcing themselves from phonological analysis of the total system of sound relations.

Varying perspectives in phonological analysis have led to the analysis of auditory qualities by some structuralists in terms of binary oppositions of distinctive features, by others in terms of articulatory components, by others in terms of the qualities *per se.* All three approaches have been exemplified by Martin (*Lg.* 27, 1951) in a single problem-oriented study. Thus he postulates nine distinctive auditory qualities, (1) nasal, (2) front, (3) high, (4) mid, (5) low, (6) labial, (7) tense, (8) contactual, and (9) fricative, for Korean phonemes; each of the nine is present or absent in a given phoneme, as shown in these examples: /p/ 6, 8 (i.e. 'labial-contactual' defines /p/); /t/ 2, 8; /c/ (a voiceless, lax, prepalatal or alveolar affricate) 2, 8, 9; /s/ 2, 9; /k/ 8; /m/ 1, 6, 7, 8; /n/ 1, 2, 7, 8. In his binary analytic example, building upon work of Roman Jakobson and John Lotz, Martin assumed for each Korean phoneme six distinctive oppositions, (1) contactual *vs.* fluid, (2) front *vs.* back (higher saturation *vs.* lower saturation), (3) high *vs.* low (acute *vs.* grave), (4) labial *vs.* nonlabial, (5) nasal *vs.* oral, and (6) tense *vs.* lax. Each phoneme, in iconic tabulation, is checked against the six sets of distinctive oppositional features; when the first, less frequent or 'marked' feature of a set is present, + is used; when the second feature of a set is present, no mark (or –, in some studies) is used; and when both features are present, ± is used: /p/ is defined by a bundle, as it were, of contactual, back, low, labial, oral, and lax distinctive features; /t/, to put it more easily, is contactual, front, low, nonlabial, oral, and lax; /c/ is both contactual and fluid, front, low, nonlabial, oral, and lax; and so on. A partial tabulation is given below.

OPPOSITIONS	p	t	c	s	k	m	n	. . .
contactual (*vs.* fluid)	+	+	+		+	±	±	
front (*vs.* back)		+	+	+			+	
high (*vs.* low)								
labial (*vs.* nonlabial)	+					+		
nasal (*vs.* oral)						+	+	
tense (*vs.* lax)						±	±	

Morris Halle has been privileged to work with both Jakobson and Chomsky. In *The Sound Pattern of Russian,* Halle integrates ideas of his associates, reflecting current concern for axiomatization in considering any sentence, for example, as a theorem derived, from a system of postulates, by applying certain 'rules of inference,' and at the same time reflecting recent binary analytic developments.

Like Martin's approach, Halle's involves some innovations when contrasted with Jakobson's earlier work. The fact remains that distinctive features have acoustic correlates, measured by various spectra and visible speech sonagrams. Vocalic phones, for example, concentrate energy in the range of 300–800 cycles per second and have concentrations of energy or 'formants' in their spectra.

The first formant is called F1, the second F2. The oppositions of Russian include (1) vocalic *vs.* nonvocalic; (2) consonantal *vs.* nonconsonantal; (3) compact *vs.* noncompact; (4) diffuse *vs.* nondiffuse; (5) low tonality *vs.* high tonality; (6) strident *vs.* mellow; (7) nasal *vs.* nonnasal; (8) continuant *vs.* interrupted; (9) voiced *vs.* unvoiced; (10)

sharped *vs.* plain. The oppositions of (3) and (4), formerly called compact *vs.* diffuse, are functions of F1; the opposition of (5) is a function of F2. *Vowels* are vocalic and nonconsonantal; other classes are *consonants,* consonantal and nonvocalic; *liquids* (*l*, palatalized *l'*, *r*, palatalized *r'*), vocalic and consonantal; and the *glide* (like our /y/ but spelled *j*), nonvocalic and nonconsonantal. Speech events are (1) segments, defined by components or distinctive features in binary sets, and (2) boundaries, described by their effects on segments. Only vowels, of those events mentioned, can be diffuse, which means that F1 is as low as possible; in Russian this feature correlates with lip rounding or widening of the pharynx.

As to (5), tonality implicates flat *vs.* natural; a flat is read from lip rounding which lowers all formants. As to (6), continuants sometimes are strident or 'noisy,' e.g. /š/, which is strident and, as a palatal, also compact and acute; /f/ is strident and also noncompact and grave; /z/ is strident and also noncompact and acute. And continuants sometimes are mellow, e.g. the noncompact and grave /p/ and /b/, the noncompact and acute /t/ and /d/, or the compact /k/ and /g/. As to (9), voiced consonants show less intensity than those which are unvoiced. In (10), sharped means palatalized.

In Russian consonants or nonvowels, diffuse *vs.* nondiffuse is unspecified; in vowels, the opposition is distinctive. An unspecified feature which is predictable from other features of the same segment (hence, nonphonemic) is represented below by 0. Here we have a partial scheme for /p/, /b/, palatalized /p'/, /b'/, and /š/, /ž/. As an abbreviation, just the first term of each opposition is indicated.

COMPONENTS	p	b	p′	b′	š	ž
vocalic	−	−	−	−	−	−
consonantal	+	+	+	+	+	+
diffuse	0	0	0	0	0	0
compact	−	−	−	−	+	+
low tonality	+	+	+	+	−	−
strident	−	−	−	−	0	0
nasal	−	−	−	−	0	0
continuant	0	0	0	0	+	+
voiced	−	+	−	+	−	+
sharped	−	−	+	+	0	0

Criticism has been directed at the interpretations of acoustic pictures, at the statements of acoustico-articulatory correlations. Such criticism is based partly on research at the Haskins Laboratories. Haskins scholars have studied acoustic cues which help hearers to perceive speech. They have used pattern playback equipment; they have synthesized speech, for example, from paintings of idealized spectrograms to study crucial components. In their view, sounds are (1) constriction sounds or point sounds, frictional /f θ s š tš v ð z ž dž/ or explosive /p t k b d g/; (2) transition sounds, also called resonance-labyrinth or channel sounds; or (3) nasal sounds. As to (1), /p t k/ have burst-frequency dimensions of difference; /s š/ have different frequency locations of friction noise. That is, frequency *level* is a cue for some consonants of the constriction class. The distinction of /f θ/ and /s š/ is a matter, in part, of intensity (more for /s š/, less for /f θ/). As to sounds of class (2), these are made by supraglottal changes, reflected in frequency *shifts* or formant transitions of F1, F2, and F3. Such shifts, it is believed, help in distinguishing stops from nasals, liquids, and semivowels. A correlation is suspected between variations in direction and extent of F2 and F3 transitions and place of production of consonants, and between such variations of F1 and manner of production of consonants.

Each consonant, excepting /k g ŋ/ before /a ɔ/, has its own locus or characteristic frequency position, where a formant transition 'starts.' Thus English /d/ 'aims' to start at about 1800 cycles per second. The locus adjusts itself to the vowel frequency-level which is anticipated.

Cues, then, are the frequency level, the formant direction, the formant extent, and also the transition duration (by which, perhaps, stops and nasals are distinguished from semivowels), and what is called the tether effect. Sometimes the formant transition begins precisely at a locus; sometimes it does not. Stops and nasals are not closely tethered; /y w r l/, however, must be.

Haskins scholars count /p b m/ as 'front,' /t d n/ as 'middle,' and /k g ŋ/ as 'back,' and observe that the coding patterns or transition cues for voiced stops, voiceless stops, and nasals are similar; the front, middle, and back elements are coded similarly, too. These scholars have not attempted to co-ordinate their research with phonological analysis of linguistic systems, and so have been unable to make contributions to the study of language comparable in importance with those of Jakobson and his associates. Acoustic analysis is not an end in itself, but simply a means toward the end of parsimonious characterization of the rules of language.

Some terminological equations will help to clarify the following demonstration of the utility of Jakobsonian acoustics, whatever refinements may be necessary before all investigators are satisfied with it. For grave, it is useful often to infer a labial consonant or a back vowel; for acute, a dental consonant or front vowel; for interrupted, a stop; for flat, sharpened; for plain, nonsharpened; for nonnasalized, oral; for tense, fortis or strong, or narrow. (Fortis consonants leave a more central, neutral position, moving further and longer. Fortes or tense consonants have greater breath pressure at the point of articulation and last longer than lenes or lax consonants. Sometimes fortes are voiceless, in contrast to lenes which are voiced; but, as in Swiss German, lenes may be voiceless, too. Subglottal pressure is less for lax than for tense vowels.) For lax, one infers lenis, weak or wide. Sometimes a raised ^{1} indicates a tense element, e.g. /e^1/, and a raised ^{2}, a lax element, e.g. /e^2/. Longer vowels are tense; lax vowels are centralized. Compact suggests more energy, and that increasing, in a spectral band both narrow and central (vowels are centralized, but consonants, especially /k g/, are narrowed and not especially centralized), and implies qualities described by back or open, implicating velar consonants and even soft palate consonants such as /k ɲ š/. Diffuse suggests less energy, and that decreasing, in the central spectral band; it suggests the terms front or close, and labial or dental consonants. Traditional accounts of assimilation of sounds, which emphasize articulatory locations, are powerfully supplemented by insights which show how close are such sounds as /p/ and /t/, where the former is identical with the latter as to diffuseness, but different where /p/ is grave and /t/ acute.

Vowel harmony involves acoustic dimensions which also would be overlooked by traditional phoneticians. Bari has this system:

$i^{1,2}$		$u^{1,2}$
$e^{1,2}$		$o^{1,2}$
	$a^{1,2}$	

If a stem vowel is V^1, the prefix or suffix has a systematically corresponding vowel, and vice versa; for example, /to¹-gi¹rja¹/ 'to make wipe,' /to²-gi²rja²/ 'to cause to cicatrize.' Ibo has:

$V_{diffuse}$	$i^{1,2}$	$u^{1,2}$
$V_{compact}$	$e^{1,2}$	$o^{1,2}$

Given as a root vowel V^1, a prefix is selected with $V_{diffuse}{}^{1,2}$; and given as a root vowel V^2, a prefix is selected with $V_{compact}{}^{1,2}$.

Jakobson observes that the simpler of two phonemic solutions is the less redundant. It is therefore better to see the French consonants /k ɲ š/ as not different respecting point of articulation (velar, palatal, prepalatal), since all three are succinctly identified in terms of opposed features, e.g. all are compact consonants: 'if certain phonemic distinctions possess a common denominator and are never observed to co-exist within one language, then they may be interpreted as mere variants of a single opposition . . . the selection of a given variant in a certain language [may be] connected with some other features proper to the same linguistic pattern.'

From Jakobson's work have stemmed binary analyses of phonemic systems such as that shown on p. 121.

Postal has pointed out that Boas, in his approach to phonetic rules, did not operate with a principle of phonemic biuniqueness; Boas was aware of grammatical restrictions on phonological rules, and of the fact that phonological rules apply to higher-order units, elements of trees whose nodes are identified by nonterminal or auxiliary symbols. That is, the constituent structure of strings is affected; a hierarchy of grammatical boundaries is implicated. Boas did not order his rules of euphony, as Sapir did; but he brought to American linguistics insights later to be expanded, with due regard for Jakobsonian acoustics, by Chomsky and Halle.

A relatively small number of Mohawk systematic segments (bundles of binary distinctive features), along with morpheme boundaries, are

	o	a	e	u	ə	i	l	r	ŋ	s	č	k	z	ǯ	g	m	f	p	v	b	n	s	θ	t	z
vocalic or nonvocalic	+	+	+	+	+	+	+	+	−	−	−	−	−	−	−	−	−	−	−	−	−	−	−	−	−
consonantal or nonconsonantal	−	−	−	−	−	−	+	+	+	+	+	+	+	+	+	+	+	+	+	+	+	+	+	+	+
compact or diffuse	+	+	+	−	−	−			+	+	+	+	+	+	+	−	−	−	−	−	−	−	−	−	−
grave or acute	+	+	−	+	+	−										+	+	+	+	+	−	−	−	−	−
flat or plain	+	−		+	−		(−)	(+)																	
nasal or oral (nonnasal)									+	−	−	−	−	−	−	+	−	−	−	−	+	−	−	−	−
tense or lax										+	+	+	−	−	−		+	+	−	−		+	+	+	−
continuant or interrupted										+	+	−	+	+	−		+	−	+	−		+	+	−	+
strident or mellow											+	−		+	−							+	−		+

available for the spelling of dictionary entries. Of these, the plus consonantal segments are defined (by Postal, *IJAL* 30, 1964) thus:

	n	r	w	y	k	p	t	s
consonantal	+	+	+	+	+	+	+	+
sonorant	+	+	+	+	−	−	−	−
vocalic	+	+	−	−				
grave			+	−	+	+	−	−
nasal	+	−						
compact					+	−		
interrupted							+	−

A branching diagram of features is useful for showing definitive components:

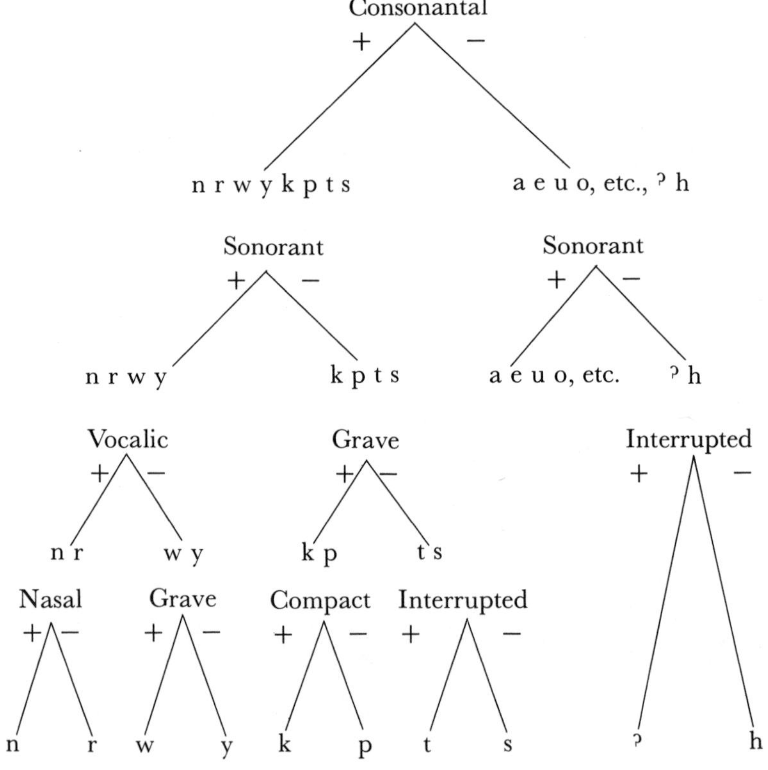

To achieve a parsimonious systematic phonological characterization, predictive generalizations over features are exploited whenever possible. The lexical redundancy rules of Mohawk, for example, include certain ordered morpheme structure rules:

1. $\begin{bmatrix} +\text{Consonantal} \\ -\text{Sonorant} \\ +\text{Grave} \end{bmatrix} \rightarrow [+\text{Interrupted}]$

(/p k/ are made interrupted.)

2. $\begin{bmatrix} +\text{Consonantal} \\ -\text{Sonorant} \\ \alpha\ \text{Interrupted} \end{bmatrix} \rightarrow [\bar{\alpha}\ \text{Strident}]$

(/t k p/ are made nonstrident; /s/ is made strident.)

The alpha symbol indicates + or −; the bar over alpha is read 'not.' Thus

$$\begin{bmatrix} +\text{Consonantal} \\ -\text{Sonorant} \\ +\text{Interrupted} \end{bmatrix} \rightarrow [-\text{Strident}], \text{ and}$$

$$\begin{bmatrix} +\text{Consonantal} \\ -\text{Sonorant} \\ -\text{Interrupted} \end{bmatrix} \rightarrow [+\text{Strident}].$$

3. $\begin{bmatrix} +\text{Consonantal} \\ -\text{Sonorant} \\ -\text{Grave} \end{bmatrix} \rightarrow [-\text{Compact}]$

(/t s/ are made noncompact.)

Some phonological rules, termed cyclic, must apply to a string more than once. Using J for any juncture, # for word boundary, and **F** for 'final,' in French, following Schane (who realizes, of course, that exceptions have to be listed, as *avec, lis, net, naïf,* etc.),

rule 1

$$\begin{bmatrix} \alpha\ \text{Consonantal} \\ \bar{\alpha}\ \text{Vocalic} \\ -\text{Stress} \end{bmatrix} \rightarrow \phi \text{ in } \_\_\_ \text{ J } [\alpha\ \text{Consonantal}], \text{ and}$$

rule 2

$$\begin{bmatrix} + \text{Consonantal} \\ - \text{Vocalic} \end{bmatrix} \rightarrow \phi \text{ in } \_\_\_ \#\mathbf{F}.$$

Using S for the plural morpheme, for *ils sont petits,*

il + S #sɔ̃t #pətit + S #**F** → il #sɔ̃ #pəti + S #**F** (by rule 1) → il #sɔ̃ #pəti #**F** (by rule 2). But for *des camarades anglais,*
deS #kamaradə + S #ãglɛz + S #**F** → de #kamaradə + S #ãglɛ + S #**F** (by rule 1) →
de #kamaradə + S #ãglɛ #**F** (by rule 2). Given the constituency

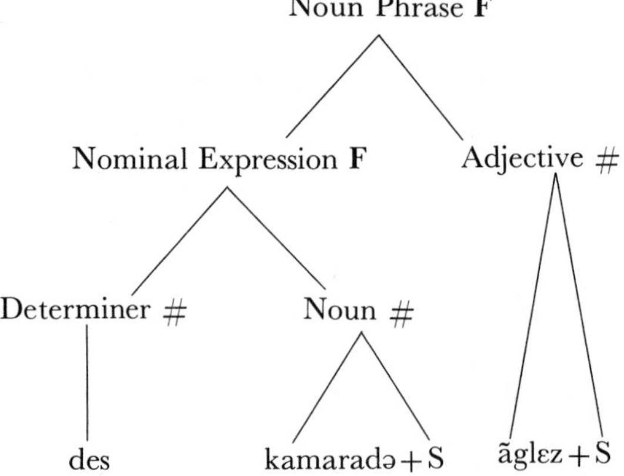

it becomes clear that phonological rules in many cases must be applied cyclically with explicit reference to a hierarchy of syntactic structures. The rules apply first to the morphemes of the inmost-bracketed words:

(((deS #)(kamaradə + S #) **F**)(ãglɛz + S #) **F**) →
(((deS #)(kamaradə + S #) **F**)(ãglɛ + S #) **F**) (by rule 1) →
(((deS #)(kamaradə + S #) **F**)(ãglɛ + S #) **F**) (by rule 2). By a reduction rule prior to the second cycle, we have
((deS #kamaradə + S #**F**)(ãglɛ + S #) **F**) →
((de #kamaradə + S #**F**)(ãglɛ + S #) **F**) (by rule 1) →
((de #kamaradə #**F**)(ãglɛ + S #) **F**) (by rule 2) →
(de #kamaradə #**F** ãglɛ + S #**F**) (by reduction) →
(de #kamarad #**F** ãglɛ + S #**F**) (by rule 1) →
(de #kamarad #**F** ãglɛ #**F**) (by rule 2) →
de kamarad ãglɛ (by reduction and deletion of junctures).

The implications of generative phonological analysis for judgments about the relationship of languages, in terms of microphonemic correspondences, form another horizon in anthropological research. Such correspondences add to evidence best provided by the matching of grammatical function, say similar formal paradigms, and morphophonemic alternations which comprise a system of some complexity.

IV

Culture: Boas

It therefore seems that almost all languages have within themselves the germ or faculty of improvement, that this is developed by the progress of knowledge and civilization, and that there is hardly any language which does not prove sufficient to satisfy all the wants of that improved state of society, whenever it occurs. Without denying some reciprocal action between the language and the mental development of a people, or that there may be some difference in degree between the several languages, I believe that their improved powers are the result and not the cause of the progress of knowledge and civilization. If there be any language the nature of which is so defective as to have impeded that progress, it must be the Chinese.

—ALBERT GALLATIN,

"Hale's Indians of North-west America, and Vocabularies of North America, with an Introduction," *Transactions of the American Ethnological Society,* Vol. II (1848).

18 «

Boas and the General Laws of Culture

We have discussed some issues and methods in linguistics. Now we may take up the question of the value of linguistics for anthropology. Anthropologists have dedicated themselves to attacking cultural stereotypes, linguistic nonsense included. They have been interested, too, in making inferences about the history of tribes, who lived where, when such-and-such peoples migrated from there to yonder, and what experiences they had at any stage along the way. The ethnoscience of tribes is another concern, to be investigated by empirical semanticists asking questions about ranges of classificatory terms. Our present concern is with attempts to recapture the past, using linguistic evidence.

The dignity in seeing models of language in the perspective of comprehensive formulations of general laws of sign behavior lies precisely in the fact that such perspective deflates extravagant claims and at the same time mocks antitheoretical conservatism. Let us review some basic concepts. A logistic system is a set of primitive definitions, rules of formation and transformation, axioms, and co-ordinating definitions or an interpretation. Contact between the system and the world comes through the interpretation. Constructs must be co-ordinated with facts; when this is not entirely possible, the constructs must be changed. That a theory may need revision spotlights the function which it serves in assembling or grouping data. The theory or model with the greatest explanatory and predictive power is best.

In Peirce's view, the best way to handle sign behavior is in terms of three kinds of signs, (1) symbols, oriented toward the future, (2) indices, oriented toward the present, and (3) icons, oriented toward the past. An icon is any image in experience which stands for some other part or parts of past experience. In a broad interpretation of Peirce's intention, an icon is not only a diagram or graph which composes data on a relatively limited scale, but also any logistical system.

Morris has proposed to develop some of Peirce's work under the heading of semiotic theory. Syntactic, semantic, and pragmatic models, and the relations among them, are to be investigated. The syntactic model deals with signs in relation to signs. The semantic model deals with signs in relation to objects or things referred to. The pragmatic model deals with signs in relation to their users. Pending final synthesis, analytic formulations must be understood to be nothing better than convenient fictions.

Language as a set of habits concerning sign behavior is part of culture. Culture is the total set of habits which man learns. Language is a subset of those habits. It is easier to work with the subset than the totality, yet from such easier work can come clues for broader generalizations.

Anthropology is the study of man as a cultured animal in possession of language. Cultural systems are structured. Because different groups of men have had different cultural structures which could be differentiated and compared, speculation arose that cultures can be ranked on a scale from primitive to civilized and that different structures produce different outlooks on experience or world views. Inferences from cultural diversity sometimes have a pernicious effect. They support notions of cultural relativism which obscure the essential homogeneity of human experience.

Values exist across cultures. Which are the enduring values? How does one approach them? Some use the artistic office. Some are idealistic, and replace rule with whim. Some follow more philosophical approaches growing from existentialism or pragmatism, as seen for example in Heidegger and the early Wittgenstein. Hegel, the ultimate idealist, held out some views interpreted by students to mean that progress toward a final stage of history will never end. Such radical historicism struck Nietzsche as having interesting implications. If one never reaches an absolute, one lives in a world of relativism, one is a creature of his time, and every belief one has is culture-bound, a product of historical 'forces.' One's thoughts are determined by circumstance, but they are relative to other thoughts determined by other circumstances. The cultural limitations which impose a character and a style upon men's thoughts and actions, in this scheme, must require unquestioning minds and limited horizons. The rule of conduct which gives a style is relative to other such rules in other places or at other times, and by other equally legitimate standards would have to be challenged and rejected.

Nietzsche did not think much of historicism. He felt that the historian is not very good at opening the way to the understanding of experience. He can show only that a rule of conduct is never objectively valid, though it may seem to be. We have to go back and look at values that once were held to be sacred and see that they are not sacred. We have to see the *relativity* of such values, reject the old ones as baseless, and find new ones which are absolute. Nietzsche saw truth to be subjective in origin, and a function of circumstance. In his solution to the problem of the relativism of decayed Hegelianism, he turned away from history to nature rather than reason, to another kind of relativism. He saw truth in a will to power, whose reflection is human creativity. Existentialism, as developed by Heidegger, tries to rid Nietzsche's alleged conquest of relativism from its nature-oriented trappings and—along with an attack on relativistic positivism—really to overcome all relativism. Yet it fails to do this.

Positivism, for its part, attempts to understand science as man's best hope and skill, as progressive, with an unpredictable future. The objects of science are open to reason, but not all at once, and so man must live with perpetual mystery. Existentialism confronts man with mystery too. Being is essentially a mystery: one cannot take a metaphysical position, because it is a falsity to assume that being can be known. Existential or 'pessimistic' relativism is antipositivistic and antiscientific; it is also committed to the false doctrine that all truths but its own are subjective. Positivistic or 'optimistic' relativism takes comfort in science, yet without any final commitment. How one approaches thought, culture, and language is a function of one's philosophical beliefs. Anthropology can only profit from increased attention to the art and purpose of rational behavior.

American linguistics was nurtured through European sap-roots. Peter Duponceau, well-enough oriented politically to become chief justice of Louisiana, was an early star of the American Philosophical Society and an early collator of linguistic data about American tribes. His work brought him fame in the early nineteenth century. Albert

Gallatin, well-enough oriented politically to become Secretary of the Treasury, an important official of the State Department, and almost a Vice-Presidential candidate, was an early star of the American Ethnological Society and the first important collator of linguistic data about American tribes. His *Synopsis* (1836) grouped languages into families on the basis of vocabularies (and the false assumption that all Indian languages have the same grammatical structure). Horatio Hale, unlike Duponceau and Gallatin, was born in the United States and was educated at Harvard. Hale's researches with the Wilkes Expedition, published in 1846, were marked by grammatical sophistication. In 1848, Gallatin published a new classification of Indian languages, doggedly ignoring Hale's use of grammar in subgrouping, though using Hale's vocabularies.

Hale, the first great native-born Americanist, lived in Canada after taking courses in law; he managed his wife's estate at Clinton as both lawyer and businessman, but he also did field work with Iroquoian and Siouan Indians. Hoping for the LL.D., which Duponceau and Gallatin both had won, Hale became active in scholarly circles. He generated such theories as one on the origin of languages which depended upon the invention by little children of private languages, the wandering away of the children into the fruitful wilds, and the development in isolation by these children of their own racial type, their own new language, and their own myths and religious doctrines. Hale never won his LL.D., but he was justifiably esteemed as a field linguist, and he was instrumental, as an official of the British Association for the Advancement of Science, in bringing the German anthropologist, Franz Boas (1858–1942), to the Pacific Northwest. Hale supervised the work of Boas in surveying tribes of that area. Boas differed with Hale in some respects, but his affection for Hale led him to curtail expression until after Hale's death.

Where did Boas stand, regarding general laws of culture? In 1899, Boas became the first professor of anthropology of the Columbia faculty. Because of a long career, and perhaps because of external factors, some contradictions may be found in his writings, for example, what seems to be a contradiction in allowing the possibility of finding general laws of culture, a view he held as early as 1896, and in disallowing the very same possibility, or the possibility of finding valid cultural laws, a view he expressed in 1932.

A careful reading, however, might resolve the issue with an assignment of priorities. Collect data first, Boas might be saying, and generalize only much later. Sweeping statements of giddy diffusionists or sober historians are generally irresponsible. To say that since many societies which give special status to men, paternal societies, derive from societies which do not, maternal societies, it follows that wherever we have a paternal society we should assume that it has originated from the breakdown of a maternal one—to say this is to beg the question. Laws based on superficial comparisons are invalid. On the other hand, laws based upon carefully collected historical data might be useful, once we overcome the seemingly insurmountable barrier offered by the unpredictable interactions of the individual and the society which he helps to shape and which helps to shape him.

It was in this context that Boas said, 'Cultural phenomena are of such complexity that it seems to me doubtful whether valid cultural laws can be found.' This opinion did not point at a substantive handicap, however, as much as at the compelling objective of a good anthropologist, to try to explain individual phenomena and their origins without establishing vague general laws so evident as to be valueless for deeper understanding. To realize this compelling objective one must study man's biological, psychological, and cultural nature in terms of historical explanations of particular features. Historical perspective, knowledge of changes of forms through time and conditions under which changes occur, protects one against mistakes, for example, the assumption that culture traits along the margins of an area always demonstrate common origin and a stable dimension of antiquity.

Boas was a vital force in the development of American linguistics. He was a pioneer in the application of linguistic insights to anthropological ends. His cautious approach to data, however, his inability to theorize, his reluctance to frame very general hypotheses whose bases are not directly observable, his disaffection for mentally interpretable theorems, all weaken his claim to purposive scientific activity.

19 «

Boas and the Classification of Languages

One cannot say that two languages are *not* related to each other. Time and custom may have erased the similarities which once were there. Such erasure may take thousands of years or relatively little time, given appropriate conditions. It *is* possible, even in the face of change, to say that two languages are *relatable*. Judgments of relatability rest on similarities of grammatical function and phonological relations so intricate that they are deemed to be beyond chance. The exact basis of formulating such judgments varies from scholar to scholar. Sometimes an impressionistic kind of inspection is all that is ventured. One simply looks at lists and gives rein to intuition. This method leads to hasty conclusions, sometimes, and to disagreements. It is well to ask in every case where a grouping of languages into a family or set is at issue: 'By which criteria was this set of languages grouped?'

Without ever answering this question, Boas nevertheless stood on the side of conservative assessment of data. He argued not so much for groupings as against them. He regarded the classification of languages as a means toward the end of tracing the history of human speech. But he felt that classification is muddied by diffusion, that ultimate blot on history.

Boas collected his favorite essays in *Race, Language, and Culture* (1940). His cautious scholarship colors these essays, and it is a kind of Baconian caution that he manifests. Among his observations is the theme that it is not quite the same to say that race, language, and culture vary in complete independence from one another as to say that racial inferences find no support in linguistic and other cultural data. Boas accordingly dismissed certain views of Brinton and Ehrenreich in 1897. Boas rejected the notion, for example, that a race can be defined in terms of linguistic criteria, a notion which

Hale had imported from Europe. It is not true that different races speak genetically related languages with fundamentally different structures. Boas had this to say in reaction to Ehrenreich's study of Brazilian Indians:

> In our investigations on the early history of mankind three methods are available, each directed to a certain series of phenomena —physical type, language, customs. These are not transmitted and do not develop in the same manner. . . . The study of the distribution of languages permits us to make nicer divisions and to follow historical changes in greater detail than that of the distribution of physical types. But often the latter give evidence in regard to phenomena which cannot be approached by linguistic methods. The distribution of the Alpine type of man in Europe, or that of the Sonoran type in North America, may be mentioned as instances of this kind. . . . The three methods . . . are all equally valuable, but since they do not refer to the same classes of facts it must not be expected that they will clear up the same incidents in the early history of mankind. . . .

In a lecture on the aims of ethnology which he gave to the Deutscher Gesellig-Wissenschaftlicher Verein von New York in 1888, Boas had offered essentially the same message. He saw value in language as one way to get at history. He was distressed by unsubstantiated and irresponsible generalizations, witness his remark that hasty theorizing is of use for 'healthy growth' and his observation that, 'Far-reaching theories have been built on weak foundations.' The student who is impelled to take these words at face value may wish to consider the possibility of sarcasm, a sarcasm to be understood in terms of Boas's audience and in the context of his further remarks on 'a relation between soil and history.' His possibly sarcastic remarks precede an attack on racist folklore.

This early lecture is interesting for several other themes. One has to do with so-called language mixture. When languages are in contact, borrowing of linguistic elements often takes place. Controversies have arisen and persist about whether and to what extent phonemes, morphemes, or grammatical rules can be borrowed or diffused from one language to another. Boas observed that when we can identify borrowed elements we learn something about cultural history; indeed, 'the history of language reflects the history of culture.' But we do not always have the good records which enable us, for example, to see English as a product of mixture (presumably mostly of Germanic and Romance elements). Later in his career, Boas was to find mixture of elements across tribal borders in America, in the Pacific Northwest or in California, for example. And he was to see here a barrier to useful inferences about genetic relationships. The doctrine that a language has a single reverse continuum is axiomatic for a majority of linguists. Heavy borrowing means heavy borrowing, not multiple reverse continua. English has borrowed heavily from French, thanks to the Norman invasion and its aftermath, but few contemporary linguists would argue that English is both a form of Latin and a form of Germanic at once. One's position on mixed languages reflects definitions and assumptions more than facts. Thus by identifying the grammatical core of a language, Hockett rules out 'mixture' of the sort postulated in the nineteenth century by Schuchardt, a German scholar much admired by Boas. The grammatical core of English is Germanic, Hockett observes, despite borrowing from French.

In linguistic contexts, the word *borrowing* serves for diffusion. Boas as a historian of culture was especially interested in diffusion, the diffusion of elements of folk tales or the diffusion of linguistic elements. He made some useful observations about linguistic elements, but in following Schuchardt and ignoring some literature which was available during his lifetime, that produced, for example, by Bloomfield, Boas fell prey, perhaps, to the ubiquity of his interests. Anthropologists for the most part no longer attempt to master the full array of anthropological branches in depth, as might have been the case in the supposed 'golden age' of anthropology when Boas was at his peak. And borrowing of traits has become less of a problem than it was in the nineteenth century. To help in the solution of the problem, researchers have resorted to various icons or models. One represents languages by continuous lines going back to nodes, points of branching. The model is familiar from organic taxonomic usage, and is called the family tree model. But languages are not like automobiles, designed on drawing-boards and issued on stipulated dates. There was no beating on pots and pans and ringing of bells on a certain night of 300 B.C., when Latin branched away from its Italic sister languages. It is more likely that when Indo-European tribesmen invaded prehistoric Italy they spoke several dialects of Indo-European, called Italic. The isolation which followed upon political considerations and which separated various groups of Italic speakers was not total. This at least is a possibility: that trading, raiding, and other relationships brought speakers of various Italic dialects, Latin, Faliscan, Oscan, Umbrian, and Sabine, for example, into contact with each other. And that borrowing of linguistic elements, linguistic diffusion, took place. The spread of elements across in-group boundaries is represented sometimes by an icon based on wave reaction. As a ripple spreads when a pebble is tossed in a pond, so in this icon an element spreads, to be shared by different culturally integral groups.

It is a widely held generalization that icons are made for iconoclasts. The family-tree icon and the wave-theory icon are useful in handling data, each in its own way. So is the atlas icon, the map on which dialect geographers chart the modal distributions of linguistic elements. But these icons are misleading for beginners who are unduly intimidated by the printer's craft. Let us consider dialect geographical work at closer range. Dialect geographers draw maps to show the recorded distributions of linguistic units (generally, phonemes, words, and grammatical usages); such records are no better than their collectors can make them. The impressionistic features of dialect atlas maps, however, are eliminated for the popular mind partly by impressive cartographic artistry. The same holds, to take another case of *majesté iconique,* for maps of supposed tribal distributions or of language areas of the Indians of aboriginal America. By thinking of an isogloss (a cartographic line which surrounds an area where a given linguistic element has great currency) as co-equal in ability to impede communication with each other isogloss—like a glass wall, as it were—it has been possible for some investigators to suppose that bundles of isoglosses indicate the boundaries of major dialect areas, and that very dense bands of isoglosses indicate the boundaries of languages. One wants to consider only languages, not dialects of a language, in comparative work and in work that demands attention to linguistic borrowing among cultural groups which have very loose ties of affiliation or none at all. It would be useful to have a system in which idiolects are grouped into dialects, and dialects into languages, and in which the relationships of language distribution to cultural and genetically determinable ethnic distributions could be described efficiently. As yet, we do not have such a system. It is convenient, however, to proceed as if we did have such a system: henceforth, the term dialect will be reserved for a collection of similar idiolects, and the term language for a collection of similar dialects if there are several, or for a single dialect if there is but one. The point at which the inexorable process of change, which transfigures a language, creates two dialects that are extremely dissimilar, so dissimilar that if there were one more change they would no longer be dialects but would be different and, to use an old metaphor, sister languages, that point we shall call the Schleicherian nodule point, in honor of the family-tree theorist Schleicher. Whenever this nodule point is invoked, it should be kept in mind that a certain assumption has been made which some day may be rejected on theoretical or factual grounds, an assumption that languages rather than dialects are being dealt with.

If the Sabines took a word from the Romans for everyday use, we would recognize an act of ordinary cultural borrowing. But when the Romans conquered the Sabines and occupied their lands, the borrowing was intimate, to use Bloomfield's term, rather than ordinary. It has sometimes happened that people have been conquered and have learned or have suffered their children to learn the conquerors' language. A case in which the language of the invaders was adopted by the subject population is that of the Gauls. Around the start of the Christian era, they lived in what now is called France and spoke a Celtic language, an Indo-European language whose common ancestor *vis-à-vis* Latin is supposed by some to have occupied an Italo-Celtic Schleicherian nodule point. Latin replaced the Gaulish language in France. A case in which the language of the invaders was lost is that of the Normans in England. By the fifteenth century, Norman French had been abandoned by most Englishmen as less useful than English. In both cases there was intimate borrowing, and then a kind of swamping.

But is there ever any mixture, rather than swamping? What about jargons, pidgins, lingua francas, and creoles? Are not these mixed languages, each with multiple reverse continua? And what about the gypsies, those wide-ranging borrowers? If by definition each new language arises at a Schleicherian nodule point, these questions lose their thorns. If masters mock the mistakes of speakers of the subject population as they attempt to become bilingual, this verbal malice produces a jargon. The jargon is an imitation of a perverted model; if used in commerce, we call it a lingua franca; in some cases we call it a pidgin; and when children learn it as their first and most useful language we call it a creolized language. In Washington and Oregon the Chinook Indians invented a jargon, a perverted model, for use as a lingua franca by speakers of English and various Indian languages. The question most properly asked is not, 'Is Chinook jargon a mixed language?' The question most properly asked is, 'Can we call Chinook jargon a different language from Lower Chinook?' Or, to shift to a creolized tongue which originated as a perverted dialect of North French, 'Can we call Haitian creole a different language from French?'

Let us expose the nerve of the problem with a Romany knife. Romany is the far-traveled language of the gypsies, with many language contacts in its history, and with the reputation of being an excellent witness to *Sprachvermischung,* language-mixture. The language comes from India, not Egypt; our word *gypsy* (from earlier *gipsyan* 'Egyptian') renders to Osiris what should be rendered to Indra. Boas (who brought his influence to bear upon Kroeber) was inclined to follow Schuchardt, Lepsius, von der Gabelentz, and Dempwolff, eminent language specialists of the nineteenth century, in espousing a doctrine of multiple roots, i.e. origins from several reverse continua. Boas suggested that

> it is not possible to group American languages rigidly in a genealogical scheme in which each linguistic family is shown to have developed to modern forms, but we have to recognize that many of the languages have multiple roots.

Boas engaged in controversy with a more optimistic Sapir, and argued that cases of morphological diffusion sometimes impose an insurmountable barrier to the demonstration of prehistoric unity.*

*This sweeping view persists into our own century: *cf.* V. Pisani's observation that 'one cannot write the history of a language, but only the history of particular elements,' in *'Parenté linguistique,' Lingua,* III 14. See Boas, 'Classification of American Indian Languages,' *Language* 5.1–7, and 'The Classification of American Languages,' *American Anthropologist* 22.367–76. Also read Harry Hoijer, 'Methods in the Classification of American Indian Languages,' in L. Spier, A. I. Hallowell, and S. S. Newman, *Language, Culture, and Personality* 9–12 (1941), and Morris Swadesh, 'Diffusional Cumulation and Archaic Residue as Historical Explanations,' *SJA* 7.1–21.

One can agree with Boas and others that sometimes morphological considerations create intricate problems of analysis. That such problems need not or cannot properly be attended to in historical perspective because of hopeless admixtures is another proposition, quite sweeping. When sweeping statements are made without immediate substantiation, it is proper sometimes to wonder if we are dealing with some sort of bird watcher-duck hunter scale, which pits the cautious empiricist like Boas against the speculative theorist and advocate of across-the-board insight such as Sapir, or with some other scale. Bloomfield wasted little time on the framers of amateurish generalizations. Confronted with such generalizations, he crisply countered with professional aplomb.

Bloomfield's treatment of what he calls aberrant borrowing ends a tradition epitomized in the assertion of H. Paul, *Prinzipien der Sprachgeschichte* (1880), that the most widespread adoption of inflectional suffixes has taken place in the Gypsy language, yielding, for example, Spanish Gypsy or English Gypsy. Paul's English commentators, Strong, Logeman, and Wheeler, in their *Introduction to the Study of the History of Language* (1891), say that gypsies have borrowed the inflectional endings of each country they have lived in. With equal carelessness, G. F. Black, in *An American-Romani Vocabulary by Albert Thomas Sinclair* (1915), refers to 'corrupt English grammatical endings' as in the plural *hevyas* 'nits' beside the plurals *kania* 'ears' and *lilya* 'papers.' In contrast, Bloomfield calls '*rukjr̩*, plural of *ruk* 'tree,' a Gypsy inflected form in English.

The student may properly feel that he is not qualified to evaluate such competing points of view as those of Paul and Bloomfield. It is for authorities to be authoritative, not students. Yet one can scarcely reject the proposition that authorities differ not so much on clarity and consistency as on adequacy of evidence. A certain quantity of factual data led Paul to his conclusion, and a certain quantity, probably a greater quantity, led Bloomfield to his. The clever student will see immediately that each person, be he a great scholar or a great baker of apple pies, has to make up his own mind about every hypothesis that he discovers. The authority who presents the hypothesis is, as it were, a native speaker, an informant: and one must never trust one's informant. Listen politely, but be ready to take an independent stance. Accumulate data to satisfy your own standards of adequacy of evidence. Bloomfield's position, when put to the test, easily replaces polite aloofness with intellectual commitment. Let us see how.

Rebolledo's *Diccionario Gitano-Español y Español-Gitano* (1909) reveals use of Spanish phonemes in Romany words; e.g. *jojoí* 'rabbit' as compared with Romany *xašói, šošói* shows *j* /x/ for /š/, not used in the majority of Spanish dialects. Also revealed are Spanish endings for verbs of Romany origin, e.g. *jelar* 'love' (cf. Welsh Romany *k^hel-* 'play, sport, gambol') has present forms *jela, jelas, jela; jelamos, jeláis, jelan* 'I play,' 'you play,' 'he plays'; 'we play,' 'you (plural) play,' 'they play' (cf. Spanish *amo, amas, ama; amamos, amáis, aman,* the set for 'love'). European Romany has these endings, with the so-called thematic vowels *a* and *e: -av, -es* (or *-eh* in Finnish, German, and Transylvanian Romany), *-el; -as* (or *-ah* in Finnish, German, and Transylvanian Romany), *-en, -en;* cf. Syrian Romany *-am, -ek, -ar; -an, -as, -and.* The contrast in systems increases in the imperfect, where Romany regularly adds *-as* to present endings: a Spanish Gypsy says *jelaba, jelabas, jelaba; jelabamos, jelabais, jelaban;* a Welsh native speaker of Romany says *k^helavas, k^helesas, k^helelas; k^helasas, k^helenas, k^helenas.* Rebolledo's work involves a typical misinterpretation of aberrant borrowing, arguing as it does that a Spanish verbal system of endings suited speakers of Romany better than the Romany system and was therefore borrowed in one fell swoop, like a whole coop of chickens.

Like the Gypsies of England and Spain, those of Armenia have been credited with wholesale morphological borrowing. Sampson reports borrowing of the Armenian present tense (*-em, -es, -e; -eŋk^h, -ek, -en*).* Vendryes more generously reports the Armenian Gypsies 'adopted the Armenian morphological system' but kept Romany words. He does, however, throw a spotlight upon the seclusive value of communication based in aberrant borrowing.

Bloomfield's observation that the inflectional system of German Romany dialects is intact bears extension to other Romany dialects, except that (as noted by Sampson) the imperfect and pluperfect were lost in the Syrian dialects and are rare in some Balkan, Transylvanian, German, and Finnish dialects. It bears extension in a double sense: Romany is intact from borrowing into the system and intact from borrowing out of the system. Part of what led to aberrant borrowing

* *The Dialect of the Gipsies of Wales* (1926), p. 187, n. 1.

was the humorous or seclusive value of Romany morphemes to Gypsy native speakers of, say, English, Spanish, or Armenian; but the borrowing, while it may have been wholesale enough to bewilder commentators for generations, was not significantly morphological.

The ample philological resources of the Indo-Europeanist make possible the clear determination of aberrant borrowing in the Gypsy case. As Americanists add to their own resources it should become possible to resolve in similar fashion at least some of their supposedly insurmountable problems of morphological diffusion.

Boas contributed to two linguistic journals which all serious students of language and culture should follow, the *International Journal of American Linguistics* (edited by C. F. Voegelin of Indiana University) and *Language; Journal of the Linguistic Society of America* (edited by Bernard Bloch of Yale University). In his introduction to the former journal, Boas shows his preoccupation with classification of languages and his awareness that divergence of sister languages is impossible to trace after enough time has gone by. He notes that borrowing complicates the issue. It can be phonetic or morphological. He observes that areas in America show diffusion of vowel nasalization, glottalization, a profuseness of laterals, absence of spirants, and absence of trills. He had in mind, perhaps, such hypotheses as he mentions elsewhere: vowel nasalization is absent in northwestern America, but is found in central and eastern plains areas; many types of *k*- and *l*-phones are found along the northern Pacific coast but are absent in California and east of the Rockies. Boas could find no correlation of phonetic distributions and morphological groupings.

It was obvious to him, nevertheless, that American morphological types have wide continuous distribution, morphological types such as incorporation of nominal object, reduplication, and vocalic or consonantal stem variations. He had in mind probably the spread of reduplication in the Great Plains, the Eastern Woodlands, and an area from British Columbia southward along the Pacific coast. While he did not exemplify all of his generalizations, Boas showed that he was against leaping to conclusions that ignore the complexity of the problem.

He raised an issue which is still with us. When does a resemblance of forms or features reflect development from a common Schleicherian nodule point, and when does such resemblance, which makes things look cognate, reflect mere accident? The same problem besets paleontologists, because evolution may be phyletic, along a given line, or it may be convergent, so that several lines meet and give a specious impression of kinship, as with the ostrich, the rhea, and the emu. Swadesh is inclined to minimize accidental resemblance. Others demur. They want more information, of a sort now generally called typological. The seeds of linguistic typology were nurtured in Europe by Jespersen and broadcast in America most vigorously by Boas. Sapir contributed to typological studies in his book *Language* (1921), and improvements of a quantificational nature have been made more recently by Joseph Greenberg. In his essay of 1917, Boas also touched upon 'categories of thought that find expression in grammatical form,' which we shall return to later.

Boas published 'The Classification of American Languages' in 1920. American Indian languages had been grouped into sets or families of related languages in the nineteenth century by personnel of the Bureau of Ethnology. Henshaw finished a preliminary grouping in 1885 and Powell used this in working up an official Bureau publication for 1891. Powell's classification postulated 58 groups north of Mexico. The method for grouping languages was based on Indo-Europeanist precedents and involved the examination of comparative vocabularies. Inspection rather than quantification, and hence impressionism, was a major ingredient. We should not be surprised, therefore, that Sapir, using greater quantities of inspected data and generalizations of the sort alluded to above, was able to reduce 58 to 6 by 1929, to see the 58 as subsets of a set of 6 super-groups which could not then be taken back to a common nodule point. When a statement that a number of languages all have an ancestral nodule point is made, it cannot be disproved. Inexorable change washes away traces of genetic relationship and washes in spurious traces, like surf on a beach: and so we cannot disprove the statement, if someone wanted to make it, that Sapir's six super-groups all go back to a common ancestor. This fact should not alarm the beginning student. A distinction has come to be made between what is said to be related and what is said to be *relatable*. Out of the work of such men as Bloomfield and Sapir, building upon Indo-Europeanist foundations, have come techniques, as we shall see, for establishing that languages are relatable.

Boas, in his article of 1920, made the point that a good linguist will work from small subgroups to larger families. Thus, to digress a moment in order to give some examples, suppose that a linguist has filled a notebook with words from various languages which he thinks are related. Let us use A, B, C, and D instead of words. A page of the notebook might look like this:

English Gloss	First Language	Second Language	Third Language
hand	A	B	A
foot	A	B	C
nose	A	B,C,D	A
go	A	A	B
find	A	B	A
tendon	A	B	A
moose	A	B	A
elk	A	B	A
one	A	A	A
two	A	A	A

In the 'hand' row, we see that a word in the first language appears to be cognate with a word in the third language, and that a word in the second language does not appear to be cognate with the other forms. In the 'nose' row, there are three words for nose in the second language, none of which is cognate as far as appearances go with the apparently cognate words of the first and third languages. In the 'two' row, the words from all three languages seem to be cognate. Given several hundred sets of this sort, it is possible to subgroup languages: we would guess that the first and third languages are to be subgrouped together in a set of two, since they share more cognates than either does with the second language represented by the middle column.

Early work in the subgrouping of putatively relatable languages often could be no better than sketchy, because of faulty and incomplete grammatical descriptions. It is fallacious, therefore, to ignore restrictions and qualifications of the input, and to act as though all subgrouping work is of equal merit. Yet this is what some anthropologists do where language classifications are at issue, since they trust their informants not wisely but too well. It is much safer to trust Hoijer regarding Athapaskan languages, for example, than Johann Buschmann, a German scholar who attempted to subgroup Athapaskan and other languages in the second half of the nineteenth century. In 1857 Buschmann printed comparative vocabularies of Tlingit, Haida, Aztec, and Athapaskan languages. Scholars disagree to this day about the relatability of Tlingit and Haida, and about the relatability of either of these to the Athapaskan group. Buschmann called Tlingit 'an entirely independent linguistic type.' Others want to group Tlingit, Haida, and the Athapaskan languages together into a Na-Dene group after Sapir. Boas wanted to settle such questions by working from smaller subgroups to larger ones.

We might begin, taking up the Na-Dene problem, by finding Athapaskan subgroups, each with its nodule point at which there would be a set of protophonemes reconstructed on the basis of available data. Relatability is partly a matter of system in correspondences of phonemes—English is relatable to Latin, for example, because of recurrent correspondences of English /f/'s to Latin /p/'s (*f*ather-*p*ater), and so on. Relatability work that involves protophonemes is slowly becoming more popular among responsible scholars than relatability work based on less carefully assessed materials. Boas, however, probably had something less ambitious in mind. Here is a short exercise for the student—by inspection of the forms given from Katchemak Bay, Iliamna, Hupa, Sarsi, Navaho, and Tlingit, what tentative hypotheses can be made about subgroups? Which two languages seem to be most akin?

EXERCISE IN SUBGROUPING BY INSPECTION

Gloss	Katchemak Bay	Iliamna	Sarsi	Hupa	Navaho	Tlingit
girl	kísoŋkʷa	q̓ísńkóya	ts'ika	t'eaxətš	-t'ééd	xat-kátsko
moon	γalǯá	γalǯáiyi	yiináγá	Wa	γoolǯééʔ	dis
rain	ełkón	ełq̓on	-tšạ	kyaŋ	-tsą́	ssīm
star	sínʔ	sínʔ	soh	tsiŋ'	sǫʔ	kotrarennehá
ground squirrel	q̓ónša	q̓ónša	tšuustł'a	—	hazéítsoh, tseek'inástánii	ssalk, ssatl
lynx	kážna	kážna	—	mind-	nášdúí-	g̣aqʿ
sinew	ts'áx̣	ts'áx̣	-ts'ìd-	kyoots	-ts'id	tāss

Gloss	Katchemak Bay	Iliamna	Sarsi	Hupa	Navaho	Tlingit
dog	łíga	łíga	tłí	łiŋ	łéétšą́ą́ʔí	kʿetł
crane	gókdil	ndáł	—	—	deł	dúł
egg	qáža	qáža	-γàs	-weeWeʔ	-γęęžii	kwat’
feather	q̓edó	q̓éto̓ʔ	t’àh	-tš’ileʔ	-t’aʔ	t’aw
club	tšíknátłe	tšíknátłe	x̣àł	—	xaał	x’ús’
fire	—	—	kòʔ	xoŋ’	kǫʔ, kon-	x̣’an, kān
stone	q̓átłnígi	q̓átłnígi	tsá	tsee	tsé	tʿe, tā
heart	kózin	q̓éq̓deʔ	-ʒàràní	-kyansʔaan	-ǯéí	tʿéx̣’
hat	-tšax̣	-tšx̣a	—	koostan	tš’ah	s’ax^w, tsāx
yellow	ídétsígi	tł’ágéldan	-tsúú	-tsow	-tso	tsexone
caribou	witšóx̣	witšóx̣	—	—	—	wαtsíx
charcoal	tázee	táziʔ	t’as	t’ehW	t’eeš	kaniit
lake	wónʔ	wóna	tuu-	məŋk’	tooh	-áku
sun	níʔi	nóyiʔ	tš’ààt’áγá	Waa	šá	gan
tongue	q̓á-tsílo	q̓á-tsíla	-tsuuʔ	saastaan	tsooʔ	kā-tluūt

Independent invention of traits also may function as a blot on history, may present one with tokens of relationship which actually reflect common solutions to universal problems rather than genetic descent from a parent language. Similar semantic categories come to be associated with verbal stems in languages which lack adverbs with such meanings as *in, out of, up,* or *down.* But diffusion of semantic categories is also possible, side by side with the possibility that similar stem categories will develop from the same antecedent conditions. ‘It is . . . characteristic of many American languages that verbal ideas are expressed by different stems according to the form of the object in regard to which the verb predicates. This feature occurs particularly in verbs of existence and of motion, so that existence or motion of round, long, flat, etc., objects, are differentiated. This feature is prominent, among others, in Athapascan, Tlingit, Kwakiutl, and Sioux.’ Without explaining the basis for his judgment of what is ‘hardly possible,’ Boas made this judgment: ‘it would hardly be possible to claim that the numerous instrumental prefixes of the Haida and those of the Shoshonean, Kutenai, and Sioux, are historically related. . . . In the same way, it would be rash to associate the strong development of glottalized sounds in Chile with the analogous sounds on the Northwest Coast of America; the distinction between neutral and active verbs among the Maya, Sioux, and Tlingit; or the occurrence of three genders in Indo-European and in Chinook.'

20«

Durkheim, Boas, and Conservative Humanism

For particular utterances, one can invoke a scale from sunshine to moonshine, from heavily exemplified and documented generalizations to generalizations, no matter how true they may be, that are not given immediate substantiation. A weighting of the writings of Boas on this scale would put him on the side away from Bloomfield or Kroeber, for example, and on the same side as Sapir or Whorf. Such a weighting, however, is dangerous, and leads too easily to false dichotomy, that most constant of methodological embarrassments.

Durkheim used Meillet in refutation of the speculations of Max Müller, a reckless scholar whom Hale esteemed and delighted to quote. Boas also read Meillet; he argued not that Meillet was wrong in citing rules for establishing relations of languages, but that we need to study the geographical spread of linguistic elements, and that diffusion is part of the history of a language. Boas was a dialect geographer of cultural traits, including language as part of culture. Nor would it be fair to condemn him for teasing Kroeber, Redfield, and others (in 1936), when he favored cautious reconstruction as opposed to sweeping fanciful generalizations. For Boas no laws of culture will be found except those of cultural universals, because of human subjectivity. No physicist's equations here, and certainly no logistical system for culture.

In 1933, Boas directed his conservative humanism at scholars who group languages into families with statements which belong on the moonshine side of the sunshine-moonshine scale. In *The American Aborigines, Their Origin and Antiquity* (ed. Diamond Jenness), in an article entitled 'Relationships Between North-West America and North-East Asia,' Boas pointed out that languages which cannot be declared relatable are numerous in America and larger groupings have not been based on adequate evidence. He supposed that languages were limited in spread in ancient times and that the diversity of languages in these areas—the Pacific coast of America, the Palae-Asian area, the Sudan, the Caucasus—such diversity in a concentrated area was the rule in very ancient times, and spreads came but recently in human history. That he failed to substantiate this view with evidence does not rob it of any integrity it may have; but we are obliged to observe where it belongs on our special scale for scholarly utterances about language and culture.

In the same article, Boas touched upon categories of thought, categories which Durkheim had so brilliantly shown to be social in origin, categories which the student will encounter under various names, 'grammatical categories,' or 'linguistic categories,' or 'logical categories.' Each encounter will have to be studied carefully, but one can predict that semantic content or reference of a probabilistic nature will be involved as a general rule. Thus Durkheim had conventional reference in mind when he said in *Elementary Forms* that logical understanding is a function of society. A given society impresses it upon its members. By the social metaphor of conventional reference, 'collective thought,' reality is made susceptible of explanation. Durkheim said:

> The explanations of contemporary science are surer of being objective [than mythological explanations] because they are more methodical and because they rest on more carefully controlled observations, but they do not differ in nature from those which satisfy primitive thought.

And so we lump and split one way, in our immediate society, and the Arunta of Australia another way, according to their own rules of folk taxonomy or ethnoscience. But the means and methods in each case are far from justifying the fiction of inferior societies so ardently propounded by men like Lévy-Bruhl. In his grand summation, Durkheim said:

> Language, and consequently the system of concepts which it translates, is the product of a collective elaboration. What it expresses is the manner in which society as a whole represents the facts of experience. The ideas which correspond to the diverse elements of language are thus collective representations . . . logical thinking is always impersonal thinking, and is also thought *sub species æternitatis*—as though for all time. Impersonality and stability are the two characteristics of truth.

Truth, then, comes from collective experience, crystallized in language. In a statement that might seem to verge on social solipsism, Durkheim said, 'In all social life, in fact, science rests upon opinion.' Beyond this position, he maintained that it is irresponsible to rank societies in terms of conceptual categories, if such ranking implicates a scale, evolutionary or otherwise, from primitive to civilized. He attacked those who, like Lévy-Bruhl in *Les Fonctions mentales dans les sociétés inférieures,* speciously assume that concepts are only general ideas clearly defined and nothing else, and that inferior societies cannot produce such general ideas. Each society, Durkheim said, uses concepts of the supposedly primitive type, and logical thought 'has always existed; there is no period in history when men have lived in a chronic confusion and contradiction. . . . To be sure, we cannot insist too much upon the different characteristics which logic presents at different periods in history; it develops like the societies themselves. But howsoever real these differences may be, they should not cause us to neglect the similarities, which are no less essential.'

In section iv of his Conclusion, Durkheim said that certain categories developed out of social realities. This view, he believed, followed from the empirical data at hand which he had gathered from ethnographic descriptions of aboriginal societies of Australia. While the adequacy of his evidence may be questioned, his view is interesting, not only in itself, but because some of the statements that he made and some of those made by Boas in various studies seem to be echoed, though at the same time distorted (or, perhaps, to be sympathetic, we ought to say subjected to metamorphosis), by Whorf in the framing of the Whorfean conceptions. Durkheim's parallels were:

CATEGORY	SOCIAL REALITY
class	human group
time	rhythm of social life
space	tribal territory
efficient force	the collective force

The categories function 'to dominate and envelop all the other concepts: they are permanent moulds for the mental life. Now for them to embrace such an object, they must be founded upon a reality of equal amplitude.' Durkheim also said:

> . . . society is not at all the illogical or a-logical, incoherent and fantastic being which it has too often been considered. Quite on the contrary,

> the collective consciousness is the highest form of the psychic life, since it is the consciousness of the consciousnesses . . . at every moment of time, it embraces all known reality; that is why it alone can furnish the mind with the moulds which are applicable to the totality of things and which make it possible to think of them. It does not create these moulds artificially; it finds them within itself; it does nothing but become conscious of them . . . If society is something universal in relation to the individual, it is none the less an individuality itself, which has its own personal physiognomy and its idiosyncracies . . . collective representations also contain subjective elements, and these must be progressively rooted out, if we are to approach reality more closely.

It is not out of the question that Boas was familiar with these views of Durkheim's. His expression of similar views, however, was more modest and less expansive. In his article in the Jenness volume, Boas said:

> The classification of experience which is the foundation of linguistic expression does not follow the same principles in all American languages. On the contrary, many different forms are found. The content of nouns and of verbs depends upon cultural conditions. What for a people of temperate zone is simply 'ice,' has many shades of meaning for an Arctic people like the Eskimo, 'salt water ice, fresh water ice, drifting ice, ice several years old.' Terms of relationship and those relating to social structure vary in their contents; classifications occur such as animate and inanimate; long, flat, or round; female and non-female. In verbs modalities of action, forms of object acting or acted upon, or local ideas may be expressed. In short, the variety of linguistic content is very great.

Boas was making the point that morphological similarities or those of grammatical categories* cannot *prove* that American and Siberian languages are related.

The relations of Asian and American tribes provided a logical set of problems for Boas to attend to. Much of his ethnographic work was carried out in the Pacific Northwest and Alaska. His grammar of Tlingit, the language of Indians of the Alaskan panhandle, was published in 1917 and helped stimulate speculation that Tlingit has Athapaskan affinities. Buschmann, of course, had identified Tlingit as an independent stock in 1857. This position is still taken by

*That is, 'categories of thought that find expression in grammatical form' (1917).

conservative linguists. But Pliny Earle Goddard, who like Boas made extensive researches in Athapaskan linguistics, asked in *IJAL* in 1917 whether Tlingit has a genetic relation to Athapaskan. Systematic correspondences of phonemes, a compelling kind of genetic evidence, are hard to find, although there are, as we have seen in the exercise near the end of Chapter 19, suspicious phonetic resemblances. There are also resemblances which typologists may eventually show are due to chance rather than common origin, resemblances in the ordering of morphemes in words and sentences. Boas, like Kroeber and many other anthropologists, saw value in linguistic research as contributing to historical reconstruction of tribal history. But he was a realist about how much time has to be invested, and how much care taken, before useless dross can be taken away from pure gold.

Boas had a special place in his heart for the Kwakiutl of Vancouver and the Canadian shores facing the island. The Nootka live on Vancouver too, west of the Kwakiutl. The two languages, Nootka and Kwakiutl, are members of the Wakashan family. Swadesh studied with Sapir after Sapir came to Yale in 1931; both men have contributed greatly to knowledge of the Nootka language and culture. And Boas, with whom Sapir studied at Columbia in the first decade of this century, has contributed greatly to our store of Kwakiutl data. Boas died before finishing his study of Kwakiutl grammar, but Zellig Harris was able to edit it for publication. Boas, then, was close to and influential in Wakashan studies; and it is not surprising that he should have expressed his conservatism with special clarity in Wakashan commentary.

In 1933, Boas reviewed G. W. Locher's work on the serpent in Kwakiutl religion in the *Deutsche Literaturzeitung;* he seized the occasion to warn that a system cannot be assumed for every mythology. He indicated that he was tired of structural-functionalist attempts to find systems; his preference was for what now some scholars should call ethnographic yields of etic fragments of culture. He saw oversimplification in the view that 'contradictions within a culture are impossible,' and would not allow what Strauss in *Persecution and the Art of Writing* has clearly shown, that sometimes a contradiction is not a meaningless part of a system. Nor did he consider the possibility of system competing with system, just as referential focus competes with referential focus. Probability curves of reference vary through time; Wycliffe says that Samson slew Philistines with the cheekbone of an ass, which helps to show that the reference of *cheek* has shifted through time from jaw to cheek after competition with the reference peak or referential focus of *jaw;* and if this is so, it is not difficult also to posit system competing with system. The serpent review shows that Boas no less than Locher could produce generalizations touched with equivocation and barren of exemplification.

Yet Boas for all of that was relatively conservative in handling cultural details and was more faithfully methodical, in comparison with audacious theorists. In 1899 ('Advances in Methods of Teaching,' *Science* 9.93–6) he said:

> The method of anthropology is an inductive method, and the science must be placed side by side with the other inductive sciences. Our conclusions are based on comparisons between the forms of development of the human body, of human language, of human activities, and must be as truly inductive as those of any other science . . .
>
> The science of linguistics is growing slowly on account of its intrinsic difficulties. These difficulties are based on the lack of satisfactory material as well as on the amount of labor involved in the acquisition of knowledge in its particular line of research.

This conservatism was reflected several years later in his discussion of the relations of Siberian and American tribes. Swadesh in the Radin memorial volume *Culture in History* (1960) has supposed that tribes entered the Americas from Siberia in many migrations over thousands of years, across the land bridges which connected the continents, or the waters which replaced these bridges at different times. Swadesh as a guess suggests that 'the great bulk of American languages form a single genetic phylum [called Ancient American, or Amerindian] going far back in time . . . the entire phylum [probably] developed out of a single speech community in America . . . [perhaps] about 15,000 years ago.' His guess implicates a monogenesis of the world's languages, much as the Italian duck-hunter Trombetti supposed, but a monogenesis which occurred as recently as 30,000 years ago. It is safe to infer that Boas would have demurred at such speculation.

His own speculations were more closely tied to palpable artifacts. Thus he observed ('Some Problems in North American Archaeology,' *American Journal of Archaeology* 6.1–6, 1902) that only Eskimos and Athapaskans made pottery in the Yukon River territory, that pottery was not made anywhere else on the north Pacific coast, that tribes of northeastern Siberia did not make pottery, but that pottery had been dug up near the northern coast of the Sea of Okhotsk, 'the only place on the whole Pacific Coast, from the Amur River in Siberia northward to Bering Strait, and along the American coast south to California, where pottery is found.' Boas saw an early connection between the tribespeople of the pottery districts.

He also made inferences about migrations in ancient times on the basis of the distribution of themes or motifs as well as of linguistic data. Athapaskan languages were spoken in Alaska, Canada, down the Pacific coast in Washington as well as Oregon and California in Boas's time, and in the Southwest. The irregular distribution of Athapaskan islands betokened 'great disturbances' for Boas. It has been observed that Boas failed to see the close correlation of race, language, and culture in the cases of the Eskimo, the Bushmen of Africa, and the aborigines of Australia. He did see, however, a great diversity of physical types down through a region encompassing several culture areas: an Arctic area with Eskimos and Athapaskan Indians, merging into a Northwest Coast area with Indians like those found in British Columbia, merging into a Columbia river type, merging into a California type. Boas held that the diversity of physical types down through this region was so great as to be ancient. It was his belief that given a set of customs over a continuous area but absent in other continuous areas, the set is indigenous. Since the Tsimshian, located just south of Alaska and on the coast extending inland and also facing the islands where the Haida live, are set off in beliefs and folklore from their neighbors [and he could have said in language], they must be newcomers in their area. He observed, in a related vein, that tales from an area near the mouth of the Columbia contain elements found east of the Rockies, and presumably the river was an avenue along which customs moved westward to the Pacific Coast.

Such inferences were pattern-setting. Anthropologists depend heavily upon linguistic data in their studies of traits in culture areas, of the prehistoric relationships and migrations of tribes, and of archaeological discoveries. It is easy to treat linguists as specialists whose work is unblemished, so that every linguistic description is like a newly minted coin, in a world in which utterances on the moonshine side of the scale gain clever issue.

21«

Sound Laws and Genetic Relationships

The reliability of linguistic judgments about genetic relationships needs to be examined before the anthropologist or archaeologist can exploit linguistic data. Occasionally such researchers refer to 'the linguistic evidence,' in demonstrating that their discoveries have corroboration in language spread or history. And often such 'evidence' turns out to be idiosyncratic. What is wanted, perhaps, is diminution of unguarded enthusiasms.

Languages change, relentlessly. When people who speak a given language move away from their old homes and lose contact with old friends, their language changes. So does the language of the people left behind. Conquering bands often wind up after a few hundred years of movement speaking daughter languages of the parent once spoken in the old homeland. Thus bands moved away from a central location west of the Black Sea, having come from the east. Those at the central location are called Indo-Europeans. In time the spreading bands of Indo-Europeans developed different Indo-European daughter languages. By about 2000 B.C. migrational activity was in full swing; contacts were lost, and new languages arose. By 1000 B.C., Indo-Europeans who had invaded India were speaking an ancient variety of Sanskrit, Indo-Europeans who had invaded the Balkans and later had destroyed Troy were celebrating victories in an ancient variety of Greek, and so it went.

When we say that Sanskrit, Greek, and English are related languages, we allude, however indirectly, to their evolution from the parent Indo-European language. This language existed in prehistoric times, that is, before written records could be made. Sumerian cuneiform writing, wedge-shaped impressions in clay, go back to business offices of about 3300 B.C., and Egyptian picture writing dates from about 3100 B.C. The invention of alphabetic writing is generally credited to Semitic peoples who were inspired, perhaps, by alphabetic glimmers in Egyptian writing practices. This invention reached the Greeks perhaps by way of the Semitic Phoenicians, probably in the ninth century B.C. Much older is a system of signs that were used in writing a very old form of Greek, a system preserved on tablets which may be something like 3400 years old. These tablets were found on the island of Crete, and the language that they preserve is called Mycenaean Greek. But written records of the parent language, sometimes called Proto-Indo-European and sometimes simply Indo-European (abbreviated IE), do not exist. Words of the parent language, however, are said to be 'reconstructed' when daughter words, called cognates, have been compared, and hypotheses about the phonemes of the original or parent words have been framed. Thus by comparing Greek *néphos,* Latin *nebula,* Sanskrit *nabhas,* and other Indo-European words for 'cloud,' and by dealing with the data in a systematic way, some scholars are led to reconstruct a hypothetical Indo-European word for 'cloud.' The fact that the word is not attested in any written record is signaled in this text by a raised star or asterisk. The postulation of IE **nébhos* as the ancestor of Greek *néphos* and Sanskrit *nabhas,* and the root morpheme *{*nebh-*} 'cloud' as the ancestor of the root morpheme {*neb-*} 'cloud' in the Latin word *nebula,* is a guarded statement, in one sense, of certain correspondences of phonemes which are represented by a starred phonemic symbol. Such correspondences are identified as sound laws. It is a sound law, for example, that IE **bh* corresponds to Greek *ph,* Latin *f* initially and *b* medially in words, Sanskrit *bh,* and English *b* or *v*. This example is incomplete and simplified, but it serves in the present context to illustrate the possibility of a rigorous demonstration of language relationships. To Indo-Europeanists of the nineteenth and twentieth centuries we owe the chief foundation for methods and techniques of dealing with languages in anything that pretends to be a respectable and competent way. Work in the New World followed work in the Old World, in classification of genetic relationships of languages.

The models which Indo-Europeanists have provided for identifying related languages demand, first of all, that cognate forms be discovered. Such forms bear some phonetic resemblance to each other, and some semantic resemblance. Just how much resemblance is needed has been a matter of dispute. Consider these forms: Greek *patḗr* 'father,' Latin *pater* 'father,' Sanskrit *pitar-* 'father'; Greek *poús,* Latin *pēs,* Sanskrit *pāt,* all 'foot'; Greek *bárbaros,* Sanskrit *barbaras* 'stammering'; Latin *dē-bilis* 'not-strong, weak,' Sanskrit *balam* 'strength'; Greek *phérō,* Latin *ferō,* Sanskrit *bharāmi,* Old English *bére* 'I bear'; Latin *lubet, libet,* Sanskrit *lubh-,* tied to English *love;* Greek *tanaós,* Latin *tenuis,* Sanskrit *tanus,* tied to English *thin;* Greek *édō,* Latin *edō,* Sanskrit *admi,* tied to English *eat;* Greek *thūmós,* meaning 'spirit' or 'anger,' Latin *fūmus,* Sanskrit *dhūmas* 'smoke'; Greek *eruthrós,* Latin *ruber,* Sanskrit *rudhiras,* tied to English *red;* Latin *vidua,* Sanskrit *vidhavā,* tied to English *widow.* Except for Greek *thūmós,* whose meaning cannot immediately be connected to that of Latin *fūmus* or Sanskrit *dhūmas,* these cognate sets are united by essential agreement on the semantic plane. A knowledge of Indo-European sound laws, however, instantly leads us to set up the hypothetical IE form **dhūmós;* its primal meaning might be elucidated if we knew something about Indo-European religious beliefs. Such semantic speculation is otiose, however, in the face of recurrent phonetic correspondences. All of the Indo-European sets given above are made up of cognate forms, or to put it more precisely, include cognate morphemes.

The problem of establishing genetic relationship is complicated partly because words or forms occasionally are borrowed by family members but may be mistaken as cognates. Consider the following forms. All have to do with 'devil.'

Sanskrit has no form which ties in with 'devil,' though it has *rakṣas-* 'demon, evil spirit.' The morpheme {*man-*} 'think' appears in the word *manyu-* 'spirit, mood, anger,' which is cognate with the *mainyu-* of Avestan *aŋra- mainyu-* 'evil spirit,' name of the Zoroastrian demon of demons, Ahriman. The words for 'devil' in Lithuanian and Lettish are *velnias* and *velns* respectively. Two symbols commonly used in historical linguistics are useful here: > and <. One can read > as 'becomes' and < as 'comes from.' Thus we interpret 'Lith. *velnias* < *velinas* < *velnas*' as a statement of events in history or a hypothesis about such events: 'Lithuanian *velnias* comes from *velinas,* which comes from *velnas.*' How do we interpret this: 'Lith. *velnas* > *velinas* > *velnias*'? Some scholars prefer to use an arrow with a shaft rather than an arrow head: → serves, for example, instead of > in '*velnas* → *velinas.*' The Baltic forms are cognates, and are related to Lithuanian *vēlē* and Lettish *velis* 'spirit of the dead, ghost.' They are not cognate, however, with the Avestan form.

In the Slavic group of languages we find some forms whose history or 'etymology' is uncertain. A set of cognates is represented by Czech *čert,* Russian *čort,* and Polish *czart,* all 'devil.' Serbo-Croatian has *vrag* 'devil,' which is cognate with Old Church Slavic *vragə* 'enemy.' Alongside these forms we have Old Church Slavic *diyavolə,* Serbo-Croatian *ðavo,* Czech *d'abel, d'as,* and Polish *djabeł.*

In the Germanic group of languages we find Gothic *diabaulus* and *diabulus,* and also *unhulþa* for 'devil.' Some students, accustomed to Gothic as an appellation for novels and architecture, are astounded to learn that Gothic is a language, too. It was spoken by a tribe called the Goths. A missionary, Wulfilas, translated part of the Bible into Gothic. Most of our knowledge of the language comes from the work of Wulfilas. He has tantalized us, interestingly, respecting the Gothic word for 'mother.' It is suggested by some scholars that Wulfilas did not want to summon up remembrance of a mother goddess who was worshiped by the Goths, so he used a word which is not cognate with our word *mother* in his translation. We say that Gothic is extinct or a dead language, because its skillful use has stopped. The word *unhulþa* may be rendered 'not (*un-*) merciful (*hulþa*).' Other Germanic words for 'devil' are Old Saxon *diuƀul,* Old Norse *djöfull* < *diaƀulz,* Danish *djœvel,* Swedish *djävul,* Old English *dēoful* < *dīobul* < *dīavol,* Dutch *duivel,* Old High German *tiufal* (perhaps with *iu* borrowed from *tiuf* 'deep') > Middle High German *tiuvel* > German *teufel.*

The Romance or Romanic languages are those which have developed from Latin. In this group, connected with Latin *diabolus,* we find Italian *diavolo,* French *diable,* Portuguese *diabo,* Spanish *diablo,* Rumanian *diavol* or more popularly *drac,* which calls to mind the fact that occasionally the devil is identified with a snake or snake-like monster. Here *drac* < Latin *dracō* 'dragon.' Albanian belongs to the Indo-European family, and in Albanian we find a parallel: *djall* 'devil' and *dreq* 'devil,' as in Rumanian. One is reminded of an Avestan comment, *ažim dahākəm yam druǰim* 'the dragon Dahaka, the lie.' The Hindus sing in the *Rig Veda* of how Indra 'slew the snake.' This monster, a villain, turns up, perhaps, in other mythologies. The ancient Egyptians had an 'endless' snake (tail in mouth) as a member, not always infernal, of their pantheon. The relationship of all these snakes and dragons is a problem for critics of literature or philologists.

Words for 'devil' in the Celtic group of Indo-European languages include Old Irish *diabul* > Irish *diabhal,* Welsh *diafol* (Welsh has an archaic form *diawl*), and Breton *diaoul.*

Are the Celtic, Slavic, Germanic, and Romance forms, or any portion of them, cognates, going back to a Proto-Indo-European word for 'devil'? Did the Indo-Europeans of 2000 B.C. reckon with the Devil?

From our records, we know that it would be misleading to set up an Indo-European word for 'devil.' Without written records, we might be tempted to do so. But our records tell us that there has been a certain amount of borrowing in historical times. The Hebrew word *sātān* 'Satan' was translated by Jewish and Christian writers for the Greek-speaking world as *diábolos.* This form meant 'slanderer, traducer' in earlier times. It was derived from the verb *diáballō* 'I cast (*ball-*) through or across (*dia-*),' or more precisely we have an adjectival form in *-os* with {*dia-*} 'through' and the /bol/ actualization of a morpheme {*bal*} 'cast, throw.' This form 'slandering' then came to be used for 'slanderer' and later 'devil.' Wulfilas borrowed the form for the Goths. The Romans borrowed the Greek form too. Romance forms then were borrowed into other languages of the Indo-European family. The distribution of forms for 'devil,' then, reflects missionary activity in many cases, as against the development of cognates from a single, ancient Indo-European form.

The student must guard against easy reliance upon certain present-day theories about the nature and quality of language relationships and language prehistory. A difficult problem in comparative work is the identification of true cognates, as opposed to putative cognates which actually reflect independent invention or diffusion, the creation of similarities by random formal or semantic changes, nursery inventions, onomatopoetic imitations, or spread by borrowing rather than genetic descent. The student must guard against theorists who subgroup languages by 'inspection'—who ignore Bloomfield's lead in the axiomatization of basic assumptions. He may be more indulgent, however, toward those whose methods are statistical and deal with percentages of shared cognates or exclusively shared innovations.

We have indicated, so far, not, as the student may discover later, that linguists group languages into sets or families, sometimes on the one hand relying upon a form of intuitive procedure called inspection, compounded of unstated assumptions, hidden steps, or other impulses born of various motives, sometimes on the other hand relying upon rigorous application of unconcealed rules of science, chiefly involving counting and calculating operations applied to cognate morphemes. We have indicated only that languages are conveniently grouped into sets or families, for example, the Indo-European family, and that the integrity of the grouping depends largely upon our ability to find regular phonemic correspondences or sound laws as proof of genetic relationship.

The term sound law sometimes means a column or row in a matrix of phonemic correspondences, together with a starred phoneme, sometimes called a protophoneme, which stands for the members of the column or row. Any member of the line is called a reflex of the protophoneme. Another way of putting it is that a sound law is a statement of the expected or regular reflexes of a protophoneme. We do not always find what we expect to find, but we assume that sound changes are regular and without exceptions, and that apparent exceptions can be explained as special cases that involve other sound laws or other systematic forces of change, such as analogical inference. A matrix based upon the forms cited above looks like this.

IE	Greek	Latin	Sanskrit	English
*p	p	p	p	f
*b	b	b	b	p
*bh	ph	f initial b medial	bh	b (v)
*t	t	t	t	θ (ð)
*d	d	d	d	t
*dh	θ	f initial b medial: next to r, before l, after u d medial (in other environments)	dh (h)	d

A seasoned Indo-Europeanist carries such a matrix in his head, extended indefinitely in both directions. He has in addition, stored in the treasure chest of his memory, sets of cognates which illustrate the various sound laws. By 'indefinitely' I do not mean that the list of phonemes is endless, or the list of Indo-European languages. I mean simply that within the theoretical limits of the matrix there is room for variation where memories are concerned. Handbooks of comparative and historical linguistics generally contain matrices which exhaust available data and supplement flagging memories.

In the prehistoric Germanic area various stops changed according to a pattern memorialized as 'Grimm's Law.' Part of the pattern is shown above. Exceptions due to accentual conditions are memorialized as 'Verner's Law.' Ignoring exceptions, the first pattern involves these shifts: IE **bh, *dh, *gh* to English *b, d, g;* IE **b, *d, *g* to English *p, t, k;* IE **p, *t, *k* to English *f, θ, h.*

Let us turn now to the New World. Scholars who work with Indian languages of the Americas have learned their basic modes of approach almost without exception from scholars well-versed in Indo-Europeanist traditions. It is not surprising, therefore, to find statements of sound laws for American Indian languages. Here is a sample for three languages in a group called Otomi. The Otomian languages are spoken in central Mexico. The family includes Northern Otomian (including Pame and Chichimeca), Southern Otomian (including Matlatzinca and Ocuilteco), and Central Otomian (including Mazahua and the Otomi group). Data are presented for three languages of this group, San Gregorio, Tlacotlapilco, and San Felipe. Only a small part of the sound-law matrix is shown.

Proto-Otomi	San Gregorio	Tlacotlapilco	San Felipe
*d	t	d	d
*tʔ	tʔ	tʔ	tʔ initial t medial
*m	m before nasal vowel mb before oral vowel	m	m

Sets of cognates which illustrate these correspondences are shown with a reconstruction for Proto-Otomi in each case: **mi̢nʔyo* 'coyote,' San Gregorio *mi̢nʔyo,* Tlacotlapilco *miiʔno,* San Felipe *mi̢ʔno,* all 'coyote'; **mʉi* 'heart,' San Gregorio *mbʉi,* Tlacotlapilco *mʉi,* San Felipe *mʉi,* all 'heart'; **dɔ* 'eye,' San Gregorio *tɔ,* Tlacotlapilco *da,* San Felipe *dɔ,* all 'eye'; **tʔẹi* 'atole, corn-meal mush,' San Gregorio *tʔẹi,* Tlacotlapilco *tʔẹi,* San Felipe *tʔi̦i,* all 'atole'; **ʔøtʔe* 'do, make,' San Gregorio *ʔøtʔe,* Tlacotlapilco *ʔøtʔe,* San Felipe *ʔøte,* all 'do, make'; **thạʔtʔi* 'regrind,' San Gregorio *hthạʔtʔi,* Tlacotlapilco *θɔ̦ʔti,* San *Felipe thạʔti,* all 'regrind.' Without questioning the validity of the reconstructions, it is fairly obvious that the languages in question are relatable. We cannot prove that two languages do not represent points on reverse continua which go back to a common origin. English, for all we know, may go back, by way of Indo-European, of course, all the way to a particular prehistoric language which was the ancestor, eventually, through various protolanguages, of ancient Egyptian, an Afro-Asiatic language. We cannot prove that this is not so. And Basque may be related in the same way to Navaho. But how can we prove such hypotheses? Some would say, adduce evidence in the form of cognate morphemes which have systematically corresponding phonemes.

In this connection, the researches of Swadesh are of interest. Following Gumesindo Mendoza, a nineteenth-century theorist, Swadesh suggests that Sanskrit and Aztec (classical Nahuatl) are related. In fact, many languages which have not been grouped together because of wide geographical dispersion seem even on superficial examination to bear interesting and by no means purely coincidental phonetic and semantic similarities. Swadesh has in mind, for example, the concordance of Spanish *yo* 'I' and Nahuatl *yoloʔ-tli* 'heart' or Spanish *este* 'this' and Nahuatl *iste-tl* '(animal) nail.' On the strength of such concordances, whose existence reflects his impressions involving representatives of many of the recognized, relatable language families of the world, Swadesh has set up twelve basic groups of world languages.

These groups have developed, in consonance with the inexorable fact that phonemic systems change as time passes (whether succeeding generations of speakers realize it or not), from daughter protolanguages of an ancient language which was spoken over 10,000 years ago, a language which perhaps had ablaut or vowel gradation (as in English *sing, sang, sung, song*) and more suffixes than prefixes in its words. It seems that in Swadesh's view all the languages of the world or at least very many of them are related to each other, by virtue of a single hoary ancestor. While he cannot claim to be the first scholar with this view, he is the first scholar to present hypothetical (starred) forms for words in the ancient language. The words represented by these forms presumably developed, according to laws of sound change, into words in different daughter languages, so that Japanese *kiri* 'cut,' for example, goes back to a prehistoric **kiri* whose meaning is approximated by 'cut here or actually.' From **kara,* an ablaut relative of **kiri,* came Totonac (in Central Mexico) *kaa* 'cut'; from **s-kiri* '*fuerte-cortar* (cut hard?)' came English *shear;* from **s-kir-ta-j* '*fuerte-cortar-parado-conjuncto*' came English *sherd* 'piece'; from **kr-ta-s* '*cortar-parado-aquel*' came Latin *curtus* 'short' (the accusative *curtum* goes back to **kr-ta-m* '*cortar-parado-junto,*' and *curtare* 'shorten' goes back to **kr-ta-j-si(t)* '*cortar-parado-hacer-sentar*'). Similarly, from **kr-na-j-mi* '*cortar-dejado-hacer-yo*' came Sanskrit *krnaami* '*hiero,*' and from **kari-ɔ-si(t)* '*cortar (alejado)-estar-sentar*' came Latin *carere* '*carecer de.*' (See item 132 in the bibliography.)

The twelve language groups are:

1. *Macro caribe* [Macro-Carib]
2. *Macro aruaco* [Macro-Arawakan]
3. *Macro quechua* [Macro-Quechuan]
4. *Macro maya* [Macro-Mayan]
5. *Macro joca* [Macro-Hokan]
6. *Vascodene* [Basque-Dene]
7. *Macro australiano* [Macro-Australian]
8. *Indoeuropeo* [Indo-European]
9. *Camiteño* [Afro-Asiatic]
10. *Sudaneño* [Sudanese]
11. *Congueño* [Congolese]
12. *Khoiseño* [Khoisan].

Branch 12 includes various languages of Bushmen and Hottentots in southern Africa. Branch 11 has representatives spoken in almost two-thirds of Africa, south of the Sahara, including the Bantu languages. Branch 10 includes languages of the African Sudan. Branch 9, popularly known as Hamito-Semitic, has five main divisions: Hamitic or Egyptian (of Biblical repute); Semitic (including Hebrew, Arabic, and the extinct Assyrian); Berber; Chad; and Cushite. Branch 8, Indo-European, is the family of languages to which English belongs; it extends geographically from western Europe to the Indian peninsula, and German scholars, counting the Germanic group of languages (with German, Dutch, English, Danish, Norwegian, Swedish, Icelandic, and others) as westernmost, often call the family Indo-Germanic. Branch 7 includes hundreds of languages spoken on and near the Australian continent. Papuan and South Pacific languages are included, such as those of Timor and the Solomon Islands. Branch 6 is most far-reaching. It includes Basque, of the western Pyrenees; it includes families of languages spoken in the Caucasus region of eastern Europe, such as Georgian and Kabardian; it includes the Ural-Altaic languages, such as those of the Uralic, Turkic, Tungusic, and Mongolian families of Europe, Siberia, and Mongolia; it includes Dravidian languages of India, such as Tamil, Telugu, Kanarese, and Malayalam; it includes language groups of southeast Asia and the Far East, such as Chinese, Tibetan, Burmese, and Japanese; it includes Chukchi; it includes the vast array of Austronesian (Malayo-Polynesian) languages of Indonesian, Melanesian, Micronesian, and Polynesian provenience; it includes the Eskimo and Aleutian languages; it includes the Wakashan languages; and it includes the Na-Dene languages of Alaska, Canada, and the United States, notably the Athapaskan languages of which Navaho is representative. Swadesh includes the language of the ancient Sumerians here, noting a resemblance to the Altaic languages. American Indian languages, mainly of southern Canada, the United States, Mexico, Central and South America, belong to branches 1, 2, 3, 4, and 5. Tupi languages and Timucua find themselves in branch 2, along with Arawakan. Branch 3 includes the Quechua family of Bolivia, Peru, Ecuador, and northwestern Argentina, Aymara of Bolivia and Peru, about two dozen other groups in South America, Tarascan in Mexico, and Zuñi and the Keresan languages of New Mexico. Representatives of branch 5 once blanketed most of what is presently the United States, as well as parts of Mexico and Central America. These include Iroquoian languages, Caddoan languages, Salishan languages, Siouan languages, Algonquian languages, and various others. Jicaque, Chontal, Mohave, and Seri, for example, find themselves together with Cherokee, Pawnee, Flathead, Crow, and Cheyenne.

The membership of branch 4 includes the Uto-Aztecan languages (such as Ute, Hopi, Papago, Comanche, and Nahuatl or Aztec), the Mayan languages (such as Maya and Quiché), the Chibchan languages, the Oaxacan languages (such as Mixteco [or Mixtec], Mazateco [or Mazatec] and Isthmus Zapotec), and the Otopame languages (grouped as Pame, Jonaz, Chichimeca, Matlatzinca, and Otomi-Mazahua).

It has been observed that transmission of this duodenary classification is bound to be challenged. For some scholars, of unquestioned eminence, have given consideration to an Azteco-Tanoan family which includes the Uto-Aztecan group and Zuñi, while Swadesh, at least, prefers to assign Zuñi to branch 3 and Uto-Aztecan to branch 4. What can the anthropologist do, when faced with such competing claims? One useful technique, in deciding about competing claims, is to see if the inclusiveness of a subgroup varies inversely with the amount of corroboration.

The possibility that all the languages of America have been derived from a common ancestral language was mentioned by Swadesh some years ago, in a study of languages of branch 4 under the rubric of Macro-Mixtecan. In this study, he brings together concordances which have impressed him from a phonetic and semantic point of view. We illustrate his collocational procedure here with two examples.

**(n-)t'uqhe/tuqe* 'top, horn, head, mountain.' It is possible that **toni/totoni* 'ear, horn' and **tumi* 'feather' are related. Morphemes meaning 'point' and 'large' may underlie all these forms. Basic to the reconstructions are such forms as Otomi of Mezquital *t'ʌhʌ*, Mazahua *t'ehe* 'mountain, woods,' Jiliapan *nt'ue* 'mountain,' Acapulco *-lˀue* 'mountain,' Chocho *tuku* 'head,' Mazatec of Huautla and Mazatlan *hku* 'head,' Soyaltepec *tku* 'head,' San Juan *sku* 'head,' Cuicatec *dutiku* 'mountain' (Swadesh thinks that *du-* is from an earlier **su*, possibly akin to a reconstructed **ši* 'protrusion'), Trique *ku* 'horn' (from an earlier **tku*), Amuzgo *skę* 'head,' Mixtec *ntɨkɨ*, *ntiki* 'head, point, horn, up.' Related forms with cognate morphemes, in languages less closely related to each other, include Nootka *t'uH-* (from **t'uqh*) 'head,' representing branch 6, Takelma *takax* 'head' and Yokuts *thuk'* 'ear,' as well as Comox *ƛaƛuxˀi* 'feather' and Klamath *tuuki* 'horn,' representing branch 5, as well as Mam *tuk'a* 'horn' and Mayan **çikin* 'ear,' both representing the Mayan subgroup of branch 4. Branch 3 is represented by Tarasco [Tarascan] *tokocɨ* 'tail.' Other forms reflecting research in Mexico and Central and South America are Fulnio *tka* 'head,' Lule *toko* 'head,' Paez *tokne* 'ear,' Atacama *tikne* 'tail,' and Arawakan **teki* 'ear.'

A second set of concordances: **qani/koni* 'bone, stone, egg, fruit.'

Huave *kang* 'stone,' Trique *ku* 'horn,' Ixcatec *ʔi-nΔa,* Chocho *nča-* 'bone,' Mazatec *nτa, nça* 'horn,' Chocho and Ixcatec *τu-,* Popoloc *tu-* 'fruit, round thing' (Mazatec *tu-* assimilated to old **to-* 'stone'), Otomi **(n)to-ʔyo,* Mazahua *ndo-dye* 'bone,' Otomi *ʔyε,* Mazahua *dyεʔε* 'hand,' Jonaz *ka-nʔi* 'hand' (**qqa-niʔye*), Matlatzinca *ni-ʔye,* Acapulco *ska-nʔia* 'hand,' Matlatzinca *ka-ro* 'bone.'

Several scholars have challenged such evidence by showing that if all one needs to support a theory of relationship are a number of concordances of phonetic and semantic material, without a priori demonstration of phonemic correspondences in regular and non-accidental recurrence in different cognate morphemes, then the sky is the limit and we can easily see kinship between Tlingit in Alaska and Shasta in California or between Tibetan in Asia and Navaho or Chipewyan in North America. Or, to mention an interesting attempt by Callaghan and Miller at a *reductio ad absurdum,* between the so-called Macro-Mixtecan languages and English: **qani/koni* 'bone, stone, egg, fruit' and English *hand* /hǽnd/ and possibly, if we see an augmentative form from **koni,* also English *horn* /hɔ́rn/.

The crux of the matter seems to involve a question whose solution will have to be left to mathematicians. Given a certain number of phonemes each for a certain number of languages, and various other kinds of restrictive information about the arrangements of phonemes in words or more precisely in morphemes, the task is to see how many cognate-like resemblances are bound to occur purely by chance. If a man in Tibet uses the word /khin/ for 'building' and a Navaho Indian in Arizona uses the word /khin/ for 'building,' are we to suspect common origin (people have been tying Tibetan and Athapaskan languages together on the basis of such concordances since the nineteenth century), or are we to chalk the concordance up to chance resemblance caused by accident and not orthogenesis? Perhaps we can suggest an answer to this question by means of a metaphor. Some anthropologists have operated like cavalry generals who outflank the enemy in a broad pincers movement, leaving it for soldiers who come later to take care of the trapped pockets of resistance. Others have attacked head-on, but with much caution and little speed. They have preferred successive approximations.

V

Culture: Sapir

These real things are called by the Latin philosophers, *entia, subjecta, substantiæ;* and by the Greek philosophers, *τα ὄντα ὑποκειμενα, ὑποστάμενα*. The other, which are incorporeal, are called by the Greek philosophers, *οὐσία συμβεβηχότα, φαντάσματα*; but most of the Latin philosophers used to convert *οὐσία* into substantia, and so confound real and corporeal things with incorporeal: which is not well; for essence and substance signify divers things.

—THOMAS HOBBES,

An Historical Narration Concerning Heresy, and the Punishment Thereof (1680).

22 «

Sapir in the Field: Rules for Beginners

Edward Sapir (1884–1939) worked as a field linguist and later as a professor at the University of Chicago (1925–31) and at Yale (1931–39). He was inspired by Boas, took his Ph.D. at Columbia in 1909, and produced a popular book, *Language,* in 1921. His enthusiasm for linguistic research was one of his most compelling and winning characteristics; as a teacher he was perceptive, pleasing, and charismatic.

As with Boas and others, it can be said of Sapir's work that it improved as he gained experience. If he blundered with the phonetics of Wishram as a youth, he made up for etic bias in maturer years with Southern Paiute. He worked without tape recorders, thus gaining in self-reliance—mechanical aids encourage rationalization and discourage vital investigation. Miraculous talent with languages is a myth; behind Sapir's field achievements were years of diligence and patience.

How does the field linguist develop insight and sharpen efficiency? The ethnologist who hopes to do even a little linguistic work should keep notebooks. Phonetic transcriptions of utterances, short ones at first, then longer ones, should fill notebook after notebook. In time, hypotheses about which phones are allophones of which phonemes will simplify the transcription, sometimes disastrously. Mistakes are to be expected. It helps in the initial stages to have the disposition of an ant repairing a damaged hill.

Once a rough notion of what the phonology is like has been arrived at, utterances or utterance-fractions should be transferred to slips of paper (3″ x 5″ and 4″ x 6″ are favorite sizes; Bloomfield cut his slips longitudinally with characteristic parsimony) and filed in shoe boxes or filing boxes or drawers. A slip with a Navaho word taken from p. 18 of notebook 4 as given by informant John Begay on May 4, 1932, might look like this:

bì·hnì·t'à·h	'we both put our heads into it'
4:18	JB 5/4/32

Slips with putative morphemes as well as those with putative lexemes like the one above should be kept; some of these will find their way into a dead file.

The collection of such data should blend with a ferment of plans for grammatical description and, eventually, publication. Is it better, before going into the field, to read everything or to read nothing about the new language? When this is not an academic question because nothing has been published at all, it would seem that much time and effort can be saved by even cursory review of the linguistic literature, especially phonetic information. At the earliest opportunity in the field one's phonetic data should be collected or checked; early transcription at best is audiovisual, a fact which lessens the value of the tape recorder in preliminary work; the informant should be induced to reveal habitual tongue positions or movements and other possibly determinative physical concomitants of his speech sounds, so that records will facilitate phonemic reinterpretations which the researcher or his readers later might want to propose.

The ferment of plans mentioned above is a function of flesh-and-blood apprenticeship: phoneticians, like grammarians, like confectioners who color ice-cream, do not take all of their skill and inspiration from books; perhaps something otiose, indeed, inheres in printed admonitions. Yet some must be made. As a heuristic rule, I prefer to plan a grammatical description which balances different sorts of information throughout. Before a generative grammar can be constructed, it is useful to have a preliminary notion of the classes of structural elements which would have to be accounted for by a less comprehensive stratificational grammar. Nothing so sophisticated as a generative grammar can be expected at present from most anthropologists whose field work has some special aim relating to cultural systems in an integrated relationship. The interest and the time are not there. Nevertheless, ethnologists should be encouraged to collect linguistic data which can later be processed or reinterpreted by specialists.

If the phonology is fairly simple and the morphology elaborate, as much as possible of the morphology might be described in the section on phonology. Hoijer illustrates this approach in *Navaho Phonology* (1945). If the constituent structure part of the syntax is lengthy, the section on morphology might be enriched with syntactic rules. Hoijer's *Navaho Phonology* is rich in morphological analysis and vocabulary, about half the study being devoted to morphophonemics (pp. 31-59). One of the problems of preliminary field work is the diversity of structuralist approaches. A word needs to be said about Sapir's role in such diversity.

Working from a Boasian base, Sapir used a variety of symbols for Athapaskan phonemes; early in his work he used *c* where later he or his students used *š*, *tc* for later *tš* or *č*, *tł* for later *ƛ*, *ts* for later *c*, *ts'* for later *c'*, *tc'* for *č'*, and so on. (The phonetic unity of glottalized consonants was reflected in some fonts by placement of the glottal apostrophe over rather than after the letter: *č̓*, *c̓*, *t̓*, *k̓*, not *č'*, *c'*, *t'*, *k'*.) For Navaho, Hoijer lists these consonantal phonemes: *b*, *d*, *g*, *t*, *k*, k^w, *t'*, *k'*, ʔ, *m*, *n*, *m'*, *n'*, *s*, *š*, *ł*, *x*, x^w, *h*, h^w, *z*, *ž*, *l*, *y*, γ, γ^w, *y'*, ʒ (*dz* in another system), *j* (*dž* or ǯ in other systems), λ (*dl* in another system), *c* (= *ts*), *č*, *ƛ*, *c'*, *č'*, *ƛ'*.

Various reinterpretations have been proposed. Sapir, following Boas and others, used *b*, *d*, *g* for sounds which are, in Hoijer's words, 'voiceless, lenis, and unaspirated stops'. Since it is customary, though not universally so, to represent such stops by *p*, *t*, *k*, I have preferred to follow such scholars as Olmsted, who for Achumawi of northern

California does not write *bətgu,* for example, for *pəthku* 'wild plum,' or *abo* for *apo* 'brother,' or *ipli* for *iphli* 'tongue.' Sapir's *t* represents [tʰ], his *k* [kʰ], his *t'* [t] with a glottalization or checking feature. Since Navaho /h/ exists already, the strong aspiration of [tʰ] and [kʰ] is taken as an allophonic manifestation of /h/, yielding in my view /th/, /kh/. Since /ʔ/ also exists already, the glottalization of [t'] or [k'], for example, is taken as an allophonic manifestation of /ʔ/, yielding /tʔ/, /kʔ/, and so forth. Now, you may say, do we not violate 'phonetic unity' in such componential interpretations? What is to be gained by rewriting a Boasian *'ahi·t'į́* as *ʔahiitʔį́*? A response which would be considered satisfactory would presuppose an understanding not only of phonological problems but also of morphological problems. Morphological facts may be important in the framing of phonological solutions.

There have been two popular approaches to the finding and grouping of morphs into morphemes, an older but by no means old-fashioned processive, morphophonemic, or internal reconstructional approach, and a more recent allomorphic or alternational approach. In the former approach, historically or theoretically earlier forms are said to change morphophonemically on contact into later actual forms. Thus one might say with Hoijer that a hypothetical **biih-ni-iid-d-ʔaah* underlies the actual *biihniit'aah* of our sample datum slip. In the latter approach, it would not be possible to say that **d-d-ʔ* yields *t'*, any more than it would be possible to say that replacives, which are processes, exist as morphs. Rather one might isolate a morph *knife* /nayf/ and two morphs in *knives,* /nayv/ and /z/. Then one would group /nayf/ and /nayv/ together as alternants or allomorphs (either label applies) of a morpheme {*knife*}, each allomorph being summoned up for duty in customary neighborhoods. Before pause, for example, I use the /nayf/ allomorph of {*knife*}; before the /z/ allomorph of {*plural*}, I use /nayv/.

Many linguists wish to simplify morphophonemic statements by adopting the method of morpheme alternants as well as a phonemicization which facilitates use of the method. The phonetician who hears the pronunciation of *cat's eyes* as [kæc'aIz]—with a [c'] differing not much from the [c'] which Sapir heard in Navaho [c'ɪn] 'bone,' written *c'in*—does that phonetician then insist that English has a phoneme /c'/? Even if he is not alert enough to count /ʔ/ as an English phoneme (and to include a morpheme of emphasis {ɔ-} in our language) at least in some idiolects, he is likely to interpret the phonetic substance, unified though it is in tempo and nature of articulation, as implicating the cluster /ts/, not /c/ (though for Hopi /c/ is preferred). Navaho verbs which preserve older transcriptional features are: *'ahiit'į́* 'we see each other,' *'ádiit'į́* 'we see ourselves,' *yiš-ˀį́* 'I see him' (the stem is set off by a hyphen which precedes it), *šooh-ˀį́* 'you see me,' *dayoo-ˀį́* 'they see him.' Componentially, considerations of phonetic unity aside, we have *ˀahiit-ˀį́, ˀátiit-ˀį́, yiš-ˀį́, šooh-ˀį́, tayoo-ˀį́*. We do not have to describe several different verb stems as allomorphs, for example, since diversity is no longer forced upon us by a doctrine of phonetic unity; nor do we need elaborate statements about reciprocal theoretical or historical changes which are generated when two particular sounds 'come together.' Clarity from re-analysis of *t'* is not an isolated instance. Re-analysis of λ as /tl/ supports this generalization. Instead of writing *ˀiiλiž* 'we two urinate' we write *ˀiitliž*. Comparison with *ˀaliž* 'he urinates' and other forms shows us that the stem is *-liž*. The prefix *iit-* 'we (two)' is seen here just as clearly as elsewhere. We do not have to theorize about an **iid-* which sometimes loses its final consonant (e.g. in hypothetical **si-iid-tééž* the *d* is lost, to yield *siitééž* 'we two lie') and sometimes has its final consonant merge or coalesce into a new consonant (e.g. in hypothetical **di-iid-ˀaaš* the *d* 'comes together' with ˀ and they coalesce to form the *t'* of *diit'aaš* 'we two start off').

Sapir was a pioneer in the interpretation of linguistic data. He was perhaps the first scholar in American linguistics to combine extensive training, decades of field experience, and un-Boasian courageousness in theorizing. His intrepidity should not obscure the fact that, for all of his field experience, he was well schooled in the art of making inferences about culture lost to time from culture still at hand.

23«

Sapir and the History of Resemblances

We can work toward an understanding of earlier stages of a language partly by using information about the phonemes and morphemes of the language, without asking what the situation is in relatable languages. The use of internal evidence supports *internal reconstruction;* when inferences are supported by comparisons with relatable languages we speak of *external reconstruction.* A key assumption of internal reconstruction is that a morpheme, with several alternants now, at an earlier stage had just one alternant or allomorph. In Navaho, to take a specific case, some stems have more than one allomorph each, and one allomorph of the set comes after a prefix while the other does not: *łiž* 'urine,' *pi-liž* 'his urine'; *łį́į́ʔ* 'horse,' *pi-lį́į́ʔ* 'his horse,' *sę̨ę̨s* 'wart,' *pi-zę̨ę̨s* 'his wart,' and so on. The morpheme {*liž*} 'urine' has two allomorphs now, but we can work back toward an earlier time when there was a single allomorph; using a star to show that the reconstructed form is hypothetical, we might posit **liž* in all positions, and similarly with the other sets, e.g. **lį́į́ʔ*, **zę̨ę̨s*. Internal reconstruction has its limitations, but it can suggest avenues of exploration using comparative data.

Americanists have profited immeasurably from the work of Indo-Europeanists. Sapir was an accomplished Indo-Europeanist as well as a brilliant Americanist, no less than Bloomfield. Both were familiar, of course, with stem alternations of Indo-European nouns, and were not surprised at all to find similar phenomena in Indian languages. In Latin, for example, the word for 'king' is *rēx,* which we might write phonemically, representing length with a vowel cluster, as /reeks/. The form is used as the subject of a sentence: *rēx leōnem edit* 'the king eats a lion'; the suffix represented by /s/ shows that the referent of the sign represented by /reek/ functions as a subject, not an object; and similarly in /leoonem/ the /em/ identifies an object, not a subject: if we say *leōnem rēx edit* or even *leōnem edit rēx* we still have to admit that 'the king eats a lion.' We can change things around by giving 'lion' in its subject or nominative form, *leō,* and 'king' in its object or accusative form, *rēgem: leō rēgem edit* 'the lion eats the king.' Note that the word for king has two stem alternants, /reek/ in the nominative and /reeg/ in the accusative (and in other cases, e.g. *rēg-is* genitive case 'of the king,' *rēg-ī* dative case 'to or for the king,' *rēg-e* ablative case 'from or by or with the king,' all singular; or the plurals *rēg-ēs* nominative 'kings' *or* accusative 'kings,' *rēg-um* genitive 'of the kings,' *rēg-ibus* dative 'to or for kings' *or* ablative 'from or by or with kings'). Just from internal evidence, what would one judge the older stem alternant of *rēx* to be? Would one say /reeg/ or /reek/? The simplest theory takes the least number of steps, and our answer must be /reeg/: to restore the paradigm with the fewest moves, namely one move, we reconstruct **rēg-* for the nominative singular form. What about *leō?* Let us look at some genitive singulars beside their corresponding nominatives: *leō* 'lion,' gen. *leōnis* 'of a lion'; *homō* 'man,' gen. *hominis; origō* 'origin,' gen. *originis; margō* 'edge,' gen. *marginis; ordō* 'rank, turn,' gen. *ordinis; errō* 'wanderer,' gen. *errōnis; volō* 'volunteer,' gen. *volōnis; caupō* 'innkeeper,' gen. *caupōnis; mangō* 'slavemonger,' gen. *mangōnis; ratiō* 'account,' gen. *ratiōnis; sermō* 'speech,' gen. *sermōnis; scīpio* 'a staff,' gen. *scīpiōnis; liēn* 'spleen,' gen. *liēnis;* and *rēx,* gen. *rēgis.* Well, what about *leō?* As with other forms just noted, but not all of them, of course, an *n* appears in the oblique (non-nominative) cases; compare *-is,* the genitive ending, after the stems *leōn, errōn, volōn, caupōn, mangōn, ratiōn, sermōn,* and *scipiōn.* In the accusative we have *leōnem, errōnem, volōnem, caupōnem,* and so forth; compare *rēg-em* for 'king.' To reconstruct a paradigm with a single-allomorph root morpheme, the simplest move is to take the form with *-ōn;* the *homō: homin-is, ordō: ordinis* type needs further explanation in terms of special sound changes environmentally conditioned. If we turn away from Latin for a moment to a sister language, easily relatable to Latin, Sanskrit, we discover that 'king' in the nominative is *rā́jā.* By well-known sound laws, Sanskrit *ā* goes back to Indo-European **ē* or **ō* or **ā.* Since the *ē* reflects **ē* in the Latin form, we may assume that the first *ā* of *rā́ja* developed from an **ē;* the *r* by comparative evidence reflects a prehistoric **r* and the *j* and *g* both go back to a palatal Indo-European **g^y^,* usually written *ĝ.* The base of the Latin and Sanskrit words for king, then, involves a reconstructed **rēĝ-;* and external reconstruction confirms the internal reconstruction which we suggested for the Latin nominative singular allomorph. Note that the second *ā* of *rā́jā* might represent an earlier **ō* akin to the *-ō* in such Latin words as *leō,* so-called *n*-stem nouns; this inference is not weakened by the oblique forms, e.g. the accusative singular *rājānam* or the nominative plural *rājānas.* Note also that what is an *n*-stem in one Indo-European language is not necessarily that in another; the word for king is an *n*-stem noun in Sanskrit but not in Latin, whose *rēgem* goes back to the base with no more nasal augmentation than the syllabic *m̥* which served as the Indo-European accusative ending: **rēĝ-m̥.*

Let us pose another question: if *leō edit rēgem* means 'the lion is eating the king (or eats the king),' how does one say that in Sanskrit? When we take the Sanskrit words in isolation, we have a nom. sg. *siṅhaḥ* 'lion' whose *-ḥ* is an allomorph of a nom. sg. suffix morpheme elsewhere represented by *-s* among other allomorphs; the root of the verb 'eat' is *ad* (from earlier **ed-* clearly seen in Latin *edit*), but when the third person sg. present active indicative suffix is added, by a process of assimilation its consonant, *t,* gives us a second root allomorph, *at,* and with the suffix we have *at-ti* from earlier **ed-ti;* because of sandhi or assimilation between words, one cannot say *siṅhas atti* but must say *siṅhootti* (usually written *siṅhotti* in texts). So we say, in response to the last question, *siṅhotti rājānam* means 'the lion is eating the king.'

The intricacy of the mental associations which Indo-Europeanists share often implies a fussy atomism. Structuralists have rejected atomistic and anecdotal analysis in the past few decades; the best structuralist work on internal reconstruction and the comparative method, in my opinion, has been done by Henry M. Hoenigswald in *Language Change and Linguistic Reconstruction* (1960). Sapir and Bloomfield, though ahead of their time in theoretical as well as practical insights, were products of their time; and both were masters of internal reconstruction and morphophonemic analysis, though not in Hoenigswald's style.

In Rice's *Methods in Social Science: A Case Book* (1931), Sapir paid tribute to Bloomfield with a chapter entitled, 'The Concept of Phonetic Law as Tested in Primitive Languages by Leonard Bloomfield.'

He described some of Bloomfield's work with sound laws which among other things show the relatability of Fox, Ojibwa, Plains Cree, and Menomini, Central Algonquian languages. Then he described some of his own work in Athapaskan comparative grammar. The lesson for social scientists in such work, Sapir finally observed, is the fact that the comparative study of languages 'emphasizes the extraordinary persistence in certain cases of complex *patterns* of cultural behavior regardless of the extreme variability of the content of such patterns.' Of particular interest to us at this point is Sapir's presentation of Athapaskan sound laws for Hupa (California), Navaho (Arizona and New Mexico mainly), Sarsi (or Sarcee; west-central Canada, the interior cordillera), and Chipewyan (to the east of the Sarsi, in the laurentian upland).

Proto-Athapaskan	Hupa	Navaho	Sarsi	Chipewyan
I. 1. *s	s	s	s	θ
2. *z	s	z	z	δ
3. *dz	dz	dz	dz	dδ
4. *ts	ts	ts	ts	tθ
5. *ts'	ts'	ts'	ts'	tθ'
II. 1. *c	W	c	s	s
2. *j	W	j	z	z
3. *dj	dj	dj	dz	dz
4. *tc	tcw	tc	ts	ts
5. *tc'	tc'	tc'	ts'	ts'
III. 1. *x̯	W	s	c	c
2. *y	y	y	y	y
3. *gy	gy	dz	dj	dj
4. *ky	ky	ts	tc	tc
*kyan 'rain'	kyaŋ	tsą	tcạ	tcą
5. *ky'	ky'	ts'	tc'	tc'

The word for 'honor' in an early stage of Latin was *honos,* acc. *honosem.* A Latin sound law required every intervocalic *s* to change eventually to an *r.* The nominative *honos* seemed out of line as far as speakers of Latin were concerned. All of the oblique cases had *r,* as in *honorem.* Why not then an *r* for *honos?* Hence the replacement, by *analogy,* of *honos* with *honor.* Frequency had something to do with the analogy, witness the untouched *s* of the rarer word for 'dew,' *rōs,* acc. *rōrem.* And how about *rosa,* you ask, why does the word for 'rose' still have an intervocalic *s* and why is it not *rora*? Perhaps the word for rose was borrowed; if it came into Latin when roses came into Roman culture, and that was after intervocalic *s*'s had turned to *r*'s, there is no mystery, and we need not be startled at *rosa* with an *s* and the imperative *rōrā* 'drop dew!' Analogy and borrowing make it impossible to prove that sound laws have no exceptions, and Bloomfield is quoted by Sapir to this effect in the chapter just mentioned, the final words of which were written in 1929. Another problem, related to the freedom with which speakers refashion their everyday discourse, begs mention here. The curious fact which we noted in comparing some Latin and Sanskrit nouns, the fact that roots may be cognate but that other elements, such as the *n*-stem element, appear now in one sister language and not in another—this fact should make us properly cautious about reconstructing hypothetical parent forms. A knowledge of morphology is important in reconstruction, though one can make a beginning at reconstruction even with a skimpy morphological understanding. Two examples, one from Indo-European, the other based on Sapir's chapter in praise of Bloomfield, are instructive. In the Indo-European language called Old Church Slavic, *kə́to* is 'who,' *číto* is 'what.' (Conventional orthography demands *kъto, čьto* in transliteration, and КЪТО, ЧЬТО in text.) Cognate with the first form is Lithuanian *kàs;* Latin *quis* is cognate with the second, the neuter form *quid* 'what' being of special importance. If we knew nothing about Indo-European morphology, we would be forced to suppose that Indo-European had a word for 'what' with parts corresponding to all of the phonemes of *číto.* But in Old Church Slavic, the *-to* is an added particle, as comparative data show. The Indo-European stems probably were **k^wo-* 'who' (masculine and feminine), **k^wi-* 'what' (neuter); from **k^wos* we get Gothic *ƕas,* from **k^wid* Latin *quid.* Sanskrit (in the Rig-Veda) has *kat,* an analogical substitute; later we have only *kim* for the *i*-stem of the neuter, in which *m* has been substituted for an earlier *t*; indeed, from Middle Indic times all pronominal neuters have *-m,* as in Pali *taṁ* for earlier *tat* 'that.' It follows plainly that predictions based on sound laws are not infallible.

Yet Bloomfield and Sapir both were able to sustain such predictions. In the table, section III, item 4, p. 177, we have Sapir's reconstruction of a word for 'rain.' He set up a table (upon which ours is based) using cognates showing recurrent phonemic correspondences. One set involved Hupa *ky* corresponding to Navaho *ts* corresponding to Sarsi *tc* corresponding to Chipewyan *tc*. Presumably he had a number of sets of cognates like this set of enclitics meaning 'big': Hupa *kyoh,* Navaho *tsoh,* Sarsi *tcóó,* Chipewyan *tcòγ*. His best guess as to the sound from which the various outcomes developed, by a process of gradual but inexorable phonetic change, was a reconstructed **ky*. Given **ky*, one then says that this was unchanged in Hupa, became *ts* in Navaho, and became *tc* in Sarsi and Chipewyan. Sapir had many words for 'rain' when he constructed his table, but not the Hupa word. In 1927 he discovered Hupa *kyaŋ-kyoh* 'hailstorm.' Lacking knowledge of the independent existence of the enclitic, he would have been forced *faute de mieux* to posit a Proto-Athapaskan word for 'rain' which was actually an expression for 'big rain' made up of two morphemes instead of one. Sapir did not make this mistake. We cannot escape the inference, however, that reconstructions based upon vocabularies, unanalyzed word lists brought back by ethnographers whose main interest is not in linguistics, invite the sort of mistake which Sapir did not make. This observation is not a criticism, since even such lists are valuable; it is rather a reminder that reconstructions are always approximations based on data at hand, tentative, and subject to revision.

The discovery of sound laws helps in assigning languages to subgroups. Indo-European *k̂* became a sibilant sound in the eastern Indo-European area, in contrast to a variety of velar sounds in the western Indo-European area: the word for 'hundred,' with initial **k̂* in Proto-Indo-European, has /s/ in Avestan /satəm/ versus /k/ in Latin /kentum/.* On the basis of a single phonological isogloss-web which developed from the history of IE **k̂*, then, some scholars decided that the Indo-European community broke into two parts, an eastern and a western, a satem and a centum group, with these 'satem' languages: *Indic* (Sanskrit; Middle Indic Pali, Prakrit, Apabhraṃśa; Modern Indic Bengali, Hindi, Gujarati, Marathi) and *Iranian* (Avestan, Old Persian), these two comprising an 'Aryan' or

*In the classical Latin of Cicero's day, /kę̄tų/ with nasalized vowels.

'Indo-Iranian' branch; *Baltic* (Lithuanian, Lettish, extinct Old Prussian) and *Slavic* (Old Church Slavic, Czech, Slovak, Lusatian, Polish, Bulgarian, Serbo-Croatian, Russian), these two comprising a 'Balto-Slavic' branch; *Armenian; Albanian;* the extinct *Thracian* and *Illyrian,* and perhaps the extinct *Phrygian.* And with these 'centum' languages: *Greek; Latin; Celtic* (extinct Gallic; Irish [Gaelic], Brittanic [Welsh, Cornish, Breton]); *Germanic* (extinct Gothic; North Germanic languages such as Norwegian or the early Old Norse; West Germanic languages such as English, German, or the early Old English, Old High German); *Tocharian* (extinct, known from remains found in Chinese Turkestan); *Hittite* (extinct, known from Anatolian remains); the extinct *Venetic.*

To take an Athapaskan example, Hoijer in 1960 set up a *Pacific Coast* subgroup of Athapaskan with two main divisions, *Californian* (Hupa, Wailaki, Mattole, Kato) and *Oregonian* (Tolowa, Chasta Costa, Galice, Coquille, Euchre Creek, Umpqua). He used sound laws in establishing subgroups, for example, 'the shift of PA [Proto-Athapaskan] **k*, **x* to *x* or *k* in PCA [Pacific Coast Athapaskan]' helps to set PCA off from Northern and Southern or Apachean Athapaskan languages. Other changes which guide the subgrouper are: 'the combining, in PCA, of PA **s* and **z* . . . the confusion, in most PCA languages, of PA **s*, **z*, **j* [the **dz* of Sapir's table], and **c* [the **ts* of Sapir's table] . . . the combining in PCA of PA **š* and **ž* [the **c* and **j* of Sapir's table] . . . the partial confusion in the Oregon languages of PA **ǰ* and **č* [the **dj* and **tc* of Sapir's table] . . . the shift of PA **L* [older *dl*] and **Ł* [often written *tł*] to PCA *l* or *ł* and *ł*, respectively. . . .'; there are also cases of $*\gamma^w > w$ and $*\gamma > g$ in Hoijer's argument. A 'provisional hypothesis' then justifies this subgrouping:

A. California Division
  1. Hupa
  2. Wailaki-Kato-Mattole
    a. Wailaki
    b. Kato
    c. Mattole
B. Oregon Division
  1. Southern group
    a. Euchre Creek-Coquille
      i. Euchre Creek

ii. Coquille
b. Tolowa
c. Chasta Costa
2. Galice (and Applegate?)
3. Umpqua

As nonphonological grammatical data become available, it is possible that this subgrouping will be modified in some ways; Hoijer's work, replacing many moonshine statements, gives us a working theory, not a reification. Not all working theories of this sort rely mainly on sound laws. How are subgroups usefully identified, in general? The classical subgrouping technique, that of inspection, has been described by Karl Brugmann. It is said of Brugmann that he 'learned' all of the Indo-European languages known to scholars of his day; Brugmann's scholarship, which drew Bloomfield to study with him early in the second decade of this century, makes the saying less than incredible. Swadesh and others have shown that more than simple or even phonologically augmented inspection is needed for efficiency in subgrouping.

If word lists are available, the ethnologist can prepare a notebook for comparative studies. He can subgroup by inspection which consists simply of scanning. Greenberg used this technique, to take a particular case, in establishing his preliminary classification of the languages of South America. What the technique lacks in rigor it gains, for some, in taxonomic progress; and most diligent scholars who use the technique reinforce their earliest intuitive inferences with phonological, morphological, and lexical evidence. There are, in other words, successive approximations to truth in subgrouping as in other areas of science; and the student must be always alert to avoid the seductions of oversimplification, particularly if he is an ethnologist and not primarily a linguist. All too often does a tentative hypothesis about genetic relationships of languages lose its tentative and uncertain nature as it moves from the linguist's article to the ethnologist's monograph! If we can justly say: *Do not reify your reconstructions,* we can also justly say: *Do not reify your subgroups!* They are, after all, only what I think Peirce would call icons.

If word lists are available, subgrouping by a so-called lexicostatistic technique is possible. This technique involves the identification of cognates and the counting of cognates which are shared. The languages which share more cognates may be said to be more closely related; those which share less, less closely related. A family or genetic tree can be drawn from such information. But there are several different lexicostatistic techniques which scholars are studying at the present time; to understand some of them, we must consider actual data. Our data come partly from three Northern Athapaskan languages of Alaska, Ingalik, Kenai, and Upper Inlet, partly from a Southern Athapaskan or Apachean language of the Southwest, Navaho. Let us consider some word-sets, those for 'louse,' 'fire,' 'lynx,' 'arrow,' 'rabbit,' and '(mountain) sheep.'

	Ingalik	Kenai	Upper Inlet	Navaho
1. louse	yoʔ	iiyóʔ	iiyóʔ	yaaʔ
2. fire	kon	tážiʔ	qanʔ	kǫʔ
3. lynx	noodog	kážna	nidyá	nášdúíłbáí
4. arrow	k̓oo	ízin	ééni	k'aaʔ
5. rabbit	gox	nq̓wáʔ	qabéé	gah
6. sheep	giłc̓aii	nóóǯi	nóóǯi	dibé

If we use a capital letter to represent similar forms which might be or might contain cognate morphemes, we can replace our Athapaskan words by letters, as follows in a 'cognation table':

	Ingalik	Kenai	Upper Inlet	Navaho
1. louse	A	A	A	A
2. fire	A	B	A	A
3. lynx	A	B	C	D
4. arrow	A	B	C	A
5. rabbit	A	B	C	A
6. sheep	A	B	B	C

One of four alternatives appears in the set for 'louse': all forms have cognate morphemes, which justifies an inference of relatability. A second alternative appears in the set for 'lynx': no form is cognate with any other form in the set, which justifies an inference of independence. The patterns AAAA and ABCD if repeated often in a large corpus of data will help us to say something useful about external relationships. In a third type of pattern, a letter is repeated so that it appears two times or more, as with 'fire,' 'arrow,' 'rabbit,' and 'sheep.' A fourth pattern requires two different repeated letters as a minimum, e.g. AABB or ABBA; an illustration is French *père,* German *vater,* Russian *otec,* Welsh *tad* 'father,' AABB. Sets of this type enable us to find 'counterindications' in subgrouping.

How many branching alternatives are possible for four dialects destined to become languages, if a speech community splits conveniently like an amoeba? Say that we have a community with dialects A, B, C, and D, represented by Figure 7(a). The first split might separate A from B-C-D, as in Fig. 7(b); or A-B from C-D, Fig. 7(c); or A-B-C from D, Fig. 7(d). After the first split, there are two languages, each on its own branch. In the case of Fig. 7(b), the next split must separate B-C from D, or B from C-D. In the case of Fig. 7(c), the next split must separate A from B and C from D. In the case of Fig. 7(d), the next split must separate A-B from C or A from B-C. These possibilities are shown in Figure 8. Figures 7 and 8 hint at the complexity of even a schematic history of four languages with an assumption of strictly binary divergence, i.e. only two paths from any given nodule point. Each tree, like any icon whatsoever, is the image of a hypothe-

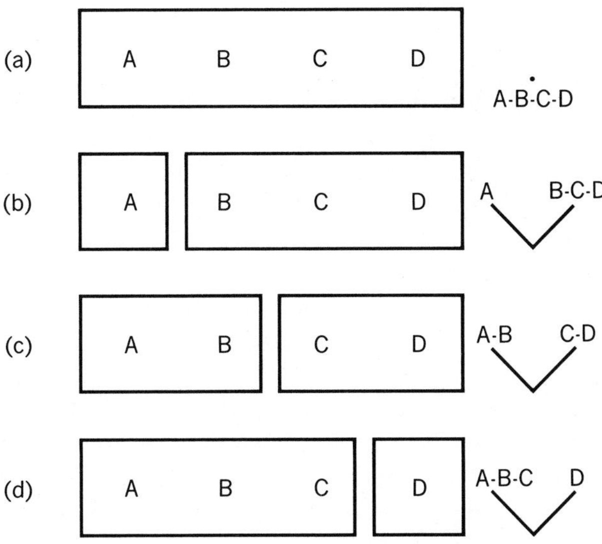

FIGURE 7 Community aggregations and genetic trees

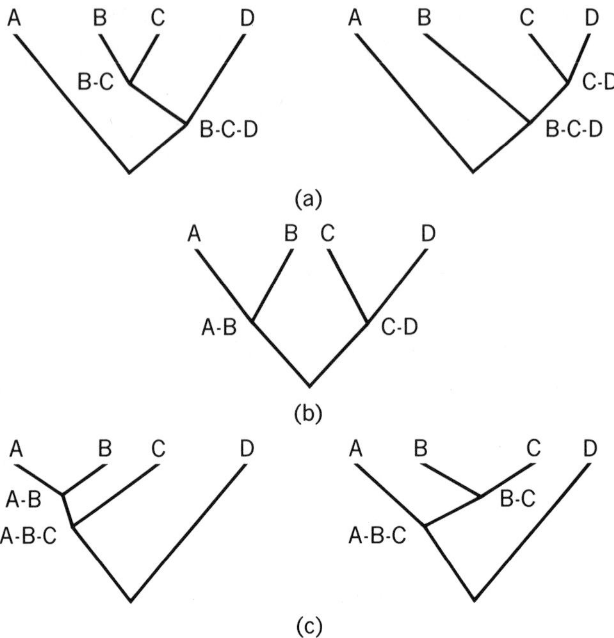

FIGURE 8 Branching alternatives of genetic trees

sis, if we follow Peirce; so that the maximum of possible schemata—over a dozen for any four languages—far exceeds in general the supply of implausible alternatives which the corrective medicine of empirical data, notably geographical information, quickly purges from serious consideration. We would not easily suppose, for example, that Welsh and Russian are more closely related than Russian and German, judging from geographical distributions. Yet the tree which represents the best hypothesis about the historical relationships of, say, French, German, Welsh, and Russian does not find its best corroboration in geography.

Without sound laws, the scholar is prey to certain kinds of possibly mistaken inference about the relatability of languages. Sapir's promise to publish sound laws linking Tlingit, Haida, and Athapaskan languages was canceled at least by his untimely death; typological resemblances and putative phonemic correspondences, said to link these 'Na-Dene' languages, do not convince the Boasian temperament, and the Na-Dene issue has not been settled. The linguist's problem is in some respects a reflection of the larger problem of the culture historian: to explain the history of resemblances. Genetic resemblances put us on the track of historical truth. Universals throw us off the track, elements common to all cultures or languages; if phonemic systems undergo pressures and seek symmetries of certain types, as some investigators suspect, we must factor them out. If all men imitate the cries of lower creatures or the sounds of elemental nature, responsively and with some accuracy, onomatopoetically, or if there are limits to chance which force convergence, giving us a sound-and-meaning element in one language which is only by chance like a sound-and-meaning element in another (Shasta *xacki* 'three,' Tlingit *notsk* 'three'; Shasta *nuk-sua,* Tlingit *šiā,* Ingalik *sis,* all 'mountain'; the end of Shasta *ʔawatíkwaa* 'man, husband,' Tlingit *kaa* 'man'; Shasta *c'ítakku,* Chipewyan *e-c'eze* 'kidney'; Shasta *ʔísaak* 'ear,' Navaho *ʔažaaʔ* 'ear')—if, in short, such things as chance resemblances exist, as the ostriches, emus, and rheas of language, and more dangerously perhaps, if resemblances by borrowing or diffusion exist, whether in the taking over of a scale model or the construction of an analogue or 'stimulus diffusional' model (English has thousands of latinical words, but its resemblances to Latin do not make it a Romance language), then chance resemblances and resemblances by diffusion are bound to throw us off the track of historical truth. Linguists have constructed word lists to avoid, if possible, any static or interference from borrowing or accidental resemblance. The hope is to avoid 'phoney' cognates, the ghosts of cognates, cognates which are not really cognates. Such hopeful lists are called 'basic' vocabularies. These have played an important role in American linguistics, both before Sapir, in the experiments of Gallatin, Hale, Dixon, and Kroeber, and after Sapir, principally in the experiments of Swadesh.

24«

The Glottochronological Experiment

Swadesh has developed more than one basic vocabulary list. His rules for collection of items must be honored. An item must be first in frequency, even if it has a competitor which is cognate with another item in a comparable language. When there are doubts of any sort, an item must be left out. One list has 200 items per language; another has 100. Hoijer modified the 100-word list in his work with Athapaskan glottochronology and did not reckon with frequency data as required by Swadesh. Hoijer's study, nevertheless, proved how difficult, and in some ways unrealistic, the initial expectations of glottochronologists were.

Archaeologists and ethnologists in search of linguistic support for theories of culture history based on nonlinguistic data have sometimes made too much of glottochronology. Various positions have been taken by linguists, from rejection on mathematical grounds (by Lees and later Chrétien), to guarded interest (manifested notably by Hymes), to unguarded devotion (particularly when archaeological data and glottochronological data seem to jibe, as sometimes happens). In a study of some of the methods and results of glottochronology, one finds a partial answer to the larger, more significant question: What is the value of lexicostatistics to students of language and culture?

The glottochronologist begins with basic vocabularies. Consider these:

Basic List	French	German	Russian	Welsh
1. all	tout	all	vse	holl
2. and	et	und	i	a
3. animal	animal	tier	zver'	anifail
4. ashes	cendre	asche	pepel	lludw

Basic List	French	German	Russian	Welsh
5. at	à	an	v	yn
6. back	dos	rücken	spina	cefn
7. bad	mauvais	schlecht	plochoj	drwg
8. bark	écorce	rinde	[phrase]*	barc
9. because	car	wegen	potomu čto	oherwydd
10. belly	ventre	bauch	brjucho	bol
11. big	grand	gross	bol'šoj	mawr
12. bird	oiseau	vogel	ptica	aderyn
13. bite	mordre	beissen	kusat'	cnoi
14. black	noir	schwarz	černyj	du
15. blood	sang	blut	krov'	gwaed
16. blow	souffler	blasen	dut'	cwythu
17. bone	os	knochen	kost'	asgwrn
18. breathe	respirer	atmen	dyšat'	anadlu
19. burn	brûler	brennen	goret'	llosgi
20. child	enfant	kind	rebenok	plentyn
21. cloud	nuage	wolke	oblako	cwmwl
22. cold	froid	kalt	cholodnyj	oer
23. come	venir	kommen	pridti	dyfod
24. count	compter	rechnen	sčitat'	rhifo
25. cut	couper	schneiden	rezat'	torri
26. day	jour	tag	den'	dydd
27. die	mourir	sterben	umirat'	marw
28. dig	creuser	graben	kopat'	cloddio
29. dirty	sale	schmutzig	grjaznyj	budr
30. dog	chien	hund	sobaka	ci
31. drink	boire	trinken	pit'	yfed
32. dry	sec	trocken	suchoj	sych
33. dull	émoussé	stumpf	tupoj	pwl
34. dust	poussière	staub	pyl	llwch
35. ear	oreille	ohr	ucho	clust
36. earth	terre	erde	zemlja	daear
37. eat	manger	essen	jest'	bwyta
38. egg	œuf	ei	jajco	wy
39. eye	oeil	auge	glaz	llygad
40. fall	tomber	fallen	past'	cwympo
41. far	loin	fern	daleko	ymhell
42. fat	gras	fett	žir	bras
43. father	père	vater	otec	tad

*The rule has been observed that phrases are not included, if there is no certainty on the part of the investigator that they are idiomatic. Clearly idiomatic phrases, on the other hand, have been listed.

Basic List	French	German	Russian	Welsh
44. fear	craindre	fürchten	bojat'sja	ofni
45. feather	plume	feder	pero	pluen
46. few	peu de	wenig	malo	ychydig
47. fight	combattre	kämpfen	sražat'sja	ymladd
48. fire	feu	feuer	ogon'	tan
49. fish	poisson	fisch	ryba	pysgodyn
50. five	cinq	fünf	pjat'	pump
51. float	flotter	schwimmen	plyt'	nofio
52. flow	couler	fliessen	teč'	llifo
53. flower	fleur	blume	cvetok	blodeuyn
54. fly	voler	fliegen	letet'	ehedeg
55. fog	brouillard	nebel	tuman	niwl
56. foot	pied	fuss	noga	troed
57. four	quatre	vier	četyrje	pedwar
58. freeze	glacer	erstarren	morozit'	rhewi
59. fruit	fruit	obst	frukty	ffrwyth
60. give	donner	geben	dat'	rhoi
61. good	bon	gut	chorošij	da
62. grass	herbe	gras	trava	gwellt
63. green	vert	grün	zelenyj	gwyrdd
64. guts	ventre	eingeweide	vnutrennosti	perfedd
65. hair	cheveu	haar	volosy	gwallt
66. hand	main	hand	ruka	llaw
67. he	il	er	on	efe
68. head	tête	kopf	golova	pen
69. hear	entendre	hören	slyšat'	clywed
70. heart	coeur	herz	serdce	calon
71. heavy	lourd	schwer	tjaželyj	trwm
72. here	ici	hier	zdjes'	yma
73. hit	frapper	schlagen	bit'	taro
74. hold	tenir	halten	deržat'	dal
75. how	comment	wie	kak	pa
76. hunt	chasser	jagen	ochotit'sja	hela
77. husband	mari	mann	muž	gŵr
78. I	je	ich	ja	mi
79. ice	glace	eis	led	rhew
80. if	si	wenn	esli	os
81. in	dans	in	v	yn
82. kill	tuer	töten	ubit'	llad
83. know	savoir	wissen	znat'	gwybod
84. lake	lac	see	ozero	llyn
85. laugh	rire	lachen	smejat'sja	chwerthin

Basic List	French	German	Russian	Welsh
86. leaf	feuille	blatt	list	deilen
87. left	gauche	link	levyj	aswy
88. leg	jambe	bein	noga	coes
89. lie	être couché	liegen	ležat’	gorwedd
90. live	vivre	leben	žit’	byw
91. liver	foie	leber	pečenka	iau
92. long	long	lang	dolgij	hir
93. louse	pou	laus	voš’	lleuen
94. man	homme	mensch	čelovek	dyn
95. many	beaucoup de	viel	mnogo	llawer
96. meat	viande	fleisch	mjaso	cig
97. mother	mère	mutter	mat’	mam
98. mountain	montagne	berg	gora	mynydd
99. mouth	bouche	mund	rot	ceg
100. name	nom	name	imja	enw
101. narrow	étroit	[?]	[?]	[?]*
102. near	près	nah(e)	blizko	yn agos
103. neck	cou	hals	šeja	gwddf
104. new	neuf/nouveau	neu	novyj	newydd
105. night	nuit	nacht	noč’	nos
106. nose	nez	nase	nos	trwyn
107. not	non	nicht	nje	na
108. old	vieux	alt	staryj	hen
109. one	un	ein	odin	un
110. other	autre	andere	drugoi	arall
111. person	personne	person	osoba	dyn
112. play	jouer	spielen	igrat’	chware
113. pull	tirer	ziehen	tjanut’	tynnu
114. push	pousser	stossen	tolkat’	pwsio
115. rain	pleuvoir	regnen	dožd’ idyot	glawio
116. red	rouge	rot	krasnyj	[?]**
117. right	juste	recht	pravyj	iawn
118. right	droit	rechts	pravyj	de
119. river	fleuve	fluss	reka	afon
120. road	chemin	weg	doroga	ffordd
121. root	racine	wurzel	koren’	gwreiddyn
122. rope	corde	seil	verevka	rhaff
123. rotten	pourri	verdorben	gniloj	pydri
124. rub	frotter	reiben	teret’	rhwbio

*German eng *vs.* schmal, Russian uzkij *vs.* tesnyj, Welsh cul *vs.* cyfing.

**coch or rhudd.

Basic List	French	German	Russian	Welsh
125. salt	sel	salz	sol'	halen
126. sand	sable	sand	pesok	tywod
127. say	dire	sagen	skazat'	dywedyd
128. scratch	gratter	kratzen	česat'	crafu
129. sea	mer	meer	more	mor
130. see	voir	sehen	videt'	gweled
131. seed	graine	same	semja	had
132. sew	coudre	nähen	šit'	gwnïo
133. sharp	tranchant	scharf	ostryj	llym
134. short	court	kurz	korotkyj	byr
135. sing	chanter	singen	pet'	canu
136. sit	être assis	sitzen	sidet'	eistedd
137. skin	peau	haut	koža	croen
138. sky	ciel	himmel	nebo	wybr
139. sleep	dormir	schlafen	spat'	cysgu
140. small	petit	klein	malyj	bach
141. smell	sentir	riechen	njuchat'	arogli
142. smoke	fumée	rauch	dym	mwg
143. smooth	lisse	glatt	gladkij	llyfn
144. snake	serpent	schlange	zmeja	neidr
145. snow	neige	schnee	sneg	eira
146. some	du	etwas	neskol'ko	rhai
147. spit	cracher	speien	plevat'	poeri
148. split	fendre	spalten	kolot'	hollti
149. squeeze	presser	drücken	tiskat'	gwasgu
150. stab	percer	stechen	zakalot'	brathu
151. stand	être debout	stehen	stojat'	sefyll
152. star	étoile	stern	zvezda	seren
153. stick	baton	stock	palka	pren
154. stone	pierre	stein	kamen'	carreg
155. straight	droit	gerade	prjamoj	union
156. suck	sucer	saugen	sosat'	sugno
157. sun	soleil	sonne	solnce	haul
158. swell	enfler	schwellen	puchnut'	chwyddo
159. swim	nager	schwimmen	plyt'	nofio
160. tail	queue	schwanz	chvost	cynffon
161. that	ce	der	tot	hwnnw
162. there	là	da	tam	yna
163. they	ils	sie	oni	n(h)w
164. thick	épais	dick	tolstyj	tew
165. thin	mince	dünn	tonkij	teneu
166. think	penser	denken	dumat'	meddwl

Basic List	French	German	Russian	Welsh
167. this	ce	dies	etot	hwn
168. thou	tu	du	ty	ti
169. three	troi	drei	tri	tri
170. throw	jeter	werfen	brosit'	taflu
171. tie	lier	binden	svjazat'	clymu
172. tongue	langue	zunge	jazyk	tafod
173. tooth	dent	zahn	zub	dant
174. tree	arbre	baum	derevo	coeden
175. turn	tourner	wenden	povernut'	troi
176. two	deux	zwei	dva	dau
177. vomit	vomir	sich erbrechen	blevat'	chwydu
178. walk	marcher	gehen	idti	cerdded
179. warm	chaud	warm	teplyj	cynnes
180. wash	laver	waschen	myt'	golchi
181. water	eau	wasser	voda	dŵr
182. we	nous	wir	my	ni
183. wet	mouillé	nass	mokryj	gwlyb
184. what?	que	was	kakoj	yr hyn
185. when?	quand	wann	kogda	pryd
186. where?	où	wo	gde	ymha le
187. white	blanc	weiss	belyj	gwyn
188. who?	qui	wer	kto	yr hwn
189. wide	large	breit	široki	llydan
190. wife	femme	frau	žena	gwraig
191. wind	vent	wind	veter	gwynt
192. wing	aile	flügel	krylo	adain
193. wipe	essuyer	wischen	vytirat'	sychu
194. with	avec	mit	s	gyda
195. woman	femme	frau	ženščina	gwraig
196. woods	bois	wald	les	coedwig
197. worm	ver	wurm	červ'	pryf
198. ye	vous	ihr	vy	chwi
199. year	an	jahr	god	blwyddyn
200. yellow	jaune	gelb	želtyj	melyn

LEXICOSTATISTIC EXERCISES

1. Make a cognation table for these data, or for as many word-sets as your instructor specifies. This exercise provides some insight into inferences which figure in preliminary lexicostatistic work.

2. In judgments about our cognates, a measure of control is afforded by records. We know, for example, that the Welsh list contains some forms diffused from Latin; for resemblances by diffusion, compare 32 *sych,* 45 *pluen,* 49 *pysgodyn,* 55 *niwl,* 59 *ffrwyth,* 113 *tynnu,* 116 *coch,* 139 *cysgu.* Other loans: 59 Russian *frukty* is from Latin, 124 Welsh *rhwbio* is from English, 134 German *kurz* is from Latin, and 143 French *lisse* probably is from German. Revise your cognation table on the basis of this information.

3. Here are some informed judgments about cognate morphemes of our lists, based upon a knowledge of Indo-European sound laws. If two words of a set are deemed cognate, say French *chien* 'dog' and German *hund* 'dog,' the word 'dog' is listed after FRENCH-*German.* Welsh *ci* 'dog' is cognate with the French and German forms; hence we find 'dog' in both the FRENCH-*Welsh* and GERMAN-*Welsh* lists.

FRENCH-*German:* dog, ear, egg, eye, father, fish, five, flower, foot, four, heart, I, long, mother, name, neck, new, night, nose, not, one, red, right (direction), salt, scratch, sea, snow, star, suck, sun, thou, three, tongue, tooth, two, who?, wind, worm, yellow.

FRENCH-*Russian:* bone, die, drink, ear, egg, five, four, give, heart, I, in, live, long, mother, name, new, night, nose, not, one, pull, salt, sea, see, snow, suck, sun, thou, three, two, who?, wind, ye, yellow.

FRENCH-*Welsh:* animal, die, dog, egg, five, flower, four, green, live, mountain, name, new, night, one, right (direction), salt, sea, sing, star, suck, sun, thou, three, tongue, tooth, two, we, wind.

GERMAN-*Russian:* animal, ear, eat, egg, five, four, heart, I, lie, long, mother, name, new, night, nose, not, one, salt, sea, seed, sit, smooth, snow, spit, stand, suck, sun, thin, this, thou, three, two, water, we, who?, wind, yellow.

GERMAN-*Welsh:* all, dog, egg, five, flower, four, know, name, new, night, one, right (direction), root, salt, sea, seed, sit, star, suck, sun, thin, thou, three, tongue, tooth, two, wind.

RUSSIAN-*Welsh:* day, die, drink, egg, father, five, four, hair, hear, live, name, new, night, one, salt, sea, seed, sit, suck, sun, thin, thou, three, two, wind.

A basic assumption of glottochronology is that in general (in the absence of special conditions, such as the ritual tabooing of words) over something like a thousand years or even longer a number of morphemes will be lost from the basic vocabulary at something approaching a logarithmic rate. On the assumption of such marvelous constancy—a constant of 81 per cent of retained words per thousand years has been proposed on the basis of work with little more than a dozen languages for which written records are available—it should be possible to estimate roughly how many years have gone by since two languages branched away from a common nodule point. The time of split *t* equals a fraction. The numerator of the fraction is the logarithm of *c*; the denominator is twice the logarithm of *r*.

How do we find *c*? Let us look at the data of 3 above. Count the cognates listed for each pair of languages.

French-German	German-Russian
French-Russian	German-Welsh
French-Welsh	Russian-Welsh

Now divide each number by 2. The French-Russian number, for example, is 34; and 34 divided by 2 is 17. We can say then that French and Russian share 17 per cent of the basic vocabulary,* and that, in decimal figures, *c*, the percentage of cognates, equals .17.

How do we find *r*? This is a constant, .81, based on the number of cognates which will be retained on any list, say the French list or the Welsh list, after a thousand years.**

GLOTTOCHRONOLOGICAL PROBLEMS

Bypassing mathematical computations and simplifying somewhat, we arrive at the tabulation of data in a form which the student may encounter in his reading of journals. The table sits neatly on the page, little betraying the work and the puzzles that lie behind it. Figures in the left-hand corner represent *c*, the percentage of cognates

*Not of any basic list (e.g. the Swadesh 100-word list or Hoijer's special Athapaskan list of 100 words), but only of the 200-word Swadesh basic list given above; other lists require other mathematical computations.

**The 'constant' is an average of a certain probability. The retention or loss of morphemes is subject to cultural determinants of which the investigator may be ignorant. The constant of .81 is more carefully specified by Robert Lees, *Lg.* 29.113–27 (1953), as .8048 ± .0176/millennium, at the 90 per cent level of confidence; *cf.* English .766, Spanish .79, French .776, German .854, Coptic .76, Athenian .836, Cypriote .829, Chinese .795, Swedish .854, Italian .839, Portuguese .806, Rumanian .764, Catalan .793.

in common; those in the right-hand corner represent *t*, the 'time depth' in centuries.

Centuries of Divergence

French	39	41.5	46.5
.19	**German**	39.5	47.5
.17	.185	**Russian**	49.1
.14	.135	.125	**Welsh**

Percentage of Cognates

To take the Franco-Russian case as an example, the 17 per cent figure would appear to correspond to 4150 years of divergence (the Italic-Slavic 'split' being set roughly at 2200 B.C.), on the basis of the 200-word list with $r = .81$. We have to specify the list and the constant, for in *IJAL* 21.121–37 (1955) Swadesh proposed a new 100-word list and a new constant of about .86. This proposal of a new list and a new constant was in part a reflection of the importance of frequency as a determinant of culture change, in part a recognition of the value for scientific progress of successive approximations to truth. Some words, of higher frequency, are supposed to be more durable, more resistant to being lost, than others: the word for 'nose,' for example, is quite frequent, quite viable, quite persistent. In an article of signal importance at the time, in *PAPS* 96.452–63 (1952), Swadesh had supposed, as some textbooks still do, that 19 per cent of the words of any list—we can think of our French list, for a concrete example—would be lost in 1000 years, and 81 per cent would be kept. And for two languages, after 1000 years of separation, the 81 per cent of the words kept by language A—say, French—would not be identical with the 81 per cent kept by language B—say, Russian. How many words would be held in common? About 81 per cent of 81 per cent, roughly 66 per cent. And after 2000 years, how many words would be held in common? By the same logic, 81 per cent of 66 per cent, or roughly 53 per cent. But this logic ignores viability. The more viable words persist and do not disappear in support of the metaphor of radioactive decay. An 86 per cent retention rate and a 100-word list presumably corrected for viability offer hope for greater accuracy of dating in the future.

But how accurate are the various glottochronological estimates now in existence? Each estimate is a problem by itself; each estimate is worth more as an independent check upon estimates arrived at by radio-carbon dating, tree-ring dating, pollen dating, and other kinds of dating, than in isolation.

We will be aided, in assessing estimates, by the following table. Given a value for *c* we may find an estimate of centuries of divergence, either by reading it directly or by extrapolation.

c	*t*		*c*	*t*		*c*	*t*	
	r.81	*r*.86		*r*.81	*r*.86		*r*.81	*r*.86
95	1.*		50	17.	19.	14	46.5	
90	2.5	5.	45	19.		12	50.	
85	4.		40	21.5	27.	10	54.	72.
80	5.	7.	35	25.		9	57.	
75	6.5		30	28.5	37.	8	59.5	
70	8.	10.	25	33.5		7	63.	
65	10.		20	38.	52.	6	66.5	
60	12.	14.	18	40.		5	70.5	
55	14.5		16	43.				

*To nearest half-century

4. The smaller the basic vocabulary list is and the smaller one's store of written records or of inferences about sound laws, which would reduce the chance of being deceived by appearances, the greater one's chances are of going astray. As a final step of our exercise, and to illustrate this remark in part, compute the time depths for French, German, Russian, and Welsh, using values of *c* which reflect ignorance of borrowing.

Centuries of Divergence

French			
.20	German		
.175	.185	Russian	
.165	.15	.135	Welsh

Percentage of Cognates

GLOTTOCHRONOLOGIC RELATIONSHIPS

Swadesh has proposed the following model for the interpretation of data.*

Term	Centuries of Divergence	Percentage of Cognates	General Character	Example
Language	0–5	100–81	Mutual intelligibility of dialects	English
Family	5–25	81–36	Relationship obvious to anyone	Germanic languages
Stock	25–50	36–12	Obvious to linguist	Indo-European
Microphylum	50–75	12–4	Striking rare agreements	Salishan
Mesophylum	75–100	4–1	Rare, rare agreements	Penutian(?)
Macrophylum	over 100	under 1	Reconstruct able	Hokan-Siouan(?)

It is now possible to consider in greater detail the most comprehensive scholarly classification of the languages of the world, wherein

* *Word* 10.306–32 (1954).

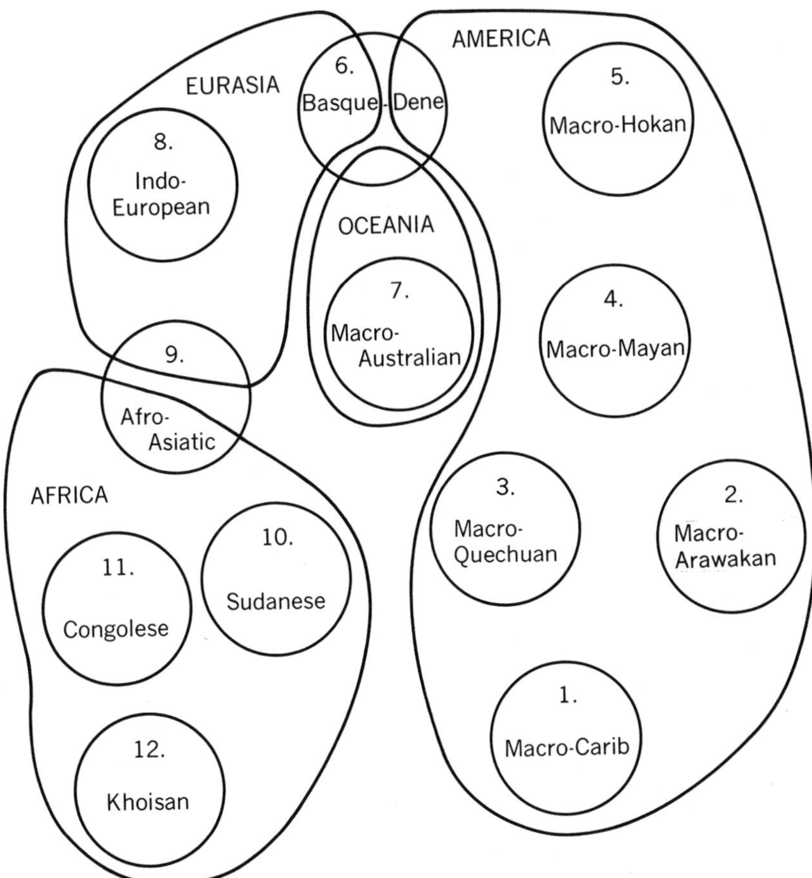

FIGURE 9 Glottochronologic grouping of the languages of the world

Swadesh revives Sapir's boldness. Figure 9, whose basis is given on p. 120 of Swadesh's *Tras la Huella Lingüística de la Prehistoria* (1960), reflects glottochronologic data and estimates of divergences in 'minimum centuries.' Inner divergences are given for Indo-European, Macro-Carib, Basque-Dene, Macro-Mayan, Macro-Quechuan, Macro-Hokan, and Macro-Arawakan respectively as 69, 85, 90, 90, 95, 96, and 100 centuries. The figure should be supplemented with the following information, showing centuries of divergence.

Macro-Carib	**1**	55	57	59								
Macro-Arawakan		**2**		59	67							
Macro-Quechuan			**3**	57	60							
Macro-Mayan				**4**	67							
Macro-Hokan					**5**	57						
Basque-Dene						**6**	?	60	60			
Macro-Australian							**7**					
Indo-European								**8**	67			
Afro-Asiatic									**9**	60	60	
Sudanese										**10**	80	
Congolese											**11**	67
Khoisan												**12**

25«

Lexicostatistical Subgrouping

Some scholars subgroup languages by phonological innovations in a move preliminary to further study, for example, Hoijer with Pacific Coast Athapaskan. Others use a method of inspection aimed at diverse innovations, lexical and grammatical as well as phonological, for example, Greenberg with the languages of Africa. Others again reinforce their opinions with lexicostatistic evidence, usually cognate percentages or their glottochronological analogs.

Let us consider lexicostatistical evidence at greater length. Do tables of cognation help one to identify subgroups in a useful way? The European data which we considered in the last section might lead one to suppose that such tables serve only to confuse. For the data seem to indicate that French and German are more closely related to each other than either is to Welsh or Russian. The same seems to hold for Russian and German as against French or Welsh. Russian and French, moreover, are closer to each other than either is to Welsh, and in fact are closer to Welsh than German is. These inferences must seem strange (except in the Russo-Germanic case) to proponents of a prehistoric Slavo-Germanic speech community from which the Balto-Slavic and Germanic communities later developed, and a prehistoric Italic-Celtic speech community from which later came the Romance and the Celtic communities. Were we to adopt the tree of Fig. 8(b) replacing A-B-C-D with Welsh-French-German-Russian, how much justification would there be for dating the first nodulation at about 2950 B.C., the Italic-Celtic or A-B nodulation at about 2700 B.C., and the nodulation of Germanic and Balto-Slavic at about 2000 B.C., all without danger of reification?

Gleason has pioneered in the interpretation of lexicostatistic evidence, particularly 'counterindications.' In Fig. 8(c) at the left, A is seen to be more closely related to B than either is to C or D, and C and D are more closely related to each other than either is to A or B. A and B in Gleason's term form an *immediately related* set of languages; so do C and D. A word-set composed of two or more sets of cognates contains a *counterindication* in each instance of evidence against immediate relationship, i.e. each instance of two different repeated cognation letters. The Athapaskan sets for 'fire,' 'arrow,' 'rabbit,' and 'sheep' contain no counterindications; our lexicostatistic set 43, on the other hand—French *père,* German *vater,* Russian *otec,* Welsh *tad*—shows the pattern AABB; and set 182—French *nous,* German *wir,* Russian *my,* Welsh *ni*—has ABBA.

Before we go further into the method of counterindications, we can serve the interests of clarity by stressing the utility of lexicostatistic subgrouping. The utility of lexicostatistic subgrouping for the culture historian who works with languages is not different from the utility of the genetic tree model as an icon or hypothesis. The utility is a working utility, not a final utility. Subgrouping by a lexicostatistic technique properly described and carried out lays bare every step, and every false step, that the investigator has made. It facilitates the reconstruction of protophonemes as an early step in external reconstruction. It makes a good beginning in a project that will outlive its initiator.

Mende, Loma, Kpelle, Maninka, Vai, Mano, and Busa are African languages of the Mande subgroup of Niger-Congo. In his discussion of Mande subgroups, Gleason presents two sets of words; here we use letters instead, with U for noncognates and code numbers for languages.

	1 Mende	2 Loma	3 Kpelle	4 Maninka	5 Vai	6 Mano	7 Busa
1. kill	A	A	A	A	A	B	B
2. small	U	A	A	B	B	U	U

There are 21 binary, or letter-against-letter comparisons, per set. There are 10 counterindications for 'kill,' italicized in this listing of possibilities: 1–2 (Mende *pàá,* Loma *páá*), 1–3, 1–4, 1–5, *1–6* (Mende *pàá,* Mano *zɛ*: a counterindication), *1–7* (Mende *pàá,* Busa *dὲ*: another counterindication), 2–3, 2–4, 2–5, *2–6, 2–7,* 3–4, 3–5, *3–6, 3–7,* 4–5, *4–6, 4–7, 5–6, 5–7,* 6–7. How many counterindications can you find for 'small'?

Fifty-two word-sets produced this counterindicative matrix:

Mende						
1	Loma					
2	1	Kpelle				
24	27	26	Maninka			
26	29	28	2	Vai		
34	37	37	21	21	Mano	
33	35	36	20	20	0	Busa

There are 24 counterindications against the immediate relation of Maninka and Mende, 27 against Loma and Maninka, 26 against Kpelle and Maninka, only 2 against Vai and Maninka, and 20 against Busa and Maninka. There are 26 counterindications against the immediate relation of Vai and Mende, 29 against Vai and Loma, 28 against Vai and Kpelle, only 2 against Vai and Maninka, 21 against Vai and Mano, and 20 against Vai and Busa. We assume from this evidence that Vai and Maninka are immediately related. What significance does the 0 have for Mano and Busa? Are they also immediately related?

Let us ask a more difficult question. What is the significance of the 1 for Mende and Loma as compared with the 1 for Kpelle and Loma? The 1 for Mende and Loma is not much smaller than the 2 for Mende and Kpelle; there are, in contrast, 24 or more counterindications against Mende and Maninka, Mende and Vai, Mende and Mano, or Mende and Busa. The 2 for Kpelle and Mende is not much greater than the 1 for Kpelle and Loma; there are in contrast 26 or more counterindications against relating Kpelle immediately to Maninka, Vai, Mano, or Busa. And what do we have to say about the 1 for Mende and Loma as compared with the 1 for Loma and Kpelle? In such straits, for want of a simpler theory, a trinary split is postulated, at least temporarily.

Osgood, an important Athapaskan ethnologist but not primarily a linguist, recorded vocabularies of several Tanaina languages, Kenai, Upper Inlet, Kachemak Bay, Tyonek, Susitna, and Iliamna. Working on a problem in Athapaskan phonology, I found it important to reconstruct the protophonemes for the Tanaina group. First subgroup, then reconstruct: this is a good rule. Though I was familiar with Gleason's approach, having applied it to 55 word-sets for 34 Austronesian languages of Formosa, I ventured a lexicostatistically simple subgrouping for Tanaina. Perhaps I was biased by data on phonologic isoglosses, which do not show up in lexicostatistic tables; at any rate, the subgrouping set up Northern Tanaina with Susitna and Upper Inlet and Southern Tanaina with two branches, Iliamna and Kachemak Bay-Kenai-Tyonek (branching into Bay and Kenai on the one hand and Tyonek on the other). Gleason reworked the data into a proposal for a four-way split from Proto-Tanaina to Proto-Bay-Kenai (whence Bay and Kenai), Proto-Susitna-Upper Inlet (whence Susitna and Upper Inlet), Tyonek, and Iliamna.

In reworking the data, in addition to counterindicative matrices Gleason used another lexicostatistic subgrouping technique, one which tabulates a weighting of exclusively shared cognates; one might call the tabulation a homotrophic matrix, or, as is more commonly done, a 'characteristic vocabulary index.' How does this weighting work? In the set AABB, which contains two sets of exclusively shared cognates, a maximum weight of 1 is given to each set, AA and BB. In AAABB the weight of 1 is maintained for each different set; but on the principle that every pair shares equally in the weight we say the weight for AA = 1, for BB = 1, but for AAA = 3/1 or .33, for AAAA = 6/1 or .17, for AAAAA = 10/1 or .1, for AAAAAA = 15/1 or .07, and so on. Gleason's African figures added up to the following homotrophic matrix; clear maxima, indicating immediate relationship, are boxed in. The matrix is a kind of count of cognates rewarded for being most exclusive.

Mende						
12.4	Loma					
11.4	16.3	Kpelle				
1.3	1.1	2.3	Maninka			
2.9	1.8	1.1	22.1	Vai		
0.2	0.5	1.2	2.7	2.5	Mano	
0.2	0.5	0.2	1.0	0.8	29.7	Busa

Extended calculations group all but Mano-Busa into a larger subgroup. Glottochronologic inferences support Gleason's tentative hypothesis. On the other hand, all lines of evidence do not always converge: Mayan Yucatec, Chol, and Chorti were counterindicated into a trinodulational model, but homotrophically indexed into a Chol-Chorti versus Yucatec model. And the Tanaina results, because of the paucity of the data, are ambiguous.

The point of our extended discussion of subgrouping by various lexicostatistic techniques is cautionary. Our point is not that true scholars get nowhere because they engage in aimless wanderings. Our point is that they refine their methods slowly and painstakingly and with infinite qualification. Only autocrats say, 'I have the truth, because I have measured it.'

A SUBGROUPING EXERCISE

In the study of Formosan languages mentioned above, in less than 15 minutes by rapid intuitional inspection, I judged that there were eight major Formosan groups; by sophisticated lexicostatistic techniques (after many tedious hours, 17 hours and 40 minutes of which were spent in counting and calculating to arrive at a counterindicative matrix with 578 items) it turned out that there were four, perhaps five, lines to Proto-Formosan; yet I think that techniques other than Gleason's might add two more.* Here is a portion of the matrix just mentioned. Abbreviations are Tok(uvul), Kai(paiwanan), Kav(iangan), Cal(aqavus), Kul(alao), Caq(ovoqoval), Coa(kachilai), Cao(vali), Rao(krik), Pac(avan).

Tok									
1	Kai								
2	1	Kav							
3	2	1	Cal						
2	1	0	1	Kul					
5	3	2	1	1	Caq				
4	5	1	1	2	1	Coa			
5	6	2	5	5	3	4	Cao		
3	3	1	3	2	2	1	5	Rao	
4	3	2	3	1	1	2	4	1	Pac

1. What subgrouping inferences are possible, from this tabulation?

**Cf.* C. F. and F. M. Voegelin, 'Languages of the World: Indo-Pacific Fascicle Four,' *AL* 7:2.1–297 (1965).

2. Tokuvul, Kaipaiwanan, Kaviangan, Calaqavus, and Kulalao are set off from the other Formosan languages by two equiranged isoglosses; the same is true of Caqovoqoval, Coakachilai, Raokrik, Pacavan, and Caovali—they also share two equiranged isoglosses. The ten languages share 14 equiranged isoglosses. What implications if any do these isoglosses have for the subgrouping inferences that you just made?

3. The language called Imulud in Fig. 10 is spoken on the island of Yami, not far from the southeastern tip of Formosa. Formosan languages spoken in the southeastern coastal area include the ten Paiwan languages mentioned in **1** and **2** above. Formosa is north of the Philippines; a language called Yami, which is identical with Imulud, is classified by some Austronesian experts as belonging to the group of Philippine languages. If Imulud is not a Formosan language, how might one account for its obvious isoglossic inclusion in Formosan subgroups?

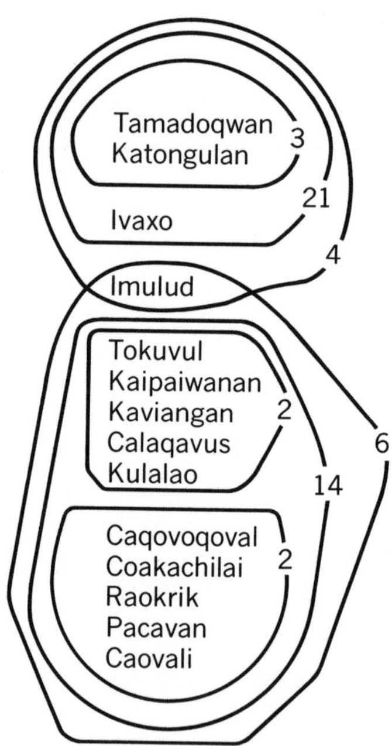

FIGURE 10 Equiranged Formosan isoglosses

4. Here is another portion of the Formosan matrix; abbreviations are Tam(adoqwan), Kat(ongulan), Iva(xo), and Imu(lud).

Imu			
49	Tam		
47	15	Kat	
48	17	8	Iva

Would this information lead one to revise one's answer to the foregoing question? How should one evaluate the fact that Tamadoqwan, Katongulan, and Ivaxo are Bunun languages of the Formosan interior, and lack speakers who live on the coast?

26 «

Sapir's American Subgroups and Theories of Migration

Sapir lived in Canada from 1910 until he left for Chicago in 1925. He was chief of the Division of Anthropology of the National Museum. He studied many languages of Canada, including Nootka, Sarsi, and Kutchin; he also studied Ingalik and Tlingit, languages of Alaska. He published on Wakashan, Athapaskan, Algonquian, Salishan, Uto-Aztecan, Hokan, Chinookan, and Penutian languages. His genius flowered in Canada. It was the period of his *Time Perspective in Aboriginal American Culture* (1916) and *Language* (1921).

In *Time Perspective* Sapir discussed the historical weighting of artifacts in the identification of subgroups. The Plains culture area, he observed, reflects the subgrouping of traits through time while nothing similar can be demonstrated for the relatively primary Eskimo or Eastern Woodlands areas. In fact, the Plains culture very likely derives from Eastern Woodlands, Southeastern, Plateau, and possibly Southwestern tribal contributions. In another sense, however, as one moves back in history, one finds more inclusive culture areas, possibly only three for all of North America—the Northwest Coast, the Mexican, and the Central. The Central area produced the Eskimo as one extreme type, the Pueblo as another extreme, and the other areas now identified. Variability is accounted for largely in ecological and diffusional terms. Cultural subgroups, then, are not strictly comparable to language subgroups.

No language possesses multiple reverse continua, though every language reflects diffusion; and no language reflects environmental streams, mountains, vegetation, or climate in the structure of its grammatical core, any more than it reflects the race of its speakers, despite vulgar tales of how the frozen lips of northern peoples or the thick lips of the Equatorial cannot form certain sounds properly. This does not mean that Sapir's cultural relativism was wasteful; culture typology and language typology have significant comparativist value: 'Are there universals in culture?'—this question cannot be answered without the kind of typological information which Sapir set out to collect.

It pleased Sapir to generalize on the basis of his prodigious knowledge of American languages, setting up subgrouping hypotheses which are still being tested. In 1929 he saw six major but provisional groups in America north of Mexico: Eskimo-Aleut, Algonquian-Wakashan, Na-Dene, Penutian, Hokan-Siouan, and Aztec-Tanoan. Let us examine the third group, Na-Dene. In 1915 Sapir had reported two subgroups for the 'most specialized' of the six major groups, Haida on the one hand and Continental Na-Dene on the other; and two subgroups for the latter, Tlingit and Athapaskan. Fang-kuei Li has assigned Eyak to the Athapaskan group, convincingly, but refuses to be rushed into accepting Sapir's inclusion of Haida and Tlingit in a group with the Athapaskan languages. Hoijer follows Sapir. Greenberg says, 'even cursory investigation of the celebrated "disputed" cases, such as Athabaskan-Tlingit-Haida and Algonkin-Wiyot-Yurok, indicate that these relationships are not very distant ones and, indeed, are evident on inspection. Even the much larger Macro-Penutian grouping seems well within the bounds of what can be accepted without more elaborate investigation and marshaling of supporting evidence.' What can the ethnologist or archaeologist do, in the face of such diversity of opinion?

He can be noncommittal, if he wishes, as a positive measure. More important, perhaps, as a negative measure, is a readiness for reflection and painstaking evaluation of authoritative views in terms of established scales. Let us narrow attention to the Athapaskan languages.

The maps of Fig. 11 bristle with a schematic impudence that reminds the reader not to take them too literally; the languages represented do not comprise an exhaustive roster and some are extinct. The maps, none the less, represent geographical relationships with a vividness not possible otherwise.

Shown are the three main Athapaskan areas, the Northern (top), the Pacific Coast (left), and the Southern or Apachean (lower right). In the Northern area, Pacific-oriented cultures lie roughly to the west

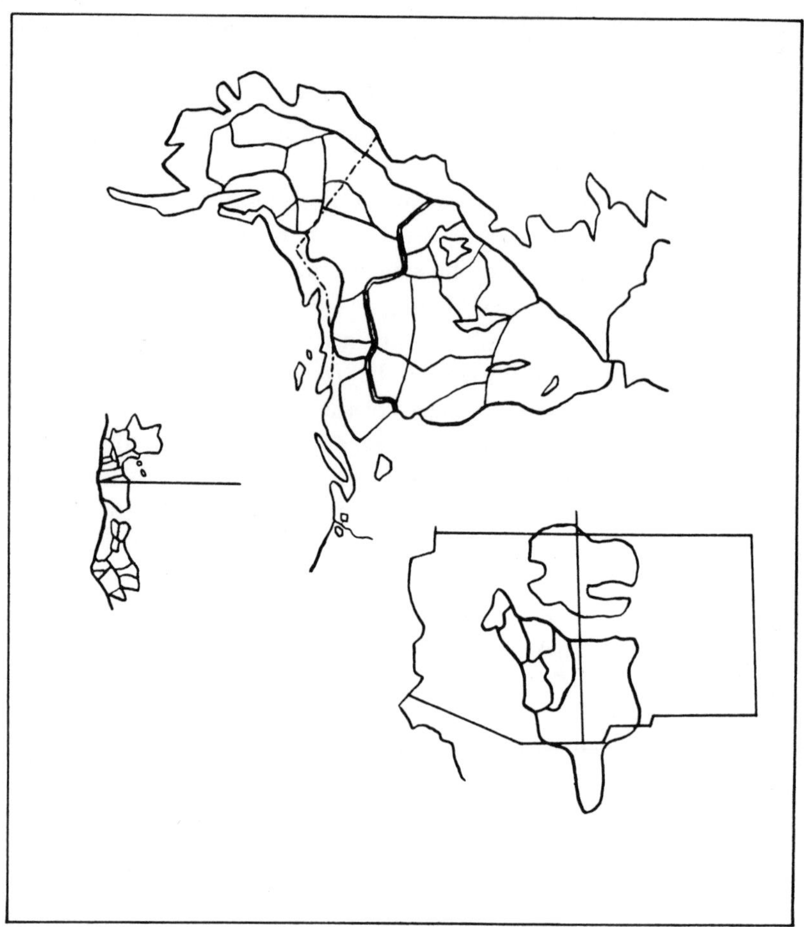

FIGURE 11 Athapaskan language distributions

of the double line, and Arctic-oriented cultures to the east. Tanaina has speakers living in Alaska along the Pacific seacoast, in contrast to land-locked groups. East of the Tanaina area are speakers of Eyak (Copper River delta, not shown), probably an Athapaskan language. Moving clockwise from Tanaina, based in Alaska we have Ingalik, Koyukon, Tanana, Nabesna, and Ahtena. From north to south, the other Pacific-oriented cultures are Kutchin, Han, Tutchone, Tahltan, and Tsetsaut;* still in Canada are Carrier and Chilcotin, and a speech island of Nicola. Two other speech islands are Kwalhiokwa north and Klatskanie south of the Columbia River, one in Washington, the other in Oregon. The languages of these three islands are extinct; Boas was able to work with them, but only sketchily. East of the double line in Mackenzie country, moving from north to south and from left to right in tiers, we find Hare; Mountain and Bear Lake; Kaska, Slave, Dogrib, and Yellowknife; and the southernmost four, Sekani, Beaver, Sarsi, and Chipewyan.

The Pacific Coast languages include some in Oregon and some in California. Moving southward and coastward, inland we have a larger area for Upper Umpqua, and a smaller one for Upper Coquille, just south of which is the Chasta Costa inland area (Sapir worked on a sketch of Chasta Costa in his Ottawa period); small islands are Galice south of Chasta Costa and Applegate south of Galice; the larger area north of the state line shows Chetco; north of Chetco, and with uncertain relative distribution, were Tututni, Euchre, Sixes, and Joshua. Tolowa straddles the line. Entirely in California, moving southward from the inland coastward, are Hupa and Chilula; south of Hupa is Nongatl, south of Chilula, Whilkut; south of Nongatl inland is Lassik and south of Lassik, Wailaki; west of Nongatl is Bear River, below which is Mattole; the last coastal unit is Sinkyone; and the southernmost inland unit is Kato, which was spoken in predominantly Yuki surroundings.

The mapping of Apachean languages is for 1850 rather than for the time of European contact. It shows Navaho in a speech island to the north, in Arizona and New Mexico and Utah and Colorado, as well. To the south, moving eastward from left to right we have Northern Tonto; Southern Tonto and Cibecue; San Carlos and White

*The non-Athapaskan Tlingit occupy the Alaskan panhandle roughly opposite Tutchone; the non-Athapaskan Haida live on islands not far away. Some accounts group names, e.g. Tanaina-Ingalik, as single languages rather than different ones. Years of study lead me to a skepticism of such accounts; criteria for calling something a 'dialect' rather than a 'language' seem never to be specified. The beginner does well to ask, 'How do you know?' when confronted with such accounts. If the answer is, 'So-and-so says so,' it is well to ask, 'How does he know?' Our knowledge of Athapaskan languages is still in an early state in many respects. Much field work cries out to be done, and done thoroughly.

Mountain; and Chiricahua extending eastward into New Mexico and southward into Mexico. Some Apachean groups are not shown, e.g. the Mescalero to the west, the Kiowa Apache (not to be confused with the Kiowa tribe) of Oklahoma, the Lipan of Texas, and the Jicarilla of northeastern New Mexico and adjacent parts of Oklahoma and Texas. Apachean groups also lived in northern Mexico.

According to Cornelius Osgood, Sapir made this estimate of Athapaskan subgroups:

> First, it appears certain that there are major linguistic divisions within the Northern Athapaskan area, which are individually equal in comparative weight to the whole Southern, or Pacific, Athapaskan division taken collectively. Linguistically, the difference between Ingalik and Chipewyan, or between Carrier and Sarsi, is as great a contrast as that between Chipewyan and Navaho. Whereas there is apparently a true linguistic unity in both the Southern and the Pacific Athapaskan divisions, the Northern Athapaskan area, as such, does not form a linguistic unit.
>
> Secondly, two languages of the Northern Athapaskan group, Kutchin and Tsetsaut, stand out from any further internal alignment as individually distinct, the former being probably the most specialized of all Athapaskan languages. Finally, it seems probable that there are relationships among fifteen other groups which resolve themselves into six divisions beside the two given above. That these eight divisions given below are exactly comparable linguistic equivalents is not to be assumed:
>
> 1. Kutchin
> 2. Tsetsaut
> 3. Tanaina-Ingalik
> 4. Carrier-Chilcotin
> 5. Tahltan-Kaska
> 6. Sekani-Beaver-Sarsi
> 7. Chipewyan-Slave-Yellowknife
> 8. Dogrib-Bear Lake-Hare

Among the inferences from language about cultures of the past which Sapir discussed in *Time Perspective,* two require special notice. Whorf, like Wilhelm von Humboldt, found great potency in dead metaphors, but Sapir did not. Sapir observed that older words are morphemically opaque where once they were morphemically transparent. *Battleship,* for example, is easily reducible to {*battle*}{*ship*}, but what can be done about the 'metaphors' dead in *arrow,* what can be said about the composition of *arrow* from a synchronic point of view except that we have a single morpheme {*arrow*}? Hence arrows are older cultural elements than battleships. Consider another example, this time from Sanskrit. We have two words, *rucirānana* 'one whose face is beautiful' and *śaṅkaḥ* 'bull'—which is older in Indic culture, awareness of facial radiance or awareness of cattle? By Sapir's method we must take the former as representing a relatively recent innovation since it can be analyzed into two main parts, *rucira* 'beautiful' and *ānana* 'face'; these constituents themselves have constituents, all transparent—{*ruc*} 'shine' + {*-ira*} 'substantive' and {*an*} 'breathe' + {*-ana*} 'substantive.' (Whorfist or Humboldtian inferences that this sort of linguistic analysis has discernible effects in the popular consciousness are based in part on a faulty assumption that awareness is sharpened by habit rather than dulled by it.) As for the word for 'bull,' it reflects a prehistoric Indo-European metonym, I think, and is probably cognate with a large family of words of which I will mention only Swedish *hingst* 'stallion.' Perhaps the metonym, a metaphor in which one distinctive feature or set of criterial attributes represents a greater number, was apparent to students of the Rig-Veda, ancient Indian religious poems, where *śaṅkuḥ* 'stick' occurs; or perhaps there were two base morphemes, one for 'stick' and one for 'bull.' Comparative grammarians would be able to connect the Sanskrit and Swedish forms by regular phonetic laws, taking them back to a set of Indo-European roots, perhaps to a root something like **k̂ok-* 'stick, peg, hook' (or with reduced ablaut grade **k̂ək-*) and a nasal infix of unknown meaning. Even lacking such inferences from external comparisons, internal comparisons would suffice to suggest that the reference of {*śaṅk*} antedates the conventions associated with the compound for 'one whose face is beautiful.' Sapir cautions against reliance simply on internal evidence by indicating that transparent compounding sometimes is a feature of and hence as ancient as the protolanguage, as with Proto-Athapaskan, which must have had hundreds of nominal expressions still reflected in daughter languages (Chipewyan *la-djis* 'mitten,' transparently meaning 'hand-bag' and Navaho *la-djic* 'mitten,' transparently meaning 'hand-bag' both go back to a Proto-Athapaskan compound transparently meaning 'hand-bag').

Sapir valued linguistic subgrouping as the chief service rendered ethnology by linguistics. Changes in structure take time, wanderings for survival and comfort take time, and *ceteris paribus* the more numerous the linguistic changes and the greater the geographical spread of related languages, the remoter in history the protoculture of the *Urheimat* or primitive culture area must have been. As a general rule each major reconstructed subgroup (questions of its internal language diversity aside) is weighted equally at a given stage. Thus Algonquian languages are found from coast to coast but with a relatively centralized upper Great Lakes area. Among the major Algonquian subgroups Sapir listed Blackfoot, Arapaho-Cheyenne, and Central-Eastern Algonquian. It was clear that two Plains tribes, the Blackfoot and the Arapaho, speak languages of different major branches and so are *ceteris paribus* more distantly related in time than the far-traveled Shawnee of the Southeast and the Naskapi of the laurentian upland of northeastern Canada, both from a single major subgroup. The Algonquian languages of the west are more highly differentiated, hence perhaps more ancient, than those found eastward, witness Yurok-Wiyot. On the basis of prehistoric subgroups diversity tips the scale toward a western homeland.

Athapaskan languages are distributed as shown in Fig. 11. Nothing in the geographical distribution indicates an ancient homeland—was it in the north or in the southwest or on the Pacific coast of California and Oregon? Sapir saw possibly four major Athapaskan subgroups in 1916, one Southern, one Pacific Coast, one Carrier-type, one Kutchin-type. The greater area occupied by the northern tribes says less about time perspective than the numerical superiority of protolanguages in the north. Eyak, not considered by Sapir, betters his case. And Tlingit and Haida, if they are Na-Dene languages, make it 'completely impossible' to suspect a homeland in the warmer latitudes. Comparative evidence, moreover, shows Athapaskan interruptions of what earlier must have been homogeneous Hokan-Coahuiltecan areas.

Sapir built upon the best of Boas's work and tempered the penchant for sweeping statements of some of his contemporaries with his own scrupulous qualifications. Sapir set the stage for what must turn out to be generations of supplementary work that aims—in some respects, whether consciously or not—at the effective axiomatization of the fields in which he pioneered. We have seen that axiomatic systems are either extremely practical or extremely theoretical, and that Bloomfield favored the former, as all that might be expected at the present time. Some supplementary work may be mentioned here.

Mary R. Haas has written two articles which beginning students should study for method and content, one dealing with the establishment of the relatability of Algonquian-Ritwan languages, the other dealing with inclusion of a Muskogean subgroup (Tunica, Natchez, Atakapa, Chitimacha) under the Algonquian rubric. In the latter, using Bloomfield's system of transcription for Proto-Central-Algonquian, Haas lists word-sets including reconstructions and then supports her statement of sound laws or systematic and predictable phonemic correspondences by reference to sets listed. For example:

	Proto-Central Algonquian	Proto-Muskogean	Natchez	Tunica	Chitimacha	Atakapa
Cut	*ki·šk-	*kač-	kec-	káhču	—	kec
Scrape	*ka·šk	*ka·s-	ko·c-	kɔ́sa	k'atka-	kau-š

The correspondence PCA *k: PM *k is obviously supported by these sets for 'cut' and 'scrape'; two sets might be a reflection of borrowing, but Haas also adduces sets for 'bloom,' 'crawfish,' 'dip,' 'dwell,' 'land,' 'negative,' 'plural,' 'shake,' 'spotted,' and 'talk,' and dozens of other sets for other protophonemes besides. Had Sapir considered Muskogean as an Algonquian subgroup, would he have altered his opinion about the western homeland of the most ancient of Algonquian speakers?*

Dyen's contribution to migration theory also adds to the constant efforts of responsible linguists, who, like Sapir, would serve ethnology. This contribution is so rich in detail that the following remarks must be taken as a report rather than a synopsis. The basic postulates of migration theory are '(1) the area of origin of related languages

*Sapir, on inspection of evidence available to him then, set up in his *Encyclopedia Britannica* article of 1929 as one of his six major groups the Hokan-Siouan, with six main groups spread out from coast to coast:

1. Hokan-Coahuiltecan
2. Yuki
3. Keres
4. Tunican (Tunica-Atakapa and Chitimacha)
5. Iroquois-Caddoan
6. Eastern group (Siouan-Yuchi, and Natchez-Muskogean with Natchez, Muskogean, and perhaps Timucua)

is continuous, and (2) the probabilities of different reconstructed migrations are in an inverse relation to the number of reconstructed language movements that each requires.' A special vocabulary is useful in migration theory. A minimal group is a set of what are called co-ordinate or equivalent languages from a single nodulation, for example, A and B in Fig. 9(b) so long as A and B, or sister languages, if there are any, are closer to each other historically than to any other language. Thus the Apachean languages may be said to form a minimal group of co-ordinate languages on a simple family tree. If all were located prehistorically in one continuous southwestern region we would be able to consider them as a 'chain' of languages. (Later, of course, Navaho, Kiowa Apache, and others were separated from the chain—if it existed—and they became 'separates.') A complex family tree has several simple family trees. A language occupies a region or discontinuous regions; the Apachean languages, for example, occupy several regions. A language move which raises the tally of regions is a migration; if the Kiowa Apache left a homogeneous Apachean region to live as an Apachean separate with the Kiowa Indians, that raised the tally of Apachean regions and must indicate a language migration. If the Hokan-Coahuiltecan region, built up by migratory expansion, was cut in two by an Apachean migratory intrusion, raising the tally of regions for Hokan-Coahuiltecan, the creation of the isolated Coahuiltecan region counts as a migrational move. A separate, like Kiowa Apache, is represented by S; a chain, like the hypothetical Apachean chain, by C. The units of distribution of a minimal group can be represented by C and S with necessary letter subscripts for particular languages: CS stands for our Apachean chain with one separate, say Kiowa Apache. Suppose that Navaho is also a separate: we write CS_aS_b. Suppose that Navaho and Jicarilla form a chain away from the others, but that Kiowa Apache is a separate: the formula is C_aC_bS.*

In *Time Perspective,* Sapir assumed a chain of Northern Athapaskan co-ordinate branches ($C_aC_b \ldots C_n$), and an earlier chain of Na-Dene co-ordinate protolanguages ($C_aC_bC_c$, Haida, Tlingit, Athapaskan); separates in the Pacific Coast and Southwestern regions extend the Athapaskan description to $C_aC_b \ldots C_nS_aS_b$, a complex distribution.

*In introducing some of Dyen's terminology, I have used extremely hypothetical examples which are not part of Dyen's paper.

A chain is a unit of distribution and so is a separate. Thus S_aS_b counts as two units. There are several possible explanations for S_aS_b, each explanation involving a certain number of moves. We know that the Athapaskan separates reflect migrations from a northern homeland; part of this knowledge rests in Sapir's work with vocabulary; we know in advance, therefore, that our inferential waters are not as muddy as they might be in other instances. But suppose that we consider the various migration theory alternatives. We need some symbols at this point. $S_a \rightarrow S_b$ means 'S_b moved from the area of S_a'—one move. We represent the homeland by H; if we equate the homeland with S_a we write $H = S_a$. If $H = S_b$, it follows on a principle of simplicity that $S_b \rightarrow S_a$; if $H = S_aS_b$, we suppose an intrusion, I; and if $H \neq S_aS_b$, each of the separates must have moved away from the homeland ($H \rightarrow S_aS_b$), giving us two moves rather than the single most probable moves of the first three cases. If 'most probable' has to mean by implication 'most probable in face of ignorance of other data,' we should be consoled at least by the step toward rigorous axiomatization. The following tabulation serves for distributions of simple trees.

Distribution	Homeland		Number of Moves	Type of Move
	=	≠		
S_aS_b	S_a		1	$S_a \rightarrow S_b$
	S_b		1	$S_b \rightarrow S_a$
	S_aS_b		1	I
		S_aS_b	2	$H \rightarrow S_aS_b$
C_aC_b	C_a		2 or more	$C_a \rightarrow C_b$
	C_b		2 or more	$C_b \rightarrow C_a$
	C_aC_b		1	I
		C_aC_b	4 or more	$H \rightarrow C_aC_b$
CS	C		1	$C \rightarrow S$
	S		2 or more	$S \rightarrow C$
	CS		1	I
		CS	3 or more	$H \rightarrow CS$

27«

Sapir, Whorf, and the Latent Content of Languages

In *Language,* Sapir insists on the complete independence of race, language, and culture. These may be correlated roughly (Melanesian race, language, and culture *vs.* Polynesian race, language, and culture, but with overlapping). But they are never *necessarily* correlated. There is no basis in fact for the 'poor kaboo,' in Whitman's *Salut au Monde,* with his 'glimmering language and spirituality!' Thought, Sapir said, is not hobbled by language.

> The latent content of all languages is the same—the intuitive *science* of experience. It is the manifest form that is never twice the same, for this form, which we call linguistic morphology, is nothing more nor less than a collective *art* of thought, an art denuded of the irrelevancies of individual sentiment. At last analysis, then, language can no more flow from race as such than can the sonnet form.

In advance confutation of Whorfean relativism, Sapir added:

> Nor can I believe that culture and language are in any true sense causally related. Culture may be defined as *what* a society does and thinks. Language is a particular *how* of thought. It is difficult to see what particular causal relations may be expected to subsist between a selected inventory of experience (culture, a significant selection made by society) and the particular manner in which the society expresses all experience. The drift of culture, another way of saying history, is a complex series of changes in society's selected inventory—additions, losses, changes of emphasis and relation. The drift of language is not properly concerned with changes of content at all, merely with changes in formal expression. It is possible, in thought, to change every sound, word, and concrete concept of a language without changing its inner actuality in the least, just as one can pour into a fixed mold water or plaster or molten gold. If it can be shown that

> culture has an innate form, a series of contours, quite apart from subject-matter of any description whatsoever, we have a something in culture that may serve as a term of comparison with and possibly a means of relating it to language. But until such purely formal patterns of culture are discovered and laid bare, we shall do well to hold the drifts of language and of culture to be non-comparable and unrelated processes.

Just as the content of Sapir's work gained quality from researches of the past, so Whorf's work cannot be isolated from its roots in any careful assessment. The practice of praising or condemning individuals or, more ambiguously, schools, rather than particular propositions or contributions, is more popular than prudent. That Sapir and Whorf had different views about the relationship of language to culture and thought is clear once false labels have been removed. Can we then move from the 'Sapir-Whorf hypothesis' to the 'Whorf hypothesis'? Or is 'hypothesis' better replaced by 'common-sense position' or 'archetypical root metaphor'? Black seems to suggest that much of Whorf's trouble stems from an interesting and suggestive position which is metaphysically naïve. Without straying too far from Sapir's Athapaskan contributions, it might be useful to show further how Whorf differed from Sapir.

Whorf survived Sapir by two years, dying in 1941, a year before Hoijer—as Sapir's chief collaborator in Southern Athapaskan field work—published *Navaho Texts by Edward Sapir, with Supplementary Texts by Harry Hoijer.* Almost a decade in advance this volume had been heralded by Gladys Reichard in her 'Introduction' to Pliny Earle Goddard's *Navajo Texts,* texts collected in 1923 and 1924 and shepherded into print in 1933, five years after Goddard's death. The Sapir-Hoijer texts were in technical excellence a culmination of Athapaskan researches given important early impetus in the United States by Franz Boas, Pliny Earle Goddard, Edward Sapir, Fang-kuei Li, Harry Hoijer, Berard Haile, and Robert Young; they were followed by a brilliant series of articles published by Hoijer in the 'forties and 'fifties. Although he had an A in Athapaskan from Sapir, Whorf used Hopi, the Uto-Aztecan language spoken in a speech island, an isolated community of pueblos surrounded by once hostile Navaho hogans, to illustrate many of his relativistic conjectures. Perhaps one should call these conjectures deterministic, since the icon of a determining mold for thought, a mold made of the plaster of language, has been suggested as Whorfean by some commentators. But suppose that Whorf had been able to use Athapaskan examples and particularly Navaho examples as freely as those from Hopi. What might he have said about Navaho?

Applying themes in Whorf's writing to a popular view of the Navaho world, we arrive at this statement:

> Reality is a timeless motionful flux composed of the impressions of raw experience, experience more basic than language, infused with a sense of becoming, a sense of the irreversible changing of relations, which serves for time.* Language in general and Navaho in particular reflects this true reality not at all, nor does the logic of any referential category. Rather, the logic, for example, of a color category or a category of motionful shape, number, or consistency encoded in verb stems,** the logic of categorization and the grammatical conventions which are associated with that logic, do not reflect true reality. On the other hand, Navaho, like any other language, embodies an

*Black, *Models and Metaphors,* pp. 255–6, mentions the possible inspiration of James's 'stream of thought,' and the paradox of the relativist whose own truth about the superficial embroidery of language upon the deeper process of consciousness can only be relative, despite his attempts to escape. (Escape to what? To the untouched, independent point of view of the naïve solipsist, some would say, where, as Bonaventure, *Breviloquium,* II, 2, 5, puts it, things are seen 'from the viewpoint of angels.') Black allows that experience flows continuously, but questions Whorf's sense of time. 'Perhaps the best to be said for Whorf's metaphysics is that in all its amateurish crudity it is no worse than some philosophical systems that have had a considerable vogue.'

**Compare *naathę́ę́š* 'it (a roundish bulky object) falls [moves downward]' with a stem for motion of a single so-called round object; *naaltsʔíít* 'they (plural roundish objects) fall' with a stem for motion of several hats or other such objects; *naatééh* 'it (a load) falls' with a burden-in-motion stem; *naatžooł* 'it (fluffy matter) falls' with a stem for motion of loosely compacted or non-compact matter; *naakhaat* 'it (liquid or solid stuff in an open container) falls' with a stem for matter in an open container, such as water in a glass or sugar in a bowl; *naateeł* 'it (a slender flexible object) falls' with a stem for such objects as a rope or whip but not a live snake; *naatłíš* 'it (a living thing) falls' with an animate-object stem; *naakhęęs* 'it (a slender stiff object) falls' with a stem for a thin rigid object; *naathęęš* 'it (mushy matter) falls'; *naaneeh* 'it (a flat flexible object) falls', used, for example, of a blanket or rug. The logic of English requires 'lumping' of attributes, association with a single form, {*move*}, where the logic of Navaho requires 'splitting' of attributes, a finely discriminatory association of attributes with stem forms, depending upon the criterial attributes of what it is that moves, the direction of motion inhering in a prefixed element that means 'downward.'

integrated fashion of speaking or background linguistic system which partially determines not only how the people who speak it organize their experience conceptually but also how they view the world and their relations to it. There is, then, a distinctive Navaho conceptual system and *Weltanschauung* or world view.

The Navaho fashion of speaking cuts across different formal systems and emphasizes events or better, 'eventing,' inspiring in every Navaho mind a microcosmic awareness or conceptualization of motionful events perceived with marvellous attentiveness. We have seen one system in the variation of stems with shapes and other attributes. Another system is that of tense, mode and aspect. In our standard average European or SAE mind, we have a past time and a time not past, viz., present and future. In the standard average Navaho or SAN mind, a different influence is felt. The Navaho verb often has a separate stem for a future, but a future delayed indefinitely; another stem for a future event on the brink of becoming, sometimes spilling over into actuality, called the imperfective; a perfective stem for past eventing; a repetitive stem for repeated eventing now and again; and an optative stem for desired eventing. A thin rigid object, for example, does not simply 'move downward' when it falls: it must fall motionfully with respect to various aspects of time which the SAE mind ignores: a Navaho cannot say 'it will fall' without specifying the nature of the object, the fact of a motionful event, and the potency with respect to future actuality of the motionful event. We say, *it will fall.* The Navaho says, *ntookhǫs* 'it will move downward eventually, as a thin rigid object,' or he says, *ntootił* 'it will move downward eventually, as a slender flexible object,' or he says *naakhęęs* 'it moves downward instantly, as a thin rigid object,' or he says *naateeł* 'it moves downward instantly, as a slender flexible object.' We say, *it will fall from time to time* or *it falls from time to time.* We cannot compress the concept of occasional eventing into a single verbal base: the Navaho, on the other hand, says *ninákhǫs* 'it moves downward every so often, as a thin rigid object,' or he says *ninátił* 'it moves downward every so often, as a slender flexible object.'

With the quality and timing of motionful activity so strongly emphasized by the background linguistic system, the presence of a dynamic theme of motionful activity in Navaho culture is no surprise. Navahos value motionful activity as a sign of power and well-being. Myths and folktales abound in accounts of motionful activity, while the tales of Apache neighbors are relatively barren of such attentiveness to verbal diversity. In the Navaho metaphysics or world view, existence is seen as a manifestation of EVENTING MOTION.

The advanced student of language and culture will, of course, recognize that it would be wrong to dismiss Whorf's contribution flippantly. If in reading the foregoing passage the questions, '*How* do you know?' and 'What do you mean?' have flitted into consciousness, these may have raised interesting points for future investigation. Whatmough, *Language: A Modern Synthesis* (1956), and Black (item 8 in the bibliography), both have doubted that native speakers or innocent outsiders would see the things that a linguist like Whorf would see. Psychologists of language, moreover, have not yet proved that cognition is affected in important ways by linguistic structures; not even in the case of the Navaho verb have results been convincing. They have been too suggestive, on the other hand, in some cases, for one to be anxious to see future psycholinguistic experimentation abandoned. What has been discovered is that some problems cannot be solved in a single lifetime, that the psycholinguistic issues which were for Whorf a lifelong attraction belong in the category of such problems, and that slow progress may be expected, provided that it has a rational and empirical basis.

Psycholinguistic research on the relation of perceptual saliency to the availability of cognitive categories has produced some interesting results. With Roberts, Lenneberg has shown that in some cases one's ability to encode an experience and one's ability to recall that experience are related. Where social usage is nearly unanimous that a certain pattern of stimuli, a color for example, be referred to by a particular name, the probability structure of reference helps in the recall of that pattern. The greater the efficiency in transmission of a sensory experience which society accords to itself, the greater the 'codability' of the experience. Brown and Lenneberg supposed that the more accurately a color can be named in a given language, the better its chance for accurate recognition. Some colors are easier to remember than others; and part of the ease relates to the peak of the probability curve, that is, to high codability. Lenneberg and Roberts worked on this problem in western New Mexico with Zuñi Indians. They discovered that while orange and yellow are highly codable in English, monolingual Zuñis have as a single color category that which is prefigured by a curve over the range of the spectrum that extends through orange and yellow; and it was striking that 'not a single monolingual Zuñi recognized correctly either orange or yellow,' thus supporting the Brown-Lenneberg hypothesis of 1954, that under certain conditions habits of naming colors affect color memory.

This hypothesis was shown by Lenneberg in 1961 to be a special case of a more powerful hypothesis which implicates the entire probability curve in successful recognition: not high codability merely, the peak of the curve, facilitates recognition, but in general 'it is our habit of structuring color material semantically which provides a number of anchoring points in a recognition task.'

That Sapir's teachings, which were grounded in empirical reality, were not always well understood even by his most ardent students is a sad fact of history. Whorf's interests and background prevented him from fully understanding Sapir's teachings. Whorf received his B. S. in Chemical Engineering from M.I.T. in 1918. Then he became a fire prevention inspector. Soon after Whorf completed a book which reflected his deep concern with religious philosophy. The book found no publisher when it was sent out in 1925; it is symptomatic, however, of the motivation which led Whorf into a study of Hebrew in 1924 with the hope that by way of linguistic sophistication he might unlock secrets of the Book of Books, and so resolve the conflicting claims of science and religion, rational progress and progress by revelation. Instead of following Spinoza in his enterprise, Whorf followed Antoine Fabre d'Olivet, author of *The Hebrew Language Reconstituted* (2 v., 1815–16). The Frenchman's searches for semantic common denominators of recurring formal segments attracted Whorf. Whether this attraction led Whorf to excess in his field work with speakers of Nahuatl or Hopi or in his faith that old metaphors scarcely fade and that their covert existence influences thought,* we cannot say; his passion for hermetic texts, at any rate, took him to the protracted study of Aztec and Maya documents. By the late 'twenties, Whorf had addressed many professional scholars for aid, and with the help of some in securing a research fellowship of the Social Science Research Council, in 1930 he went to Mexico to study Milpa Alta, a variety of Nahuatl. When Sapir came to Yale

*Whorf would not say this for English, that the *b-* in *butterfly, bug, beetle* signifies 'insect,' and the utter in flight is achieved by the *b-utter-fly;* but this imaginative style of analysis is explicit in Fabre d'Olivet's method. This method has been criticized as a manifestation of translator's ataxia by those who take as the best model of thought a spread of constituents, not a segmented progression, supposed morpheme by supposed morpheme.

from Chicago in 1931, Whorf, who had encountered Sapir at meetings of learned societies if not in Sapir's volume of 1921, matriculated as a graduate student to study American Indian linguistics with him. Carroll notes that Sapir gave Whorf an A for a study called 'The structure of the Athabaskan languages.' In dedication if not in insight Whorf joined the small coterie of scholars who felt Sapir's influence at Yale in the 'thirties; some of these scholars are now eminent. Whorf for his part attained to the eminence of a lectureship at Yale, and planned to write a hermeneutic textbook on language and culture, inscribed to the memory of Edward Sapir and Antoine Fabre d'Olivet. And in another kind of eminence, Whorf's name has been entwined with Sapir's, entwined, buttressed, and associated with Sapir's, in what has been called the 'Sapir-Whorf' hypothesis.

This association of the name of Sapir with the name of Whorf issues in part from the transduction or transfer of Sapir's language into a description of Whorf's system. The words a man uses take color from their context; in the transduction, contexts linking Sapir to Durkheim and other sociologists of knowledge were dismissed, and new contexts were supplied. Sapir read a paper on 'The Status of Linguistics as a Science' to a joint meeting of learned societies in New York in 1928. This paper was published in the journal *Language* in 1929. Here, Sapir said that the comparison of Indo-European languages and attendant efforts at reconstruction of prehistoric stages of Indo-European languages contributed to the initial scientific worth of linguistics. He noted that Indo-Europeanist methods had been applied to other groups of languages, and observed that the regularities of language change were not fictions but had been confirmed by his work with Athapaskan and Bloomfield's work with Central Algonquian. He moved on to consider the value of linguistics for anthropology and culture history. He criticized attempts to 'master a primitive culture' without knowledge of its language as 'amateurish.' Part of the amateurishness reposes in a denial of the relativity of referential conventions.

The relativity of logical categories, as Durkheim called them, is a social reality which must not be overlooked. In this context, Sapir made certain remarks which appealed to Whorf as a literary craftsman. In the summer of 1939, Whorf composed a paper called 'The

Relation of Habitual Thought and Behavior to Language.' Whorf's epigraph was a quotation from Sapir's 'Status' paper of 1928:

> Human beings do not live in the objective world alone, nor alone in the world of social activity as ordinarily understood, but are very much at the mercy of the particular language which has become the medium of expression for their society. It is quite an illusion to imagine that one adjusts to reality essentially without the use of language and that language is merely an incidental means of solving specific problems of communication or reflection. The fact of the matter is that the 'real world' is to a large extent unconsciously built up on the language habits of the group. . . . We see and hear and otherwise experience very largely as we do because the language habits of our community predispose certain choices of interpretation.

In 'Linguistic Relativity: The Views of Benjamin Lee Whorf,' Black, before identifying deftly and incisively certain types of oversimplification in Whorf, such as naïve solipsism, says that obstacles to testing and criticizing 'what Whorf called "linguistic relativity"' include inconsistent variant formulations of central points, exaggeration, and 'a vaporous mysticism'; but the 'dominating thought is happily expressed in the quotation from Sapir that Whorf himself used as an epigraph for his best essay. . . .' The ellipsis indicates the part of the epigraph which precedes Whorf's own ellipsis. After quoting the epigraph without its last sentence, Black says, 'This has been called the "Sapir-Whorf hypothesis."' It is to Black's credit that he restricts himself in his article to Whorf's relativistic propositions, without sharing with Whorf in the unhappy transduction of Sapir's words.

That it was transduction, a twisting of one sort of physical energy into another, is shown by the perspective which has been provided earlier in this chapter, and also by an examination of specific details which Whorf in his epigraph replaced with ellipsis. The material represented by three dots constitutes in part these opening sentences which build up to the topic sentence which Whorf kept as an unexemplified generalization:

> The understanding of a simple poem, for instance, involves not merely an understanding of the single words in their average significance, but a full comprehension of the whole life of the community as it is mirrored in the words, or as it is suggested by their overtones.

> Even comparatively simple acts of perception are very much more at the mercy of the social patterns called words than we might suppose. If one draws some dozen lines, for instance, of different shapes, one perceives them as divisible into such categories as 'straight,' 'crooked,' 'curved,' 'zigzag' because of the classificatory suggestiveness of the linguistic terms themselves.

Also withheld from the epigraph were the closing words of the preceding paragraph (whose opening words were not given either):

> No two languages are ever sufficiently similar to be considered as representing the same social reality. The worlds in which different societies live are distinct worlds, not merely the same world with different labels attached.

The precise meaning of these oft-quoted and much-misunderstood words lies in the insight that Sapir was echoing Durkheim and the social psychologists who gave Durkheim some of his inspiration.

28 «

The Causal Relations of Language and Culture

Language is a social institution. Nineteenth-century sociologists knew this to be so. Durkheim gave great impetus to this idea. For Durkheim, social conventions are based on social models. Children, that is, learn the meanings of words by narrowing down possibilities and by learning probabilities. Society helps the child to play what Brown has called 'the original word game.' The child sees a canary in the home and learns to associate certain distinctive features or criterial attributes of the bird with the word *canary*. His successes are marked, perhaps reinforced, by social adulation. Then he is taken for a walk and sees a sparrow and, pointing with expectation, says: 'Canary!' Children are allowed to be eccentric in this way. They stand in danger of being accused of primitive mentality for such eccentricities; but all we have here is lack of experience. As a kindness, the child is corrected. He learns very early that competence counts.

The child must learn which attributes are shared by sparrows and canaries and which are proper to sparrows alone or nearly so and canaries alone or nearly so. Socioculturally structured associations have to be internalized. A tissue of memorized and easy to recall associations grows and spreads with age. Secondary associations vary from culture to culture. For some college students, *canary* is sweet, white, and intoxicating, a liquid treat from the Canary Islands; and Chaucer says that the *sparrow* is lecherous. The Kwakiutl may have words for canary and sparrow, but his secondary associations are different.

The individual's mistakes during his socialization, his errors, his driftings, or his wanton fluctuations from conventional norms or models, partake of a dynamic process of historical change. If the existence of this fluctuational dynamism is ignored for a time by the synchronically oriented specialist at description, it has been chastened by the scientific policy of divide and conquer; but it cannot be ignored forever. Linguists may ignore the probabilistic structure of form and meaning, the frequency dimension of cultural traits, as a tactical maneuver. But in the final axiomatization, the implications of frequency for stability and change will be spelled out in full. At present, investigators have made only a small start in this direction, largely in the field of color words.

The color spectrum moves from invisible waves at the infra-red end through red, orange, yellow, green, blue, indigo, and violet, and continues into invisible waves at the ultra violet end. Bees can see flowers which are colored ultraviolet though we cannot. Porpoises can hear ultrasonic waves at pitches out of reach of the human ear. We are limited by our neurological equipment to the reception of only part of the universe as stimulus. And by cultural conditioning we restrict and limit our attentiveness to only a fraction of the stimuli which bombard us all the time. Whether and to what extent learned expectations about words and their meanings direct our attention to the world around us is one of the central problems in the study of language and culture. Sweeping generalizations cannot solve this problem, if those who frame them are hasty and careless about empirical substantiation. By restricting attention to stimuli which can be controlled, such as specially prepared chips of color, psychologists of language have hoped to make a modest but rigorously scientific move toward responsible generalizations.

The use of such color chips with monolingual English and Navaho informants has resulted in the construction of probability curves which give us the likelihood that a given spot on the spectrum, identified by a so-called Farnsworth-Munsell number, will be named with a particular color word. It should be apparent from Figure 12 that some speakers of English cut a spectrum section into *green, blue,* and *purple* in such a way that color 45 has a 50-50 chance of being called either *green* or *blue.* We cannot realistically set up an iconic diagram with nice vertical borders between colors: | green | blue | purple |. The Navaho word /thátłˀit/ corresponds roughly in range but not in frequency to the English *green.* The reference of /tootłˀiž/ corresponds roughly but not exactly to that of *green, blue,* and *purple.* Psycholinguistic experimentation of the sort reflected in our curves, which show that reference has a probability structure, gives us graphic and useful information about the language expectations of various societies. The probability that color words are exactly equivalent across cultures, that /blúw/ in English, for example, is exactly equivalent to Navaho /tootłˀiž/, a probability which seems to be assumed by naïve translators, is no more certain than the probability that all cultures share the same expectations and have in their membership experienced the same kinds of socialization. This probability, of course, is nil: to argue otherwise is to bring oversimplification into the confessional.

In a color recognition test described by Burnham and Clark (1955), mistakes were made not randomly but with a bias. Greenish hues were shifted toward 'blue,' bluish toward 'green.' Color 13, perhaps the most ambiguously named color for speakers of English, was best remembered. In a color recognition test described by Lenneberg (1961), it was found that intercept colors are memorable. Note in Fig.

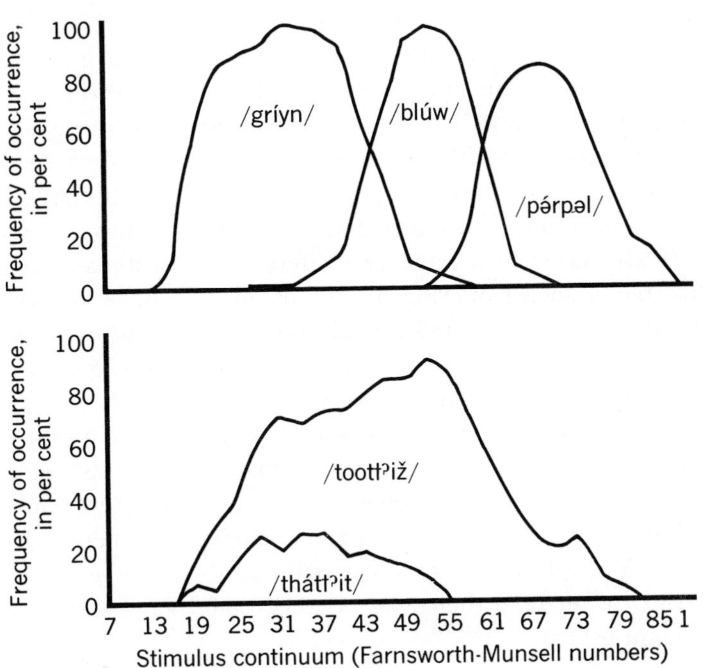

FIGURE 12 The probability structure of selected ranges of English and Navaho color reference

12 that color 13 lies at the left toe of the frequency polygon for 'green.' There is a place at color 46 where the polygons for 'blue' and 'green' intercept each other: 45 is the next greener color and 47 the next bluer color. Lenneberg found that the intercept color was easy to remember, despite variation in instructions to subjects, after a 30-minute delay. He says, 'High communality of verbal response to a given color (Brown and Lenneberg's "codability") appears to be only *one of several* possible ways in which naming and linguistic categorization may affect recognition. Burnham and Clark's data show that the very opposite, singularly low communality, may also provide anchoring points, provided the experimental stimulus universe is such that the majority of its constituents cannot be labelled unequivocally by precise color terms. Semantic habits provide no absolute, invariable means of distinguishing stimuli, but serve as a device for classification or articulation of a continuum and thus help us in many situations to find points of reference, "anchorage," for judgments, whatever they may be.'

From a psychological vantage point it might be argued that the meaning of a language sign is the total disposition of the individual to respond to that sign. This is an interpretation in terms of neurological mechanisms. A different interpretation is possible from a sociological vantage point, apart from neurological psychology. The institution of language has a social basis in which supposedly or axiomatically same forms are associated with distinctive features or recognizable elements of criterial dimensions. We have seen that as a descriptive tactic Bloomfield postulated for such features a stability which he admitted they did not have. He spoke of 'same' meanings. But social conventions are variable, variable as the waves of the ocean. There is no guarantee that the curves of Figure 12 if accurate in the 1950's will be so ten or twenty years later. Just as sounds shift and change through time, so meanings shift and change. And just as sounds have cultural vitality when they belong as phonemes or points in a network of relationships, so too referential categories are not universals but rather take their essence and have their being in oppositional relationships.

This view of semantic categories is rejected by some philosophers. Durkheim, in questioning such rejections, revealed his dedication to the notion of cultural (and hence linguistic) relativity. In doing so, he also revealed his application to the views of social psychologists of the nineteenth century in the arena of what has been called 'folk psychology' or 'the psychology of peoples' but which might better be called ethnosociology. Durkheim mentioned certain rational and universal categories which are treated according to different social conventions by different tribes or cultures with different languages: time, space, number, cause, class, force, personality, efficacy, and even contradiction, which is part of mythological thought. He said: 'These variations through which the rules which seem to govern our present logic have passed prove that, far from being engraven through all eternity upon the mental constitution of men, they depend, at least in part, upon factors that are historical and consequently social.'

In Durkheim's sociological theory of knowledge the logical life is regulated and organized by the socially determined categories of human thought, which are as changeable and unstable as language itself. Durkheim chastened Kantian apriorists for saying that reason comprehends the logical aspect of the world, wherever reason is exercised. 'But for all that,' he said, 'it is necessary for them to give the mind a certain power of transcending experience and of adding to that which is given to it directly; and of this singular power they give neither explanation nor justification.' And so Durkheim, who was sophisticated in philosophy, dismissed the oversimplified apriorist view that the categories are given as artificial constructions and on the other hand the view of classical empiricism that the categories are natural but not relative. 'To know what these conceptions which we have not made ourselves are really made of, it does not suffice to interrogate our own consciousnesses; we must look outside of ourselves, it is history that we must observe, there is a whole science which must be formed, a complex science which can advance but slowly and by collective labor.'

It was part of Durkheim's method to mention the theories current in his day which bore upon a particular thorny issue, according even the weakest the dignity of scholarly refutation. Among the weakest were some formed by Friedrich Max Müller (1823–1900). Max Müller was born in Germany and was educated in Germany and France. He moved to England in 1846 and eventually became the chief Sanskrit scholar at Oxford University. His works include an edition of the Rig-Veda (6 vols., 1849–74), *Lectures on the Science of*

Language (1861–64), *Lectures on the Science of Religion* (1870), and *Sacred Books of the East* (51 vols., 1875 *et seq.*). Durkheim was especially upset by Max Müller's views in *The Science of Thought.* Reacting to them, he took up this argument, that human nature is formed in part by the physical environment of all creatures, but also and uniquely in part by the social environment. 'Language,' Durkheim said, 'is not merely the external covering of a thought; it is also its internal framework. It does not confine itself to expressing this thought after it has once been formed; it also aids in making it. However, its nature is of a different sort, so its laws are not those of thought. Then since it contributes to the elaboration of this latter, it cannot fail to do violence to some extent, and to deform it.' Max Müller had supposed that he could reconstruct ancient institutions by using linguistic evidence; he oversimplified and came up with nonsense. He equated thinking with classification by naming. Language, he observed, is a classificatory instrument. When men of a certain culture framed a religious theory, he thought, their language marked the system of ideas with deterministic finality. Hence to know the Indo-European religion, one had to study the meanings of the reconstructed roots. These meanings, he found, were generic and not specific, and betokened actions not objects. Men, he concluded, generalized and named actions before they named objects. The derivation of substantives led to metaphors which were confused with reality, and nature was transformed by language. The view that primitive thought was tyrannized by language, until science provided civilized men with a degree of independence, was of course a myth, and had the same origin and function that Plato describes for other myths. This modern myth was accorded some currency in nineteenth-century Europe and still hangs on. Max Müller's elaborations were given short shrift by Durkheim, who had read Meillet's *Introduction à l'étude comparative des langues indo-européennes.* Meillet was an astute Indo-Europeanist. His work wins respect even now as important and inspirational. In setting Meillet against Max Müller, Durkheim showed superior insight. Like others who have made contributions to the sociology of knowledge, Durkheim knew that a community of insight links men of different ages and cultures, though not all of them, in a way which cuts across social models and their attendant conventions. If scholars like Lévy-Bruhl, who wrote about 'mental functions in inferior societies,' or Frazer, a romancer of customs, wanted to impute a thoroughgoing idiocy to primitive thinkers, Durkheim was bound to issue a warning: beware of typological work based on superficial knowledge; the hasty assembling of facts leads some men into 'tumultuous and summary comparisons.'

Nowhere in Sapir's researches is there any disagreement with the search that Durkheim proposed, a search for comprehensive theories ranging over great areas of human experience. Boas shrank from abstractions, particularly from the formulation of rules having predictive power. What Sapir has to say about social reality surely must be qualified by the ideal of rational method which Durkheim proposed:

> The first task of science is to describe the nature of the things which form its subject matter. But if they are so dissimilar among themselves that they do not form a *genus,* it is not possible to attempt their description by the use of rational means, as in this case each one of them would have to be examined and defined separately from the others. But in each individual thing reside innumerable properties, among which it is not possible to choose; how is one to define the infinite? There is in that case but one issue: to handle them as do the poets and literary people who describe things as they seem to be, without any rational method.

Sapir held that whatever may be shown presently on a rational and empirical basis about the covariation of verbal and nonverbal behavior, or the relations of signs, in Peircean perspective, will be only suggestive and, if promising, still insubstantial. He held that language and culture are not causally related in any 'true' sense. Is there then no hope that the work of the linguist will be of value for the seeker after truth? Perhaps Sapir's answer would lie in the optimism of scientific progress.

APPENDIX to II «

Construction of a scientific system makes certain demands upon the formulator. Ordinarily his system has some propositions called axioms, and others which are called theorems. I have in mind something which goes beyond the goals of Bloomfield (1926, 1939). Basing his approach on the models of the mathematician J. W. Young and the psychologist A. P. Weiss, Bloomfield refers to a postulate as an assumption or axiom, allied to a set of definitions. By framing postulates in correspondence to facts, assumptions are made explicit, and we are rid of truisms and foolishness.

Let us consider axioms and theorems in a more precise way. Such propositions have various classifications. Suppose that a linguist presents as a system a set of propositions of two kinds. Some propound a so-called higher-level hypothesis or theory, and some are deduced from the first. At least some of the propositions, testable axioms and theorems, deal exclusively with properties or relations that can be observed, and which form part of one's experience. The linguist's system is then a scientific deductive system. It permits the explanation of empirical generalizations, which are deduced from higher-level hypotheses according to rigorous logico-mathematical rules of deduction.

These rules of deduction give the system its basic logic. If the rules are complex, they may stun the reader; and even when rules of deduction are relatively simple, as in the case of a propositional calculus with the rules of finite Boolean lattices, expressed as a Boolean calculus with certain logical constants and elements of union, complementation, intersection, class inclusion, class identity, and the universal and null classes, the reader may have a bad time with them. This means only that the rules are difficult, not that the rules are useless. The value to anthropology of difficult rules is another question.

The rules of deduction which give the system its basic logic operate upon axioms which fall into two sets: a subcalculus of axioms needed for the basic logic, *if* these are needed, and a calculus, that is, a formal axiomatic system, of so-called proper axioms containing constants. The proper axioms relate to proper theorems. Proper axioms and proper theorems contain constants called primitive terms. A subset of primitive terms, if they belong to directly testable initial propositions, is distinguished as composed of so-called observable terms.

Some scientists limit themselves to directly observable phenomena. Others set up systems of a more problematic sort, attempting to generalize in a grander and more powerful way. The more problematic systems have initial propositions which involve concepts not directly observable. The axiomatic calculus includes primitive terms called theoretical, as opposed to observable, terms. Their validity is established in an indirect way, through relationship to testable theorems.

Some proper axioms have only observable terms as their primitive terms. Others have only theoretical terms. A third kind has both types of primitive terms. Axioms of the second sort are called Campbellian axioms, and these are used in formulating highest-level hypotheses called Campbellian hypotheses. Axioms of the third kind are called dictionary axioms, a simple instance of which, the so-called identificatory axiom, sets an observable primitive term into an equation with some theoretical primitive terms. The axiomatization of a scientific theory usually includes Campbellian axioms among its proper axioms. The 'mentalism' of Chomskian theorists can be identified with Campbellian sophistication, a sophistication lacking in most stratificational linguistic theories and allied anthropolgical researches.

The place of Campbellian hypotheses in the scientific study of language and culture has not yet been fully explored. Some investigators are beginning to explore implications of systems using Boolean logic and identificatory proper axioms, without actually going into axiomatization in the most efficient and technical sense. How far a very simple basic logic, such as that of finite Boolean lattices, can be pushed in respect to systems comprising Campbellian hypotheses and using more powerful basic logics, is another salient problem scarcely touched.

Morris (1955) argues for synthesis of data from three analytical perspectives: the syntactic, the semantic, and the pragmatic. A sign, whether signal or symbol, relates to other signs to form compound signs; such relations are syntactic. A sign also relates to things signified, sometimes called referents; such relations are semantic. Insofar as a sign activates a total disposition to behave in a certain way, and is meaningful, room is left for the study of the origins, uses, and effects of signs, apart from but not exclusive of the other aspects of semiotic; such study is pragmatic. In earlier axiomatic work, attempts were made to limit linguistics to syntactics, but the range of phenomena to be studied has recently been extended. At the same time, metalanguages of Carnapian design are being constructed on the tripartite Peircean icon.

Let us suppose, in the context of such research, that the basic logic of a scientific theory of grammar might be expressible by a calculus with axioms and theorems interpreted as mathematical propositions. Then the theorems would have no extralogical constants, and the use of one of these theorems in the derivation of a proper theorem of the scientific calculus would require an intermediate step, the application of a logical theorem to the primitive terms concerned. And if the logical subcalculus used the device of variables, it would be necessary, in applying the logical theorem to these primitive terms, to make substitutions of primitive terms for some or all of these variables. The derived proper theorem, containing primitive terms as extralogical constants, would belong, then, neither to the calculus nor to the logical subcalculus.

Suppose, however, that we decided to count applicational theorems as belonging to the scientific part of a theory, as opposed to the basic logical subcalculus. Usually we can count them as premises from which, together with proper axioms, we derive proper theorems; they are not in this case derived from anything in the scientific part. We then have for our proper axiom section some pseudo-axioms. When the primitive terms concerned in these pseudo-axioms are theoretical terms, they simulate Campbellian axioms. If an observer takes it into his mind that all of the proper axioms of the calculus are identificatory and hence not really genuine hypotheses, he may decide, in the style of Eddington's *Philosophy of Physical Science* (1939) that he is confronted with a calculus whose Campbellian hypotheses are logically necessary a priori.

The danger is always present, in other words, that one will mistake applicational pseudo-axioms for Campbellian axioms which represent logically necessary Campbellian hypotheses. Eddington, influenced perhaps by the exoteric teachings of Kant, held that the basic laws of physics are given a priori. His efforts to construct a unified theory for physics with a priori hypotheses have been interpreted by some as a contribution, because of his having mistaken applicational pseudo-axioms for Campbellian axioms, to the construction of a system of physics entirely free of any Campbellian hypothesis and represented by a calculus having only proper axioms of the identificatory sort, an ironic achievement indeed.

Eddington's move, once discovered, served to prompt a flurry of speculation about the relative value, in point of explanatory power, of Campbellian and identificatory systems, as far as such social sciences as psychology, sociology, or anthropology are concerned. A system with Campbellian as well as identificatory axioms would seem to be more valuable than a system whose axiomatization comprises only identificatory proper axioms, since the former would be helpful in explaining new empirical generalizations, while the latter would be best for economical explanation of a closed set of empirical generalizations.

That an explanatory theory or explicational system, a formal account or system whose theoretical concepts occur only in hypotheses which identify the observable concepts and from which testable consequences can be deduced, may for the present purposes of anthropologists turn out to be quite respectable and satisfactory, even when Campbellian hypotheses are lacking, has been suggested. In this connection, the contribution of Lounsbury (1964) is important.

PROBLEMS «

Problem 1. If it is proper to say that the meaning of Egyptian *kꜣ ỉmntt* (Kai Imentet) is 'Bull of the West,' why is it not proper to say that 'Bull of the West' is *the* meaning of *kꜣ ỉmntt?*

Problem 2. In some of his writings, Plato has Socrates talk to a young man who might want to become a philosopher, or lover of wisdom. Plato uses the literary device of irony, and indicates the existence of at least two levels of understanding, one which concentrates on the message as code and one which takes meaning from insight into context, the social matrices of the message. In his awareness of the philosophical value of context, Plato contributed to modern theories of language and the sociology of knowledge. He underlined the difference between the truth functions and the ideological functions of language. He put social philosophy in his debt by establishing a theory of knowledge in terms of social groups. He threw light on myths by showing their relation to power, the way in which the mythic process supported the claims of aristocratic elites.

The theory has been put forward that Plato was especially ironic in his regard for myths about language. Given that Socrates could be sober even if not serious in his assertions, how should one interpret his remarks to young Philebus that the Egyptian god Thoth may not have been a god but a godlike man, one who saw that sounds came in unlimited variety and who engaged in linguistic analysis, separating vowels from consonants?

Problem 3. 'He was a prince, Nala by name, mighty son of Virasena, full of wanted virtues, handsome, and a knowing horseman.' Thus opens adhyaya 50 of book III of the Mahabharata, the story of Nala and Damayanti. In romanized form the opening lines run:

āsīd rājā, nalo nāma, vīrasenasuto balī,
upapanno guṇāir iṣṭāi, rupavān, aśvakovidaḥ.

Given the Indic syllabic writing

आसीद् राजा नलो नाम वीरसेनसुतो बली ।
उपपन्नो गुणैर् इष्टै रूपवान् अश्वकोविदः ॥१॥

the opening lines of the Nala episode, and

नाम	*nā́ma*	'a name'
नाम	*nā́ma*	'a name'
नाम्ना	*nā́mnā*	'by a name'
नाम्ने	*nā́mne*	'for a name'
नाम्नस्	*nā́mnas*	'from or of a name'
नाम्नि नामनि	*nā́mni, nā́mani*	'at a name'
नामन् नाम	*nā́man, nā́ma*	'oh, name'

different forms of 'name,' inflected according to case (respectively, nominative, accusative, instrumental, dative, ablative-genitive, locative, vocative), the basic, so-called derivative stem in *-an* being नामन् *nā́man* 'name,'

(a) Write the signs which have the transliterations shown.
ma (as in *nā́ma*)
na (as in *nalo* 'Nala')
n (as in *nā́man*)

(b) Having discovered the value of the subscript slant, the *virāma* or 'stop,' write the constellation of signs which would indicate:
s rather than *sa* (as in *nā́mnas*)
m rather than *ma*
d rather than *da* (as in *āsīd*)

(c) Find the sign for *rā* in *rājā,* and compare it with the sign for *r* in *guṇāir.* The sign for *r*, all things considered, should be what?

Problem 4. In the *Book of the Dead,* ch. 183, Thoth, the god of reason, is equated with the moon in the Underworld. What relation does Stevens's use of the moon as a symbol of the imagination or supreme rational light, in *'Esthétique du mal,'* II, bear to the ancient Egyptian symbolism?

Problem 5. This problem requires a preliminary remark on Tylor and Frazer. Frazer identified two kinds of associational magic. When the association is substitutive so that *A* and *B* belong to the same class the magic which affects them is said to be imitative or homeopathic. When the association is one of contiguity so that *A* and *B* belong to different classes but have been in contact with each other in an especially intimate fashion the magic which affects them is said to be contagious. 'Homeopathic magic is founded on the association of ideas by similarity: contagious magic is founded on the association of ideas by contiguity.'

For magicians the occasion of contact guarantees the effects of contact even when objects are distant. Once in contact means always in contact and if you do thus and so to an object *B* which once was in contact with *A*, then you do it also to *A*. If the soul and the body once were intimately fused, the soul can be attracted or recalled to the body if the body is mummified; and life goes on after life has gone. Similarly, if you name a departed soul or dangerous creature in Tonkawa or Navaho society the name, whether proper or common, draws the demon.

Tylor and Frazer were able to organize their simplistic ethnographic details around important insights. For Tylor to see that all human sign behavior involves relations of two basic types, identity or paradigmatic relations and contiguity or syntagmatic relations, was a notable advance in the history of anthropology. And for Frazer to take up this thread, extend it to the classification of magical sign behavior, and generalize normatively about magic and science (which set up silly or correct rules to control powers, as the case may be) on the one hand, and religion (which worships revealed powers that exist beyond control) on the other hand, was a further demonstration of the intelligent use of ethnographic data. Anthropologists, however, have discovered that in spite of the universality of paradigmatic and syntagmatic relations, those two key principles of sign behavior, the 'logical hold' of language is structured variously for different cultures.

In view of the foregoing remark, consider this problem. In a word association test, for the stimulus word *pillow* the responses *soft* and *cushion* are given. Does the first response represent the principle of identity? Does the second response represent the principle of contiguity? Discuss those paradigmatic and syntagmatic considerations which are important in analyzing the response word *rose* when it follows the stimulus word *red.*

Problem 6. Discuss the relative merits of the statistical model which represents the meaning of *blue* or *green* with a frequency polygon (Fig. 12) and the static model which contrasts color categories as follows:

<table>
<tr><td>ENGLISH</td><td>purple</td><td>blue</td><td>green</td><td>yellow</td></tr>
<tr><td>HOPI</td><td>coro</td><td colspan="2">sak^{w}a</td><td>sika</td></tr>
</table>

(a) Is one better than the other in all circumstances? In which circumstances might one model be superior to the other? (b) How might these Hopi words and phrases affect one's conception of the English-Hopi color diagrams? *moki napna* 'green shirt,' *mokiŋ·pɨ* 'green color,' *sak^{w}a napna* 'blue shirt,' *sak^{w}a tokpela* 'blue sky,' *sak^{w}a tɨsaqa* 'green grass,' *pala napna* 'red shirt,' *coro napna* 'purple shirt,' *sikaŋpɨ* 'yellow color,' *sika* 'yellow, sour.'

Problem 7. It has been said that Sapir, committed to the Durkheimian position, holds that he cannot believe 'that culture and language are in any true sense causally related.' Whorf, committed to the position of a decadent social psychology, holds that language has a 'behavioral compulsiveness' which comes from words and phrases and also from 'large-scale patterning of grammatical categories, such as plurality, gender and similar classifications (animate, inanimate, etc.), tenses, voices, and other verb forms, classifications of the type of "parts of speech," and the matter of whether a given experience is denoted by a unit morpheme, an inflected word, or a syntactical combination.' Whorf also holds that the need for 'substantives in certain sentence positions' imprisons European scientists in the illusion that 'substance' is necessary, and the need 'for verbs in certain other positions' does the same 'for forces, attractions, etc.'

(a) Is there a vital contradiction or only an apparent one between Sapir's view that language does not insidiously or otherwise cause a group and each of its members to behave, i.e. act or think, in a given fashion, any more than what a society does and thinks causes it to use a given type of language, and Whorf's view that language insidiously causes a group and each of its members to behave in specifiable ways, even though the reverse—for all of Lévy-Bruhl's belief in the futility of the primitive mind—is not demonstrably true? Support your opinion with convincing evidence.

(b) Account for the popularity of the phrase 'the Sapir-Whorf hypothesis' in view of the contradiction just noted. What sociological and classificatory insights are pertinent in establishing your claim?

Problem 8. This and the statements of problems 9–17 are entirely or partly false, or else in need of clarification. Correct mistakes, or show how a specific fact or facts can be used to support the statement. If qualifications are needed, supply them.

'Languages cut up experience in different ways, just as they differ phonologically, morphologically, and syntactically. It is not known if non-linguistic behavior varies with the rules of reference for a language, though much speculation about possible inter-relationships has been generated by the Whorfean hypothesis. Perhaps the more codable a referent category is, the more available it is for psychological use. This tentative hypothesis does not justify wild speculation about supposed world views of primitive cultures, as they relate to grammatical elements and categories.'

Problem 9. 'We have no truly primitive language in a psychological sense. Moreover, modern researches in archaeology have indefinitely extended the time of man's cultural past. It is vain, therefore, to go much beyond the perspective opened up by the study of actual languages, particularly in view of the limitations of our knowledge respecting symbolic processes in particular and psychology in general, in trying to unravel the mysteries of the emergence of speech, and of the origin of language.'

Problem 10. 'An Englishman is a member of the Anglo-Saxon race, whose genius has fashioned the English language and the Anglo-Saxon culture of which the language is the expression.'

Problem 11. 'Primitive tongues are formless, concrete, inefficient vehicles of emotion, which prevent their speakers from thinking the way we do, or seeing the world in its proper light.'

Problem 12. 'The function of a cultural institution is only a purpose or relation which the members of the culture are unaware of but which the anthropologist or linguist is clever enough to discern.'

Problem 13. 'Linguistics has had no appreciable impact on anthropology.'

Problem 14. 'No one who is aware of the problems Whorf failed to solve searches for cultural categories outside of the investigator's own cultural frame of reference.'

Problem 15. 'It is better to say "language *in* culture" than "language *and* culture."'

Problem 16. 'It is impossible to trust generalizations about culture based on lexicostatistical or other linguistic inferences.'

Problem 17. 'Science is autonomous and exists outside of any particular human context. Linguistic science similarly exists outside of contexts supplied by the social sciences.'

Problem 18. Suppose that the lists of Chapter 24 are revised or annotated as follows.

1. Welsh *i gyd* [igí:d].
10. North Welsh *bol,* South Welsh *bola.*
12. Welsh *deryn,* pl. *adar.*
13. North Welsh *cnoi* 'chew,' *tamaid* 'bite.'
23. Welsh *dod* [dó:d] is the ordinary form, from *dyfod* [də́wod].
27. Welsh *marw* is an adjective; no verb exists for 'die.'
46. Welsh *ychydig* 'little, few'; *rhai* 'a few, some.'
47. Russian *borot'sja* 'fight (in general)'; *sražat'sja* 'fight (in battle).'
54. North Welsh *hedeg* [hέdag], South Welsh *hedfan* [hέdvan].
62. Welsh also has *glaswellt* or *gwelltglas* for 'green grass.'
64. Welsh *perfedd* 'middle, entrails,' competes with *colludd(ion)* 'bowels, intestines.'
65. Welsh also has *gwelltin,* derived from *gwellt* 'grass' and *tin* 'tail, rump.'
67. Welsh [é:v] or [vé:]; North Welsh [vó:].
75. South Welsh *sut;* also *pa sut* 'how?' and *pa fodd* 'how?'
78. Welsh *yfi* [əví:]; *cf. myfi* 'I (myself).'
79. Welsh *iâ* 'ice'; *rhew* means 'frost, ice.'
87. Welsh *chwith* 'left (side), strange, sad, sinister' competes with *aswy* 'left (side).'
91. Beside *iau* [yɑ:y], Welsh also has *afu* [ɑvi:] 'liver.'
96. North Welsh [ki:k] 'meat,' [knɑŬd] 'flesh.'
101. German *eng,* Russian *uzkij,* Welsh *cyfing* are to be preferred.
103. Welsh also has *gwddwg.*
107. Welsh *na* is dependent; *ni* is independent.
111. Welsh has borrowed *person* from English; North Welsh, however, uses *rhywun.*
115. Russian *dožd'* 'rain' is a noun; the phrase *dožd' idjot* means 'rain goes.' Welsh *glaw* 'rain' is used similarly with *bwrw* 'throw'; the resultant phrase competes with the verb *glawio.*
116. Welsh *coch* is preferred.
117. Welsh also has [kuwí:r] 'correct.'
121. Welsh also has [gwrɑ́ið].
123. Welsh *pydri* is a loan word from Latin.
133. Welsh *llym* means 'sharp (of wind)'; an alternative *brwnt* means 'harsh (dirty, cruel).'
136. North Welsh has [istɑ].
138. Welsh *wybr* 'sky' is literary; *awyr* 'air, sky' is colloquial.
143. Welsh *llyfn* 'smooth' is probably literary; an alternative is *esmwyth,* which also means 'comfortable, quiet.'

144. Welsh *neidr* competes with *sarf,* borrowed from Latin.
148. The Welsh and German forms are cognate, *assuming* an ancestral **spolto-* 'split.'
151. The Welsh form is cognate with the German and Russian forms.
155. Welsh *union* means 'direct, straightaway'; *syth* means 'stiff, straight, erect, rigid.'
167. Welsh also has [(ə)má] 'this (here)' after nouns.
178. The Russian and Welsh forms are cognate.
184. Welsh *beth* 'thing?' is preferred. Lenition is here ignored in respect to cognation.
186. Welsh *ple* or *lle* 'place?' is preferred.
188. Welsh *pwy* 'who?' (cognate with the French, German and Russian forms) is preferred.
197. Welsh *pryf,* a literary word, applies to insects in general; [prí:génwɑer] is preferred. The French, German, Russian, and Welsh forms are here deemed to be cognate; but the French and German forms might go back to **wr̥mi,* the Russian and Welsh forms to *k^{w}*r̥mi.*
198. The Welsh form is cognate with the French and Russian forms.

Which of the foregoing observations are relevant to lexicostatistical operations? Explain your choice in each case. Why are some of these observations irrelevant?

Problem 19. Assume that cognation for the lists is shown as follows.

1. FW
3. GR
5. GRW
12. RW
17. FW
26. FRW
27. FRW
30. FGW
31. FRW
35. FGW
37. GR
38. FGRW
39. FG
43. FG/RW
49. FG
50. FGRW
53. FGW
56. FG
57. FGRW
60. FR
65. RW
69. RW
70. FGR
78. FGRW
81. FGRW
83. GW
89. GR
90. FRW
92. FGR
97. FGR
98. FW
100. FGRW
101. GRW
103. FG
104. FGRW
105. FGRW
106. FGR
107. FGRW
109. FGRW
110. FW
116. FG
118. FG
121. GR
125. FGRW
128. FG
129. FGRW
130. FR
131. GRW
135. FW
136. FGRW
143. GR
145. FGR
147. GR
148. GW
151. GRW
152. FGW
156. FGRW
157. FGRW
165. GRW
167. GR
168. FGRW
169. FGRW
172. FGW
173. FGW
176. FGRW
178. RW
181. GR
182. FW/GR
188. FGRW
191. FGRW
197. FGRW
198. FRW
200. FGR.

On this interpretation, the years of divergence are:

FG 3845, FR 4150, FW 3900, GR 3845, GW 4150, RW 4000.

These figures provide rough estimates. Marija Gimbutas, 'The Indo-Europeans: Archaeological Problems,' *AA* 65.815–36 (1963), has this to say (pp. 834–5): 'In Europe a number of new cultural groups of Kurgan origin arose soon after the beginning of the second millennium B.C. . . . Best archaeologically and linguistically proven are: 1) the Proto-Germanic in northern Germany and southern Scandinavia; 2) the Proto-Baltic between eastern Pomerania in the west and the upper Volga and upper Oka basins in the east; 3) the Proto-Slavic north of the Carpathians; and 4) the Proto-Dacian (Monteoru) in eastern Rumania. The cradle of the Celtic, Italic, Venetic, Illyrian, and perhaps even Phrygian cultures must be looked for in the Corded and the Early Bronze Age Unětice culture of central Europe. The great expansions of the central European culture at the end of the 15th [century] or *ca.* 1400 B.C. and at the end of the 13th [century] or *ca.* 1200 B.C. diffused Illyrian and Venetic to the Apennine Peninsula and the Balkans, Italic to Italy, while Phrygian and Armenian spread to Anatolia. The Late Bronze Age-Early Iron Age expansion of the western central European Urnfield group brought Celtic to France, Spain, and southern Britain.' Can it be argued that the rough estimates provided by our glottochronological computations nicely support the archaeologically determined conclusions of Professor Gimbutas? Defend or counter the proposition that, 'In this case, the coincidence of linguistic and archaeological data cannot be accidental.'

BIBLIOGRAPHY «

NOTES

On the sociology of knowledge, see Simmel (1950), Parsons (1951), Strauss (1952), and Horowitz (1961). Hymes (1964) contains valuable bibliographic notes; our abbreviation for this work is *LCS*. For notes on writing and verbal art, see *LCS* 325–9, 341–3, 352–5; on more or less philosophical aspects of cultural relativism, LCS 150–53. On theories and models, see *LCS* 82–5 (primitive languages, evolution of languages, origin of languages), 364–71, 381 (technical analysis of texts), 403–6 (style and level of diction).

Popular textbooks in linguistics include Gleason (1961), Hockett (1958), and Bach (1964). For advanced theory, see esp. Chomsky (1955, 1957, 1962, 1965); three papers in the *Handbook of Mathematical Psychology*, Chomsky and Miller (1963), Chomsky (1963), and Miller and Chomsky (1963); various papers in Fodor and Katz (1964); Halle (1959, 1962); Katz and Fodor (1963); Postal (item 114 below); and Katz and Postal (1964). Dingwall (1963) has a useful bibliography. Data on Mohawk in Chapter 17 are from Postal (item 113); on French, from Sanford A. Schane, 'Cyclic Rules in French Phonology,' a paper read to the Linguistic Society of America in 1964.

Two dominant and contradictory styles of research are typified by the figures of Boas and Sapir. For background reading that will vivify Chapters 18–28, no better bibliographic basis is available than that provided by Hymes. The General Bibliography of *LCS* 711–49 does not include works cited elsewhere in the anthology. A brief note therefore is in order.

Hymes's Introduction to *LCS*, in ten sections, provides a broad, panoramic background. The sections may be read continuously, on pp. 3–14, 73–7, 115–20, 167–70, 215–20, 291–4, 385–90, 449–54, 567–73, and 667–9.

Bibliographic notes touch upon Boas, Sapir, Kroeber, and Bloomfield, and issues of field work (23–6), relations of linguists and anthropologists, sociologists and psychologists (32–5), language diversity (97–8), translation (98–100), language universals and general linguistics (108–9), the functional analysis of communication (109–11), the scholarship of semantics, componential semantic analysis, vocabulary, semantic rules, and folk taxonomy (161–3, 176–81, 184, 207–11, 225–7, 233, 244), aspects of socialization and language (248–50, 260–63), expressive language (280–88), word-play (299–300, 303–4, 310–11), the variety of subtle relations affecting levels of language (424–8), linguistic change (464–6), bilingualism (506–8, 517–20), creoles and similar forms of speech (543–6), areal linguistics (651–3), and typologies and genetic groups (659–63).

On Whorf's Hopi field work, see Voegelin and Voegelin (1957), p. 8. Also see *LCS* 481–2 (dialectology), 583–4, 597–8, 609–11, 622–3, 636–7 (comparative and historical linguistics and linguistic prehistory, including lexicostatistics).

Eric Hamp's Welsh field notes were made available to me through his generosity; he is, of course, not responsible for the use I have made of them.

ABBREVIATIONS

AA	American Anthropologist
AL	Anthropological Linguistics
AT	Anthropology Today. *See* Kroeber
CA	Current Anthropology
HMP	Handbook of Mathematical Psychology, Vol. 2. *See* Luce
IJAL	International Journal of American Linguistics
IUPAL	Indiana University Publications in Anthropology and Linguistics
JASP	Journal of Abnormal and Social Psychology
KASP	Kroeber Anthropological Society Papers
LCS	Language in Culture and Society. *See* Hymes
Lg.	Language
PAPS	Proceedings of the American Philosophical Society
RCAFL-P	Indiana University Research Center in Anthropology, Folklore, Linguistics, Publication
RL	Readings in Linguistics. *See* Joos
RLC	Race, Language and Culture. *See* Boas

RRT	Report of the Fifteenth Annual (First International) Round Table Meeting on Linguistics and Language Studies. *See* Stuart
SJA	Southwestern Journal of Anthropology
SW	Selected Writings of Edward Sapir in Language, Culture, Personality
YUPA	Yale University Publications in Anthropology

Allen, Thomas G.

1. Egyptian Stelae in Field Museum of Natural History. Field Museum of Natural History. Anthropological Series. Vol. 24, No. 1. Chicago, 1936, p. 29.

American Mathematical Society

2. Structure of Language and its Mathematical Aspects. Proceedings of Symposia in Applied Mathematics. Vol. 12. Providence, R.I.: American Mathematical Society, 1961.

Bach, Emmon

3. An Introduction to Transformational Grammars. New York: Holt, Rinehart and Winston, 1964.

Beals, Ralph L., and Harry Hoijer

4. An Introduction to Anthropology, Third Edition. New York: Macmillan, and London: Collier-Macmillan, 1965, pp. 604–42.

Bergsland, Knut, and Hans Vogt

5. On the Validity of Glottochronology. CA 3.115–29 (1962). Nineteen evaluations and a reply follow this article, through p. 153.

Birdwhistell, R. L.

6. Kinesics and Communication. In Explorations in Communication: An Anthology. Boston: Beacon Press, 1960. *See* Carpenter.

Black, Max

7. Language and Philosophy; Studies in Method. Ithaca: Cornell University Press, 1949.
8. Linguistic Relativity: The Views of Benjamin Lee Whorf. In Models and Metaphors; Studies in Language and Philosophy. Ithaca: Cornell University Press, 1962, pp. 244–57.

Bloch, Bernard

9. Japanese Phonemes. Lg. 26.86–125 (1950). In RL 329–48.

Bloomfield, Leonard

10. A Set of Postulates for the Science of Language. Lg. 2.153–64 (1926) = RL 26–31.
11. Language. New York: Henry Holt, 1933.
12. Linguistic Aspects of Science. International Encyclopedia of Unified Science. Vol. 1, No. 4. Chicago: University of Chicago Press, 1939.

Bloomfield, Morton, and Leonard D. Newmark

13. A Linguistic Introduction to the History of English. New York: Alfred A. Knopf, 1963.

Boas, Franz

14. Introduction. Handbook of American Indian Languages. United States. Bureau of American Ethnology. Bulletin No. 40, Pt. 1, pp. 59–73. Washington: Government Printing Office, 1911. *Cf.* LCS 15–22, 121–3.

15. History and Science in Anthropology: A Reply. AA 38.137–41 (1936). See item 16, pp. 309, 311.
16. Race, Language and Culture. New York: Macmillan, 1940. *Cf.* p. 279 (1896) and p. 257 (1932).

BRAITHEWAITE, Richard B.
17. Scientific Explanation; A Study of the Function of Theory, Probability and Law in Science. Cambridge: Cambridge University Press, 1953.

BROWN, Roger
18. Words and Things. Glencoe: The Free Press, 1958.

BROWN, Roger, and Marguerite Ford
19. Address in American English. JASP 62.375–85 (1961) = LCS 234–44.

BROWN, Roger, and Eric H. Lenneberg
20. A Study in Language and Cognition. JASP 49.454–62 (1954).

BRUGMANN, Karl
21. Zur Frage nach den Verwandtschaftsverhältnissen der indogermanischen Sprachen. Int. Zeitschrift für allgem. Sprachwissenschaft 1.226–56 (1884).

BUCK, Carl D.
22. Comparative Grammar of Greek and Latin. Chicago: University of Chicago Press, 1933.

BUETTNER-JANUSCH, John
23. Boas and Mason: Particularism versus Generalization. AA 59.318–24 (1957).

BUREAU OF AMERICAN ETHNOLOGY. Smithsonian Institution
24. List of Publications of the Bureau of American Ethnology, With Index to Authors and Titles, Revised to December 31, 1961. Washington: Government Printing Office, 1962. Much early 'rough and ready' work in language and culture was carried out under the auspices of surveys and expeditions. Exploration of the Colorado River was authorized in 1869. The Geographical and Geological Survey of the Rocky Mountain Region was established in 1872. In 1879, Congress consolidated various surveys into the United States Geological Survey. At that time, the Bureau of Ethnology, a product, as it were, of the Rocky Mountain Survey, was made an office of the Smithsonian Institution. The Bureau has published an extensive series of studies in linguistics and ethnography.

BURNHAM, R. W., and J. R. Clark
25. A Test of Hue Memory. Journal of Applied Psychology 39.164–72 (1955).

CARPENTER, Edmund, and Marshall McLuhan, editors
26. Explorations in Communication: An Anthology. Boston: Beacon Press, 1960.

CARROLL, John B.
27. Language and Thought. Englewood Cliffs: Prentice-Hall, 1964, *see* Whorf.

CARROLL, John B., and Joseph B. Casagrande
28. The Function of Language Classifications in Behavior. In Readings in Social Psychology. Edited by E. E. Maccoby *et al.* New York: Holt, Rinehart and Winston, 1958, pp. 18–31.

CHOMSKY, Noam
29. The Logical Structure of Linguistic Theory. Cambridge: Massachusetts Institute of Technology Library. Mimeographed and Microfilmed, 1955.

30. Syntactic Structures. The Hague: Mouton & Co., 1957. As companion and sequel, see Aspects of the Theory of Syntax. Cambridge: M.I.T. Press, 1965.
31. A Transformational Approach to Syntax. In Proceedings of the Third Texas Conference on Problems of Linguistic Analysis in English. Austin: University of Texas Press, 1962, pp. 124–58.
32. Formal Properties of Grammars. HMP 323–418.

CHOMSKY, Noam, and George A. Miller
33. Introduction to the Formal Analysis of Natural Languages. HMP 269–321.

CONKLIN, Harold C.
34. Hanunóo Color Categories. SJA 11.339–44 (1955) = LCS 189–92. Evaluated in item 83.

COOPER, William S.
35. Set Theory and Syntactic Description. The Hague: Mouton & Co., 1964.

DINGWALL, William Orr
36. Transformational Grammar: Form and Theory (A Contribution to the History of Linguistics). Lingua 12.233–75 (1963).

DIRINGER, David
37. The Alphabet; A Key to the History of Mankind. New York: Philosophical Library, 1948.
38. Writing. London: Thames and Hudson, 1962.

DURKHEIM, Émile
39. The Elementary Forms of the Religious Life. Glencoe: The Free Press, 1947. Translated by Joseph Swain in 1915, from Les Formes élémentaires de la vie réligieuse, 1912. See pp. 145, 147.

DYEN, Isidore
40. Language Distribution and Migration Theory. Lg. 32.611–26 (1956).

FODOR, J. A., and J. J. Katz, editors
41. The Structure of Language: Readings in the Philosophy of Language. Englewood Cliffs: Prentice-Hall, 1964.

FRAKE, Charles O.
42. The Diagnosis of Disease Among the Subanun of Mindanao. AA 63.113–32 (1961) = LCS 193–206. Frake, Metzger, Williams, Stefflre, and others are exploring the application of theorems of decomposition to vocabulary as an inventory of culture. Their work is a major contribution to the field of empirical semantics.

FRAZER, James G.
43. The Golden Bough; A Study in Magic and Religion. London: Macmillan, 1919–22. 12 vols.

GELB, I.
44. A study of Writing; The Foundations of Grammatology. Chicago: University of Chicago Press, 1952.

GLEASON, Henry A., Jr.
45. Counting and Calculating for Historical Reconstruction. AL 1:2.22–32 (1959).
46. A Note on Tanaina Subgroups. IJAL 26.348–51 (1960).
47. An Introduction to Descriptive Linguistics. Revised Edition. New York: Holt, Rinehart and Winston, 1961. The Workbook which accompanies this text was published in 1955.
48. The Organization of Language: A Stratificational View. RRT 75–95.

49. Linguistics and English Grammar. New York: Holt, Rinehart and Winston, 1965.
GOODELL, R. J.
50. An Ethnolinguistic Bibliography with Supporting Material in Linguistics and Anthropology. AL 6:2.10–32 (1964).
GOODENOUGH, Ward H.
51. Language and Property in Truk: Some Methodological Considerations. Revised from Property, Kin, and Community on Truk, YUPA 46.61–4 (1951). In LCS 185–8.
GREENBERG, Joseph
52. Languages of Africa. IJAL 29 II/IUPAL 25 (1963). On subgroups, see pp. 1–5.
GUDSCHINSKY, Sarah C.
53. The ABC's of Lexicostatistics (Glottochronology). Word 12.175–210 (1956). Abridged in LCS 612–22.
GUMPERZ, John J.
54. Speech Variation and the Study of Indian Civilization. AA 63.976–88 (1961) = LCS 416–24.
HALLE, Morris
55. The Sound Pattern of Russian. The Hague: Mouton & Co., 1959. *Cf.* item 70.
56. Phonology and Generative Grammar. Word 18.54–72 (1962).
HALLIDAY, Michael A. K.
57. Syntax and the Consumer. RRT 11–24.
HARRIS, Zellig
58. Structural Linguistics. Chicago: University of Chicago Press, 1951.
59. Transformations in Linguistic Structure. PAPS 108.418–22 (1964).
HARVARD UNIVERSITY
60. Catalogue of the Library of the Peabody Museum of Archaeology and Ethnology, Harvard University. Boston: G. K. Hall & Co., 1963. Authors, 26 vols. Subjects, 27 vols. For linguistics, see Subjects, Vol. 13, pp. 79–163. Coverage of this longest of anthropological bibliographies extends through 1962.
HAYS, David G.
61. Dependency Theory: A Formalism and Some Observations. Lg. 40.511–25 (1964).
HOCKETT, Charles F.
62. Two Models of Grammatical Description. Word 10.210–31 (1954) = RL 386–99.
63. A Course in Modern Linguistics. New York: Macmillan, 1958.
HOIJER, Harry
64. Navaho Phonology. Albuquerque: University of New Mexico Press, 1945.
65. Introduction. In Linguistic Structures of Native America. Edited by Cornelius Osgood. By Harry Hoijer and others. Viking Fund Publications in Anthropology, No. 6. New York: Wenner-Gren Foundation for Anthropological Research, 1946, pp. 9–29. A conservative survey of language families, which does not endorse speculative theories, Hoijer's Introduction has been separately printed by Bobbs-Merrill for their Reprint Series in Language and Linguistics.

66. Cultural Implications of Some Navaho Linguistic Categories. Lg. 27.111–20 (1951) = LCS 142–9 (with the addition of bibliographic notes).
67. Language in Culture; Proceedings of a Conference on the Interrelations of Language and Other Aspects of Culture. Comparative Studies of Cultures and Civilizations, No. 3. Edited by Harry Hoijer. American Anthropological Association, Memoir 79, Vol. 56, No. 6, Pt. 2. Chicago: University of Chicago Press, 1954.
68. The Chronology of the Athapaskan Languages. IJAL 22.219–32 (1956). A pendant to this article is Lexicostatistics: A Critique. Lg. 32.49–60 (1956).

HOROWITZ, I. L.
69. Philosophy, Science and the Sociology of Knowledge. Springfield: Thomas, 1961.

HOUSEHOLDER, F .W.
70. On Some Recent Claims in Phonological Theory. Journal of Linguistics 1.13–34 (1965).

HYMES, D. H.
71. A Note on Athapaskan Glottochronology. IJAL 23.291–7 (1957).
72. Language in Culture and Society; A Reader in Linguistics and Anthropology. Edited by Dell Hymes. New York: Harper & Row, 1964.

JAKOBSON, Roman
73. Selected Writings. Vol. 1–. The Hague: Mouton & Co., 1962–.

JAKOBSON, Roman, and Morris Halle
74. Fundamentals of Language. The Hague: Mouton & Co., 1956.
75. Phonology in Relation to Phonetics. In Manual of Phonetics. Edited by L. Kaiser. Amsterdam: North-Holland, 1957, pp. 215–51.

JAKOBSON, Roman, C. G. M. Fant, and M. Halle
76. Preliminaries to Speech Analysis; The Distinctive Features and Their Correlates. Cambridge: Massachusetts Institute of Technology. Acoustics Laboratory. Technical Report No. 13, May 1952.

JOOS, Martin, editor
77. Readings in Linguistics: The Development of Descriptive Linguistics in America Since 1925. Washington: American Council of Learned Societies, 1957.

KATZ, J. J., and J. A. Fodor
78. The Structure of a Semantic Theory. Lg. 39.170–210 (1963).

KATZ, J. J., and P. M. Postal
79. An Integrated Theory of Linguistic Descriptions. Research Monograph No. 26. Cambridge: M.I.T. Press, 1964.

KROEBER, A. L., editor
80. Anthropology Today. Chicago: University of Chicago Press, 1953.

LAMB, Sydney
81. On Alternation, Transformation, Realization, and Stratification. RRT 105–22.

LANDAR, Herbert
82. Tanaina Subgroups. IJAL 26.120–22 (1960).

LANDAR, Herbert, S. M. Ervin, and A. E. Horowitz
83. Navaho Color Categories. Lg. 36.368–82 (1960).

LENNEBERG, Eric H.
84. Color Naming, Color Recognition, Color Discrimination: A Re-Appraisal. Perceptual and Motor Skills 12.375–82 (1961). See pp. 377–8.

LENNEBERG, Eric H., and J. M. Roberts

85. The Language of Experience. IJAL/IUPAL Memoir 13 (1956). See pp. 20–21.

LÉVI-STRAUSS, Claude

86. Structural Analysis in Linguistics and in Anthropology. Translated by Dell Hymes. In LCS 40–52. From Anthropologie structurale, ch. 2. Paris: Plon, 1958.

87. Totemism. Translated by R. Needham. Boston: Beacon Press, 1963.

LOUNSBURY, Floyd G.

88. Field Methods and Techniques in Linguistics. In AT 401–16.

89. Language. In Biennial Review of Anthropology, 1959. Edited by Bernard J. Siegel. Stanford University Press, 1959, pp. 185–209.

90. Language. In Biennial Review of Anthropology, 1961. Edited by Bernard J. Siegel. Stanford: Stanford University Press, 1962, pp. 279–322.

91. A Formal Account of the Crow- and Omaha-Type Kinship Terminologies. In Explorations in Cultural Anthropology: Essays in Honor of George Peter Murdock. Edited by Ward H. Goodenough. New York: McGraw-Hill, 1964, pp. 351–93.

LUCE, R. D., R. R. Bush, and E. Galanter, editors

92. Handbook of Mathematical Psychology. New York: Wiley, 1963. 2 vols.

MANDELBAUM, David G., Gabriel W. Lasker, and Ethel M. Albert, editors

93. Resources for the Teaching of Anthropology. Berkeley and Los Angeles: University of California Press, 1963.

94. The Teaching of Anthropology. Berkeley and Los Angeles: University of California Press, 1963.

MARTIN, Samuel

95. Speech Levels in Japan and Korea. LCS 407–15.

MARTINET, André

96. Structural Linguistics. AT 574–86.

97. The Foundations of a Functional Syntax. RRT 25–36.

MATHIOT, Madeleine

98. Noun Classes and Folk Taxonomy in Papago. AA 64.340–50 (1962) = LCS 154–61.

MCQUOWN, Norman A.

99. A Planned Auxiliary Language. Review of H. Jacob, A Planned Auxiliary Language. Lg. 26.175–85 (1950) = LCS 555–63 (with the addition of bibliographic notes).

MEILLET, Antoine

100. Introduction à l'étude comparative des langues indo-européennes. Alabama Linguistic and Philol. Ser. 3. University: University of Alabama Press, 1964.

MILKE, Wilhelm

101. Athapaskische Chronologie: Versuch einer Revision. IJAL 25.182–8 (1959).

MILLER, George A., and Noam Chomsky

102. Finitary Models of Language Users. HMP 419–91.

MORRIS, Charles

103. Foundations of the Theory of Signs. International Encyclopedia of Unified Science. Vol. 1, No. 2. Chicago: University of Chicago Press, 1938.

104. Signs, Language and Behavior. New York: Prentice-Hall, 1946.

OSGOOD, Charles E., and Thomas A. Sebeok, editors, and A. Richard Diebold, Jr.

105. Psycholinguistics: A Survey of Theory and Research. Edited by Charles E. Osgood and Thomas A. Sebeok, with A Survey of Psycholinguistic Research, 1954–1964. By A. Richard Diebold, Jr. Indiana University Studies in the History and Theory of Linguistics. Bloomington: Indiana University Press, 1965.

Osgood, Cornelius

106. The Distribution of the Northern Athapaskan Indians. YUPA 7.21–2 (1936). It was thought that Ahtena might be a division by itself, and that Koyukon, Tanana, Nabesna, Han, and Tutchone were likely to be consolidated under 3, 5, and 7 (see remarks on Athapaskan in the text). Marsh groups Han with Kutchin (personal comment). Voegelin, KASP 25.170 (1961), accepts 3, 4, 5, 6, 7, and 8 as single languages and composes Tanana-Han-Tutchone.

107. Comparative Tanaina Vocabulary. In The Ethnography of the Tanaina. YUPA 16.208–21 (1937).

Parsons, Talcott

108. The Social System. Glencoe: The Free Press, 1951.

Pedersen, Holger

109. The Discovery of Language: Linguistic Science in the 19th Century. Translated by John Webster Spargo. Bloomington: Indiana University Press, 1964.

Permanent International Committee of Linguists

110. Linguistic Bibliography for the Year 1962 and Supplement for Previous Years. Utrecht: Spectrum, 1964. This is the seventeenth volume of a series begun in 1949.

Pike, Kenneth L.

111. Towards a Theory of the Structure of Human Behavior. LCS 54–61. See also item 114, pp. 33–51.

Pittenger, Robert E., Charles F. Hockett, and John J. Danehy

112. The First Five Minutes: A Sample of Microscopic Interview Analysis. Ithaca: Paul Martineau, 1960.

Postal, Paul M.

113. Boas and the Development of Phonology: Comments Based on Iroquoian. IJAL 30.269–80 (1964).

114. Constituent Structure. IJAL/RCAFL-P 30 (1964).

Pulgram, Ernst

115. Introduction to the Spectrography of Speech. The Hague: Mouton & Co., 1964.

Sapir, Edward

116. Time Perspective in Aboriginal American Culture: A Study in Method. Memoir 90, Anthropological Series No. 13, Geological Survey, Dept. of Mines, Canada. Ottawa, 1916 = SW 389–462.

117. Language: An Introduction to the Study of Speech. New York: Harcourt, Brace, 1921.

118. Sound Patterns in Language. Lg. 1.37–51 (1925) = SW 33–45, RL 19–25.

119. The Status of Linguistics as a Science. Lg. 5.207–14 (1929) = SW 160–66.

120. The Psychological Reality of Phonemes. In SW 46–60. First published as La Réalité Psychologique des Phonèmes. Journal de Psychologie Normale et Pathologique 30.247–65 (1933).

121. Internal Linguistic Evidence Suggestive of the Northern Origin of the Navaho. AA 38.224–35 (1936) = SW 213–24.
122. Selected Writings of Edward Sapir in Language, Culture, Personality. Edited by David G. Mandelbaum. Berkeley: University of California Press, 1958.

SAPIR, Edward, and Morris Swadesh
123. American Indian Grammatical Categories. Word 2.103–12 (1946) = LCS 101–7. Sapir remarks on the 'naïveté of imagining that any analysis of experience is dependent on pattern expressed in language.'

SAPORTA, Sol, and Jarvis Bastian, editors
124. Psycholinguistics: A Book of Readings. New York: Holt, Rinehart and Winston, 1961.

SCHOECK, Helmut, and James W. Wiggins, editors
125. Relativism and the Study of Man. Princeton: D. Van Nostrand, 1961.

SEBEOK, Thomas A., Alfred S. Hayes, and Mary C. Bateson, editors
126. Approaches to Semiotics. The Hague: Mouton & Co., 1964.

SIMMEL, Georg
127. The Sociology of Georg Simmel. Edited by Kurt H. Wolff. Glencoe: The Free Press, 1950.

STRAUSS, Leo
128. Persecution and the Art of Writing. Glencoe: The Free Press, 1952.

STUART, C. I. J. M., editor
129. Report of the Fifteenth Annual (First International) Round Table Meeting on Linguistics and Language Studies. Washington: Georgetown University Press, 1964.

SWADESH, Morris
130. Diffusional Cumulation and Archaic Residue as Historical Explanations. SJA 7.1–21 (1951). Cf. LCS 624–37.
131. Linguistics as an Instrument of Prehistory. Revised from SJA 15.20–35 (1959): LCS 575–83.
132. Tras la Huella Lingüística de la Prehistoria. Supplementos del seminario de problemas cientificos y filosoficos, No. 26, 2d Ser. Mexico: Universidad Nacional de Mexico, 1960. Item 133 contains a more recent discussion.
133. Linguistic Overview. In Prehistoric Man in the New World. Edited by Jesse D. Jennings and Edward Norbeck. Chicago: University of Chicago Press, 1964, pp. 527–56.

TAX, Sol, editor
134. Horizons of Anthropology. Chicago: Aldine Publishing Co., 1964.

THIEME, Paul
135. The Comparative Method for Reconstruction in Linguistics. LCS 585–97.

TRAGER, George L.
136. Paralanguage: A First Approximation. Studies in Linguistics 13.1–12 (1958) = LCS 274–80.

TYLOR, Edward B.
137. Primitive Culture; Researches into the Development of Mythology, Philosophy, Religion, Language, Art, and Custom. Third Edition, Revised. London: Murray, 1891. The first edition of this work appeared in 1871, as the sequel to a volume recently reprinted: Researches into the Early History of Mankind and the Development of Civilization. Chicago: University of Chicago Press, 1964.

VOEGELIN, C. F.

138. Influence of Area on American Indian Linguistics. Word 1.54–8 (1945) = LCS 638–41 (with the addition of bibliographic notes).

VOEGELIN, C. F., and F. M. Voegelin

139. Hopi Domains: A Lexical Approach to the Problem of Selection. IJAL/IUPAL Memoir 14 (1957).

WHITE, Carl M., and T. M. Little

140. Anthropology. In Sources of Information in the Social Sciences: A Guide to the Literature. Edited by Carl M. White. Totowa, N.J.: Bedminster Press, 1964, pp. 229–72.

WHITE, James H.

141. The Methodology of Sememic Analysis with Special Application to the English Preposition. Mechanical Translation 8.15–31 (1964).

WHORF, Benjamin Lee

142. The Relation of Habitual Thought and Behavior to Language. In Language, Culture, and Personality; Essays in Memory of Edward Sapir. Edited by L. Spier *et al.* Menasha: Sapir Memorial Fund, 1941, pp. 75–93. Reprinted in item 143, pp. 134–59.

143. Language, Thought, and Reality; Selected Writings of Benjamin Lee Whorf. Edited by John B. Carroll. Cambridge: Technology Press, and New York: Wiley, 1956.

INDEX «